Also by C. S. Giscombe

Postcards
At Large
Here
Giscome Road
Two Sections from "Practical Geography"

Into and Out of Dislocation

Into and Out of Dislocation

C. S. Giscombe

North Point Press

A division of Farrar, Straus and Giroux

New York

North Point Press
A division of Farrar, Straus and Giroux
19 Union Square West, New York 10003

Distributed in Canada by Douglas & McIntyre Ltd.
Printed in the United States of America
Designed by Jonathan D. Lippincott
First edition, 2000

Library of Congress Cataloging-in-Publication Data
Giscombe, C. S., 1950–
    Into and out of dislocation / C. S. Giscombe. — 1st ed.
        p.   cm.
    ISBN 0-86547-541-5 (alk. paper)
    1. Giscombe, C. S., 1950–   —Journeys—Canada.   2. Poets, American—
20th century—Biography.   3. British Columbia—Description and travel.
4. Jamaicans—British Columbia—Biography.   5. Giscome, John Robert,
19th cent.   6. Afro-American poets—Biography.   7. Blacks—Canada—History.
8. Canada—Race relations.   I. Title.

PS3557.I8 Z469   2000
818'.5403—dc21
[B]
                                                    99-051763

Parts of this book appeared, in different form, in *Epoch*, *The Hudson Review*, *The Iowa Review*, and *Diverse Landscapes* (University of Northern British Columbia Press, 1996).

Permissions appear on page 344.

For my mother and father

Into and Out of Dislocation

Three Locations

Grande Prairie, Alberta

Sometimes when I'm driving up Veterans Parkway, the boulevard that traces the eastern and southern edges of my city, Bloomington, Illinois, if the light's right or close to right, I'll suddenly remember Grande Prairie, Alberta, where I spent a night at the beginning of the summer of 1995. I'm never startled, really, to recall Grande Prairie at those times—the road into that town had made me think of Bloomington when we arrived there dirty and tired after several days on the various northern highways—and I *like* remembering the place, Grande Prairie, and will tease the memory, once it's arrived on its own, and pretend between the banks of stoplights that it's Alberta I'm crossing instead of downstate Illinois and that I'm heading for the Peace River instead of Kinko's copies or the Schnucks superstore; or that I'm driving out to Fort Dunvegan or Fort St. John instead of off to teach my afternoon class at Illinois State University.

I was with my wife and our nine-year-old daughter. We'd been in northern Alberta for two days and I'd been surprised to discover how flat that part of the province was. I didn't

3

know Alberta well (and still don't): before this trip, I'd only crossed it by train once, thirteen years earlier, and all I'd recalled of the province from that trip was the railroad track snaking through the incredible snowy mountains west of Calgary—Katharine and I had sat up at the top of the carpeted stairs in the coach's observation dome for hours staring into the infinity of white peaks. And here were planted fields, the look of agribusiness, a landscape that should have been familiar to me because of Illinois. But until we came into the little city, Grande Prairie, it hadn't felt like Illinois—the light we were encountering in the country was different from the light I was used to cutting through on the drive to Peoria or the drive to Champaign: there was a hazy quality to it, probably owing something to the forest fires that year, but that quality was disconcerting because I could see a great long way *through* the haze, out to where the horizon did blur into the sky. The surface of the earth there in Alberta seemed to be dishy, slightly concave in its flatness way into the distances, and the light seemed to exist not as a series of gradual, far-off wanings but as an ever-present, if less distinctly visible, entity. It seemed to be pooling in the fields.

We'd driven into Alberta—from Fort St. John, British Columbia—through that and come eventually to the Peace River at Dunvegan, where the landscape changed; we went down into the forested hills that rose above the water and camped in a provincial park. We spent the next day, which was cloudy, in some small towns along the Peace River and along the Smoky. Katharine was constructing a photo-essay about our travels along these rivers, and this low grey day was a challenge, she said, because of the kind of film she had in the camera. She photographed the Smoky from the spindly girder bridge at Watino and the Peace from the five-car ferry on which we crossed it for a third time—the first had been on the peculiar, curving span at Fort Dunvegan itself and the second was the long bridge that led into Peace River, Alberta, the town named for the water. Then we got over to Rycroft, where the rain started, and followed the straight road to Grande Prairie, dropping into town from the north.

At the eastern edge of Bloomington, Veterans is the long artery of upscale commerce. The east side's the most profoundly white side of town and there Veterans Parkway is garlanded with frontage roads and has a grassy median strip and "smart" traffic signals that allow you to turn onto the access roads for the malls or for one of the McDonald's or appallingly ridiculous Jumer's Chateau, the huge restaurant-hotel built according to a fantasy of stuccoed Europe. Beyond Veterans the "good" suburbs are extending—town marches farther east into the cornfields and soybean fields each year—and the boulevard's swath is a rough boundary between the older upper-middle-class neighborhoods (giant maples, straight streets, Prairie-style houses with recent additions) and the stark, newly built homes of surgeons and people in the insurance business (Bloomington's the corporate headquarters for State Farm), these in neighborhoods with names like Harbour Pointe. Unlike other urban boundaries the parkway doesn't separate discrete socioeconomic communities—its several lanes separate only styles. The sky, though, seems to well up above Veterans more than it wells up at any other place in Bloomington. Hardly anything is tall on the horizon and perhaps because of that the sky is simply most visible there, from along Veterans, from one's automobile—during the afternoons, the light and clouds are incredible, nearly static presences, towering in fat vertical contrast to the divided lines of traffic. But the *location* of the light is different there: it's specific and diverting and profoundly a thing. Yet even so, Veterans Parkway looks like a lot of places I can think of, effortlessly, in the East and Midwest—Far Hills Avenue in Dayton, Ohio, for example, or Erie Boulevard in Syracuse, Adlai E. Stevenson Drive in Springfield, Illinois, Central Avenue between Albany, N.Y., and Schenectady, etc. Some days I remember Grande Prairie but usually, if I'm thinking about location at all as I drive up Veterans, I think about how I could be at the edge of anywhere.

And because of that I *had* been surprised—as Katharine and Madeline and I came into Grande Prairie that evening in June—to be reminded so strongly of Bloomington's strip; it had rained, as I mentioned, earlier in the afternoon, but that had stopped and the day had cleared and the air was bright and free of haze and here we were coming into an unexpectedly big town with a lot of traffic lights, restaurants, and motels. The sky was a presence. We were grubby—we'd camped the night before, as I said, at old Fort Dunvegan on its wild little hill above the Peace and we'd spent the night before that camping in the Rockies, in prosaically named Summit Pass, in B.C. The previous evening we'd tented at Mighty Moe's Campground in the Cassiar Mountains near McDame Creek; that was one of the nights during this trip that it never quite got dark—twilight had lasted and lasted and swelled outside the tent. The air had seemed to become increasingly granular but it never really got dark.

We were actually making a long, wide circle—a two-week car and ferry trip—and Grande Prairie was the last stop before we arrived back at the starting point, Prince George, British Columbia, where we'd been renting a house near the Nechako River. Prince George is in the geographical center of the province, it's the place where the north–south highway and the north–south railroad cross the ones going east and west. The Nechako flows into the big Fraser River at Prince George; the confluence is visible from Cottonwood Park downtown. It's a hub, a lumber and railroad town, the only city of any note for several hundred miles in any direction. I had a Fulbright that year and this was where I needed to be—I'd wanted to figure out some ways to document the travels in northern British Columbia of the Jamaican miner John Robert Giscome. He'd flourished there, as they say, in the latter half of the nineteenth century and he was, perhaps, a relative of my—and Madeline's—ancestors. He'd arrived in Prince George in the November of 1862, when it was Fort George, a Hudson's Bay Company outpost; he was on his first prospecting trip north from Quesnel, the village seventy miles south of Fort George where he'd been living, and he was accompanied by Henry McDame, a man from the Bahamas. They were headed for the Peace River country, where there was supposed to be a great quantity of gold, but the ice on the Fraser River stopped them and they hunkered down for the winter in Fort George. He was thirty-one years old then, I don't know how old McDame would have been.

We'd arrived in Prince George in the winter too, or partway through it, in January, and were due to go back to the States at the end of June, so this would be our last trip out of town before that. Madeline was missing a little chunk of third grade but her teacher had agreed with us that this would be a worthwhile experience for her and that she could learn to multiply by seven later. It had been a pretty good jaunt—we'd taken the Yellowhead Highway west to the Pacific at Prince Rupert and caught the ferry from there up past Ketchikan and Wrangell and Juneau to Skagway, Alaska. From Skagway we'd made a detour to Whitehorse, the nearest city, the capital of the Yukon Territory, because Katharine was sick and needed a doctor and maybe was going to need a hospital. But it turned out all right and we were able to get back on the road after a couple of days in a motel and drive down into the Cassiar and through the Rockies and so forth. The Cassiar and the Rockies and the Peace River and Wrangell, Alaska, were important to the project because they were places John Robert Giscome had got to; Grande Prairie was not—it was a convenient juncture for us to clean up in and relax in for the last evening before the last day of travel, before we'd drive over Pine Pass and come down the Hart Highway back into Prince George. (And then we'd start packing up to really go home, to return to Bloomington.) Grande Prairie was on the flats, as its name suggests, on a high dry plateau devoid of the sorts of undulations that rivers provide, and John R. had gotten everywhere he went by water.

After the ice broke up on the Fraser in the April of 1863 Giscome and McDame had set out for the Peace River goldfields on the roundabout way that was standard then—eighteen miles on the winding Fraser north to the Salmon's mouth and then northwest for twenty-some miles up the Salmon to a short, marshy portage to what's now called Summit Lake. From there they were going to descend the Crooked River to McLeod Lake and the Parsnip River and eventually get to the Peace. But when they arrived at the place where the Salmon River flows into the Fraser they found the Salmon high and dangerous and their guide—a local man, an Indian—suggested that they go a little farther up the Fraser and take a short path he knew to a lake from which they'd be able to reach McLeod by canoe. That was in April. Much later, around Christmas, John R. would be down in Victoria talking about all this to the *British Colonist*, the newspaper there. The long front-page article, "Interesting from the Rocky Mountains," in the December 15 issue is the main source for my knowledge about his trip; it's the main print source for what I can begin to know—or guess, really—about him. The paper notes that he and McDame "made a portage of about nine miles to a lake, leaving the canoes behind," and at that lake they picked up another canoe—"from an old Indian Chief"—and came down the Crooked River (as it's called now), getting eventually to McLeod Lake. There were no towns then, of course, only those forts dotting the landscape, sitting on the shores of lakes and rivers. At the fort at McLeod Lake "a salute of about 20 shots was fired, with firearms, in honor of the arrival of that party through that route which had never been traversed by any others than Indians." The route that Giscome and McDame had used—that "portage of about nine miles"—was a more dependable route to the north than the standard, one not subject to the vagaries of high water; by 1871 the path was known as the Giscome Portage and it appeared prominently on maps until the age of highways began after the First World War, at which point travel past the new city, Prince George (built at the townsite adjacent to old Fort George), began to stop meaning travel via lakes and rivers. Up until that point it was the *way*. That first lake that the partners came to after the portage, Summit Lake, is the beginning of the Arctic watershed; the Fraser flows south and enters the Pacific at Roberts Bank in Vancouver, but Summit Lake drains into the Crooked and the Crooked flows north into other rivers and lakes and, eventually, all that water gets to the Arctic Ocean. According to the *Colonist* story, John R. noted, as he and McDame left Summit Lake, that they were in a north-flowing river—he must have known he'd crossed the divide. The two of them did eventually make it to the Peace on their 1863 trip but found little there in the way of gold and, after some adventures, moved on to other sites in B.C. where they fared better.

Now, there's something black people, or American black people of certain generations, say: we say that no matter where you go, no matter how far, no matter to what unlikely extreme, no matter what country, continent, ice floe, or island you land on, you will find someone else black already there. (In Fairview, Alberta, when I went into the 7-Eleven to ask where we might camp in the vicinity it was a big chocolate-colored man in blue overalls who said that he'd just driven his truck over from Fort Dunvegan, where there was a provincial park, and that we could be there in twenty minutes.) And maybe white people do something similar but on a grander scale, make a similar claim but one so unironically tied to civic identity and national consciousness as to be invisible, as to require no particular thought or *self*-consciousness: the local case in point is that most histories—casual and published—of B.C. start by mentioning the same fact, the same luminous detail, they all start off with Alexander Mackenzie being the first white man to enter what is now the province. The story is not indicative of some vicious racism on the part of its tellers but its presentation as a flat fact reveals the tendency that we all have to go along with things, to not question the conventional. When John R. and Henry McDame strolled into Fort McLeod, the Hudson's Bay Company lads there at the fort fired off those shots in their honor, or in what John R. *reported* as honor, "in honor of the arrival of that party" over that trail "which had never been traversed by any others than Indians." I imagine that when people read that description in the newspaper they assumed that our heroes were two white guys; and I imagine John R. smiling as he or the newspaper reporter, or the two of them together, came up with that phrase, "any others than Indians." I imagine him smiling; I don't know if he did. Who was the first black man to enter B.C.? Who was the first Giscome and how did he or she spell the name?

And all my life I've been struck by how the world's staked out by names—that the path between the Pacific and Arctic watersheds became the Giscome Portage, that's the thing that brought me to Fort George a hundred and thirty-three years after John R. had wintered there. Of course, the name's a spelling variation of my own family name, Giscombe, and all the handful of Giscomes and Giscombes I'd ever met or heard of up to the point of my own arrival at Fort George had been, as I am, black Jamaicans (by birth or by ancestry); Giscome or Giscombe is not the sort of name that one associates easily with the Arctic, with ice and snow. And British Columbia is a land of white people (who've written the place's history, starting that book with A. Mackenzie), Chinese people, and Indians—that's the standard racial breakdown in the province and white history in B.C. is an even more recent series of events than it is elsewhere in North America; "pioneer" appears with great frequency in the names of businesses and organizations in the province and various other white firsts (after Mackenzie's) are casually mentioned in most conversations about the landscape. Photographs abound of the early days of the province—history is close by. But into that history, from the Bahamas and Jamaica, come Henry McDame and John Robert Giscome. They came into Fort George that winter and the latter's black name got affixed to the geography around there: the portage wasn't the only thing named for him—there's also a town, thirty miles out from Prince George, and a canyon and a rapids, both on the Fraser, and a spate of other designations as well. And into that history—and into the land of ice and snow—came I and my little family; it wasn't the first time we'd come to Prince George but it was the first time we'd arrived to dig in.

I finally went to Jamaica for the first time in the spring of 1996, after we'd been back from Prince George for almost a year. I went there rather specifically to interview John Aaron Giscombe, Jr., who was ninety-three years old then and who is the great-nephew of John Robert Giscome. He lives just outside of Prattville, a tiny place which is itself in the hills above Mandeville, a big market town in the center of the island. These hills are no region of Giscombe family origins, they're where his wife's people were from. All the Giscombes trace back to the parishes of the northeast coast, the northern side of the Blue Mountains: Buff Bay—where my grandfather was born—, Belcarres, Portland Parish, etc., places I've still never seen. Or that I've not seen yet. I suspect there's a blood connection in all that geography, a link that's out there waiting to be found between my grandfather's people and that family, John R.'s. Or I imagine that there is; names rise in a number of different ways and if we do share some ancestry—if the same coupling long ago produced both John Robert Giscome and myself—I've certainly not discovered it, marked it, located it; I've been concerned, so far anyway, more with the peripheries than with a core.

And John R. is himself, in Canadian history, a peripheral character—that is, he appears, or his name does, in a variety of contexts, but almost never as the central focus. The articles and descriptions and paragraphs are rarely about him—they're about the countryside or the route through it that bears his name or about the business ventures of a white man for whom he's reputed to have worked once. There are a couple of exceptions to this, though—one is that long article in the *Colonist*, "Interesting from the Rocky Mountains," and the other is a videotape, made in summer 1994, at a Giscombe family reunion in Melbourne, Florida. The tape contains an extensive interview with old John Aaron and it was sent to me a year or so after the fact by Lorel Morrison, who lives in Maryland and is himself one of John Aaron's great-nephews: there's a relatively tight family group descended, it turns out, from John R.'s brother Peter, who stayed in Jamaica while John R. went on to Canada, and Lorel's part of that group. I don't know whether or not I am: there's a coincidence of some first names but they're fairly common first names and there are enough holes and guesses in the family trees to make me dubious or at least cautious and qualifying in my embrace. But on the tape the old man was sure about some things—he called the names of people long dead and told stories about John R. and Peter, who was, of course, his own grandfather.

My grandfather, for whom I am named, left Buff Bay suddenly one afternoon near the turn of the century and never went back: the story goes that one of his brothers was shipping out on a United Fruit boat to Costa Rica and that he—my grandfather—had gone down to the docks to see the brother off and decided or had decided (impulsively, that is, or by design) to join him. He picked bananas for a while in Costa Rica and saved money and came to the United States and went to Clark, the black school in Atlanta, and then on to Meharry Medical College in Nashville. He settled in Birmingham, where my father was born, and practiced medicine there until the week before he died in 1962, when I was eleven. He was a short man with coppery skin and high cheekbones, he was fierce and calm at once in his demeanor; he had an accent, of course, and I can remember the sound of that much more vividly than I can recall anything he ever said. He said rather little. When he died we all went down to

Birmingham on the overnight train (from Dayton, Ohio, where I grew up and where my parents still live) and I played with the neighborhood boys while my father closed up his office. Small mysteries were discovered among the papers— nothing scandalous but things he'd never mentioned: a medal and an accompanying citation for his work with the Selective Service signed by Harry Truman, a handful of stock certificates from shady-sounding oil ventures, and a 1921 letter from the Provincial Board of Medical Examiners telling him what he'd have to do in order to practice medicine in British Columbia.

Years later, when I found out about John R., I immediately thought of that letter—it's now ensconced in a little cardboard envelope in my top desk drawer here in Bloomington. I suppose I don't really know what to do with it on any level: it's an arti-fact all right but I'm not sure what it represents. I do see that it's no dotted line on a map connecting my grandfather's forty-some years in Birmingham to John Robert Giscome's forty-some years in B.C. I don't know what was in my grandfather's mind when he wrote to the medical examiners and I don't know what set of circumstances stopped him from going out there. Like much else in the family history it's locked up in the head of someone who's died. Papers don't reveal much, I think, for most of us, especially when it comes to our desires—we're not scrupulous about maintaining a trail that would reveal us, we're more busy getting through life than documenting it. At the funeral my grandfather was laid out in his tuxedo and my mother whispered to me that he had last worn that at her wed-ding to my father, fourteen years earlier. He'd been *entertaining* them, she said, during the reception and, because I'd never before heard the word used in that context, I imagined him fiercely doing magic tricks. I knew where British Columbia was when I was a child because I was interested in maps.

I didn't know a thing about John Robert Giscome, though, until I was thirty—I was an editor then, at *Epoch* magazine at Cornell University, and I was publishing work by a Vancouver poet, George Bowering. In one of his letters he included something odd: he circled my name on the line of salutation and scrawled a question across the top of the sheet—"Do you know that there's a town in northern B.C. that has this name?" I didn't know but when I went home that evening there it was in the world atlas I'd had since I was thirteen—a black dot on the map outside Prince George, on the red line of the Canadian National Railways. The name itself, Giscome, was in the sans serif typeface Rand McNally uses to indicate very small towns; the index listed the population at 575. A patient little time bomb, in my possession, waiting to go off. I typed a note of inquiry to the Chamber of Commerce in Prince George and got a letter back that quoted *1001 British Columbia Place Names*, the guidebook by G.P.V. and Helen B. Akrigg: "Named for John Robert Giscome, a negro miner who entered the district in 1860 and died about 1910 in Victoria." This was something real. The next afternoon I went over to the Olin Library at Cornell and took the elevator up to the sixth floor and found a copy of the Akriggs' book and read the one-line description again. I looked out the window at Inlet Valley and West Hill—it was winter and the line of the hill was jagged against the sky. The Olin ventilation made its constant whoosh and the dry, sweet stink of leather bindings drifted in the air. Here was something real indeed and eventually, because of that, I made it out to British Columbia. But I've always, all my life, been going on into Canada, going up to Canada, over into Canada.

When Katharine, Madeline, and I got to Jamaica we rented a car, a Toyota Tercel, and drove the hundred miles from

Kingston out to Mandeville. The ride was harrowing—people went fast and passed one another on curves and on hills and I was, of course, unused to driving on the left side. We got through Spanish Town, Old Harbour, and May Pen and, as the country began to get steep and the traffic got less intense, we stopped for lunch at a roadhouse called the Healthy Eaters Café. The place was full of truck drivers, African-descended and Indian men, who spoke, as we waited in line to place our orders, in an accent that stopped me from understanding whatever they were telling me; but I was finally able, after some false starts, to joke with the women at the counter about the price of Pepsi-Cola. One brought our lunches out to us in the dark little dining room and my barbecued chicken was quite delicious. We came into Mandeville a little after that and found our hotel, and the next morning I got up early and went off alone, with my new tape recorder, to see John Aaron Giscombe in Prattville.

Lorel Morrison had provided me with directions to John Aaron's house and the hotel owner's husband augmented those by drawing me a very detailed map of the way out of Mandeville. With all that on the seat beside me I headed up over the shoulders of the edge of town, passed some big estates, and suddenly town all fell away and I was on a narrow road that looped through a lush, open country. I felt a certain ebullience at driving alone through this, through Jamaica, in the morning—the road was deserted and on either side were hills that were thick and a brilliant green color and the sunlight too was thick without being either hazy or bright. This was certainly the country of joy, of resonance—but with what? The road was beautiful but it reminded me of many other trips on many other roads—one memory yielded effortlessly to another, the road was that basic in its climbs and in the way it went into the sunlight. All was a scattering, nothing cohered. And in that scattering, or rolling alongside it, I was headed for an almost arbitrary location, a place where I hoped to find some information, a crossroads, as it were, at which I was to meet an emissary from something bigger, something more specific—it was the classic literary situation, almost a cliché. But this landscape was specific too, this was Jamaica—the land of my *fathers*—and I was on my way through it to Prattville in a rented white Tercel.

After a while Newport, where I was to turn, hove into view: it was an intersection with some two-story buildings and a police station, and I found my left turn in a grove of big trees and made that and went on toward the hills in which Prattville was situated. Trees shaded the way for the first quarter mile or so, and I saluted an ancient man with a cane who was walking in the road there, tottery on his bare feet, and he returned my wave shakily with his free hand. The skin was profoundly black, the beard and hair were bright white. Actually, many people were walking in the road and there were goats too, and cows, and a plague of white egrets—all of our driving thus far in Jamaica had involved an unnerving proximity to people and animals. Lorel had asked, in one of our phone conversations, if I'd ever traveled in the Third World, fretting over me a little bit, I think, on the eve of my departure for the island of his birth, and I'd answered, half-joking, that I had been to New York. And England—where we'd lived for half a year when Madeline was a baby—had outfitted me with a series of handy comparisons: as I climbed toward Prattville I became mindful of the road I'd bicycled on over the Malvern Hills near the Welsh border—like that road it ascended and descended very sharply (much more so than the one I'd taken from Mandeville down into Newport), plunging into and out of some deep shade, and it was often gravel and there were the "washed-out interrupted raw places" too that Theodore Roethke named in his great last poem, in the section that begins "In the long journey out of the self . . ."

But all that's metaphor—literary bric-a-brac—and metaphor's heavy on any road. All around me Jamaica roiled in the sunlight and jutted out onto the pavement and seemed a lot like itself. My comment about New York was merely clever and England hadn't really prepared me—this was the land of some of my fathers and it was at least as strange to me as England had been when I'd arrived there.

Lorel's instructions had called for me to begin asking, at some point, for the way to Mr. Giscombe's house. At what felt like the outskirts of Prattville I stopped two men who were walking by and asked them and the bald man said that he lived up in Nonperel, up at the top of a hill, and asked, "You he grandson?" I'd noticed, once we left Kingston, how dark-complected almost everyone was and because of that, I think, I stuck out some—I've never thought of myself as being particularly light but in comparison to the people I ran into in the country I was. I am. Old John Aaron—whom I'd seen in the videotape—has skin roughly the same color as my own and I suppose that this was enough to base the question on. A young man named Martin appeared and one of the men I'd been speaking with arranged for him to act as guide. We drove up the potholed hill to Nonperel, which was a group of houses in among some trees; I steered around a young one-armed woman in a sleeveless blouse who was walking with children—hers?—, carrying a gallon jug of milk, and Martin pointed out Mr. Giscombe's driveway and accepted the couple of dollars I offered for his trouble. I parked at the bottom of the hill and climbed up to the house, where I was met by

Noel Giscombe, John Aaron's son. I'd written and so was expected.

The old man came out of the back room then and I introduced myself to him, using my first name—Cecil—and my last name, which was, of course, the same as his. "I knew a Cecil Giscombe," he said but I couldn't get him to elaborate. He rambled for a long time, repeating, word for word, snippets of his talk on the tape Lorel had sent me. I'd try to guide him, but everything about John R. came back to him having "found a gold mine in Canada" and that, when he died, "his property was worth twenty-five *t'ousand* dollars"—he'd emphasize the "t'ousand" the same way each time, just as I'd heard him emphasize it when he told the story on the videotape, and finally his son said, "Forget it, man," and went on to say I should have been there last year; he'd been sharp then, Noel said, and could've told me everything I wanted to know. But during the intervening winter he'd fallen sick and Noel and his other sons had thought he was going to die; he hadn't, of course, but he'd emerged from the illness frail and disoriented. "His mind's gone, man," Noel said; "you're about a year too late." The old man sat on the couch next to me staring out the open window. The tops of trees were visible and from somewhere else in the house music was playing. There was a picture of Queen Elizabeth on the wall. I get tangled up in language myself sometimes and often will remember things I've said or should have said and repeat them later, turning them over again and again in my mind. I teach in a largely windowless building named after the Bloomingtonian Adlai Stevenson and have identified a malaise I call Adlai Stevenson's disease, the first sign of which is talking to yourself in the stall in the fourth-floor washroom, the one English shares with Accounting and Philosophy. It's a joke ailment of course, garden-variety depression crossed with the fear of Alzheimer's. The question on the road had been whether or not I was a grandson, but I was forty-five then, about the same age as Noel. What'll I be like in half a century? The videotape had been made at a family reunion in Florida and the old man had been casually encyclopedic about the tribe—the range of skin colors, his father's experiences in Panama, his own adventures when he'd lived in Chicago. Some of those adventures had had a sexual tinge and John Aaron had flirted, a little, on the tape with some of his young, distant cousins, trim good-looking Giscombe women in their fifties and sixties.

I've never been terribly interested in the costume drama that most imaginations of the past seem to entail. Which is to say that I regard devotion to family trees with a mix of suspicion and uninterest—there's something irritatingly civic about the enterprise, something that verges on a kind of boosterism. One wishes to find and then capture the connection as though it were a trophy. It'll settle this or that, it'll confer status. I recently met a white man in Indiana who made a point of telling me that he'd traced his lineage back to Abraham. When I do think of the past and family trees and so forth I imagine copulation—the romance of sex, the inevitability of bodies producing another body, the grandparent suddenly youthful and randy. The delights of being naked. Or I imagine the ancestor wasting time doing this or that or being sullen or fearful or, as Auden said, just walking dully along. Eating. Working for someone. Asleep. Or waiting for something to happen.

I came back to Mandeville, picked up Katharine and Madeline, and we drove down to Treasure Beach on the south coast and went swimming in the Caribbean. It was March and the water was warm. We sat on the sand and watched pelicans, birds none of us had ever seen before except in pictures.

Above the Schnucks parking lot in Bloomington nighthawks are a presence in the spring. Schnucks is the biggest supermarket in town and its lot has the best arc lights of any of the lots in town and the birds come because of those, in pursuit of insects. Their wings jiggle, light catches on their bellies, the calls are high-pitched and piercing as they swoop. I found a dead one recently, when I was bicycling outside of town, at a country intersection, and it was cause to stop and take a close look. They're not really hawks, of course, they're goatsuckers; the name sounds vampirish and oddly sexual in other ways as well—it comes from the astounding width of their open mouths, big enough, the notion goes, to fit around a goat's teat. The beaks are very small, though, in terms of length. I leaned over the handlebars and poked it with my foot: it was perfect, as we say of dead creatures, it had probably been struck glancingly and died of shock—even dead it looked sleek and capable. I'd never seen a nighthawk close up before.

A mile south of our house on Vale Street is the edge of town and I'll often make for that when I'm out for a quick before-dinner bike ride; town stops, at least for right now, at a little subindustrial copse—something having to do with Olin Corporation, Stahly's Truck City, Owen Nursery—bordering the Norfolk Southern tracks and there's a twelve-mile loop I do that commences just beyond that: it follows a relatively hilly road along the railroad, skirts the edge of a freestanding subdivision that's popped up beyond town, and crosses I-74 twice. In the fields outside Bloomington live thirteen-lined ground squirrels—handsome rodents, they have a bad time with cars—, moles, voles, the inevitable raccoons and woodchucks. Pheasants, a couple of varieties of owls, kestrels, redtail hawks, casual flocks of pigeons. Nighthawks. "An enormous added dimension is given a country by its game," said Edward Hoagland in his book about B.C. Deer occur in the little clumps of woods around Lake Bloomington and some of the other man-made lakes. I recently saw a bald eagle above the Illinois River at Peoria and I've encountered four coyotes in the last few years. Once I saw a fox run across the parking lot of the Super 8 Motel.

I said something in a poem once about "all locations being temporary" and, later in the same long poem, that they—locations—are "emphatic and come to know one place," counting on the reader to hear "know" as both itself and "no." Locations are provisional: we're in Bloomington because of my job with the university but there's no origin for us here—or anything that might remind us of any place of origin, this is not any-place that one might aim at or make for deliberately—and no resonance in the shape of the countryside past town which stretches unambiguously to the horizons and is owned by a corporation. But locations are where you happen to get to and then, as the joke goes, there you are.

I went to British Columbia to see and live in the remote, unlikely place that the family, people with this Jamaican name, arrived at. Being in British Columbia—living there—was like going along a ridge, like being on a path that follows the top of the ridge for a long time and offers a view of myriad this and that below. It was like having *gained* the ridge, as they say. (When I went back to Prince George, in June of 1996, I climbed up Teapot Mountain with Vivien Lougheed and John Harris and Barry McKinnon; when we got to the top we were able to see a great distance into the west—valleys, the plume of smoke from a lumber mill, two or three lakes, and a town. Nothing terribly exciting except for the conjunction and the fact of distance. And the presence of height, or the presence of a change in height, in elevation, someplace to see from. Still, it's pretty much what I'd expected to have a view of, those valleys and that town and some water. But my metaphors come, if sometimes too easily, from that sort of thing, there being geographic sites on the earth. And on the body—the recollection of this erotic adventure, that injury, that little surgery. Old places where the hair doesn't grow.)

Grande Prairie was not a special place, it was a coincidence of light that makes our approach to it stick in my memory. Or it was the prescience that came along with the light—soon it was going to be time to go back. Once we'd got to the motel and lugged our stuff into the room we began arguing about something stupid: there was only one towel in the bathroom and Katharine and I went around and around about who was going to call the front desk to ask for more so we could all shower before going out for dinner. I can't recall now which one of us finally made the call, and though we both apologized and chalked our behavior up to travel fatigue, the argument had soured my mood some and dinner didn't make it better. We ate at a Greek restaurant downtown—it had a nice tile decor and the sun slanted in through its big windows but the food was unmemorable—and wandered back to the motel. I was feeling a slow sad irritation that I now think had more to do with the end of our life in British Columbia becoming visible to me than it did with being tired and having carried on about towels. We'd be eating soon at one of the chain restaurants on Veterans—Chili's or Applebee's or the Olive Garden. Katharine agreed to take Madeline to the swimming pool and I went out to try to walk off my unhappiness in whatever was behind the strip of motels and eateries.

The road went across the CN tracks and up a little hill:

there was a newly built school on the right-hand side but to the left was a wide expanse of bushes and trees and a paved footpath leading off into them. I thought again of Bloomington: we have a series of connected walking and cycling paths that, together, are called the Constitution Trail; the trail's situated on the old railroad beds that wind through town and one leg of it traverses an interesting little undeveloped area by Veterans Parkway—it follows the curves of a creek with low, scruffy sides in between Jumer's Chateau and Pier One Imports. Someone said recently, in a letter to *The Pantagraph*, the Bloomington paper, that she'd seen otters there but I suspect she really saw a muskrat. Whatever she saw, it's one of my favorite places in Bloomington. But this was Grande Prairie—or an edge of Grande Prairie—and I followed the path off into the trees and bushes, and ten or so minutes later I was surprised to arrive at a body of water. A sign told me it was Crystal Lake.

A dock stuck out from a marshy corner of the lake and, as I walked out onto it, I saw the whole place was alive with birds. I've never been so close to more shorebirds, or more different kinds of shorebirds, at once than I was at that long moment when I stood out at the end of that dock. A pair of ruddy ducks did a courtship display and a tern divebombed me so repeatedly that I had to take several steps back—I suppose the bird's nest was nearby. I saw scoters and great numbers of Bonaparte's gulls. A muskrat swam nearby and female redwings with nesting materials in their mouths clung to reeds just as they do in Peterson's. It was a brilliant, noisy place and I stood there and watched and listened for half an hour. I don't know if the lake was natural or man-made, I don't know how often people visit it, whether it was a feeding site or not. It was a place where I wanted to surrender, a place I'd come to unexpectedly, an uncomplicated center. I was still in my funk but I'd seen birds. They won't save you but they're beautiful and necessary.

Finally I turned away from that, turned to go back to the motel down the path I'd come up on, and I realized, once I'd regained the bushes, that the light had changed a little; it wasn't dark or even near dark but the light had shifted. Dark was coming—"black like me," Langston Hughes said—, it was going to get dark. I walked on, thinking about the birds and the muskrat and about this place, and suddenly I knew, there on the path, that I wasn't quite sure where I was. I mean I knew I was on the path back to the road back to the motel, but I didn't know what the country right here was. It touched me the way understandings do in the dreams that are not nightmares but that have an interesting, menacing edge to them, that entangle the dreamer, me, in a slow cognizance not of danger but of the fact of danger probably existing, somewhere that I the dreamer can't quite see. I mean I suddenly realized that in the bushes beyond the path there might very possibly be bears.

Winter in Fort George

The deal was that we were to meet in Seattle on the first of January, the first day of 1995, and then be on our way north. Katharine and Madeline were coming on the train, the Empire Builder, from Illinois and I was flying up from the Modern Language Association convention in San Diego. We were going to stay a few days with friends in town and then depart for Prince George in our new vehicle, a green Willys-Overland wagon, in time for the beginning of Madeline's spring semester in third grade. I'd bought the truck a couple of months earlier when I was in Seattle on a reading tour: I'd had a poetry book come out that fall—1994—and spent three weeks in November visiting bookstores and colleges in Washington, Oregon, and British Columbia. Knowing that we were going to be living in northern B.C. in January, I figured that we were going to want something with four-wheel drive; my recollection of Prince George was that everyone there had such a vehicle and, besides, I had nostalgic feelings about the International Scout I'd owned when I met Katharine twenty years before, when we were in graduate school in upstate New

York—we'd gotten into a number of fixes with it, predictable mirings in mud and snow, and had had to walk out of some interesting places, this is what our courtship was like.

So when I was going around in Seattle giving readings downtown and in the 'burbs, and visiting with our friends Kathryn MacDonald and Jim Snydal, I found a couple of ads for Jeeps and light trucks in *The Seattle Times* and made the phone calls but nothing worked out. But then I picked up a sheet called the *Lucky Nickel* and there was someone selling a Willys and I called and found out it was in a place called Beaver, Washington—way west of Seattle, out on the Olympic Peninsula—and Kathryn and Jim and I drove out to look at it. The road—U.S. Route 101—got narrow after we passed through Port Angeles, the big rough-and-tumble lumber town where Jim was raised and where his family owns the Pepsi-Cola bottling plant. It's a beautiful road, really, but it does zig and zag and there's not much leeway to it, hardly any shoulders; the state's put up signs warning bicyclists about the lumber trucks—they essentially advise you to abandon hope. Jim had worked for the family business when he was in high school and college and when we got to the stretch of road that follows the long shore of Lake Crescent he pointed out the place where he'd lost the brakes on a Pepsi truck and, because he'd had a choice, driven into a tree rather than the lake, which is, for all practical purposes, bottomless. Eventually we came to the turnoff the directions had described and went up a winding driveway that ended at a new house in a clearing; there were scrubby woods rising behind the house and losing themselves in the perpetual mist of the peninsula—the ocean was near, as were the Olympic Mountains. The Willys stood in the middle of the yard, boxy and green and old, and dogs came from somewhere and surrounded Jim and Kathryn's van, barking. A woman stepped out onto the porch of the house and she and Kathryn yelled to each other—we should watch out for the skinny one because she'd go for our ankles when our backs were turned, the woman said, but other than that they wouldn't hurt us. We left Calvin, Jim and Kathryn's dog, in the van and made it into the house, watching our backs. The woman's husband, who was selling the truck, was out guiding a fishermen's party, she said, but he would be back soon, any minute, and we were welcome to wait. We settled into her couch and she and Kathryn, who runs the animal welfare outfit on Bainbridge Island, talked about pets—cats and dogs were much in evidence both inside and outside the house. The woman, Patty Piggott, said that she and her husband, Bob, had lived on Bainbridge a long time ago and she compared houses and locations and views with Kathryn and Jim; the island's just across the water from downtown Seattle and a lot of people commute via ferry. This was different, Patty said—she liked it but there were some downsides, one of which was the mountain lions—"They want to eat my kitties," she said, matter-of-factly. Suddenly then there were gunshots on the TV and our eyes all fixed on it—it was a crime show on the Fox channel from Denver (they had a satellite dish) and a group of black men on a catwalk above a factory floor was opening fire with automatic weapons on a group of white men who'd been working below at machines. The white actors ducked and dodged appropriately.

It was getting dark and Bob still wasn't home and Jim and Kathryn and I talked about it, deciding to go out and get dinner and come back. There was a place up the road in Beaver but Patty said that they weren't "clean," so we went to the Chinese restaurant out in Forks instead. Forks, according to legend, is where a group of Hell's Angels tangled with a group of unemployed loggers and lost and ran. Or rode, I suppose.

The waitresses in the Chinese place were skinny blond women and the food was dull—it was a well-lit place, garish actually, the sort of restaurant where families would go, and in the booths around us white families were hunched over their dinners. Establishments describing themselves as family restaurants, I've recently realized, tend to be brightly lit. Jim said there'd been one black family in Port Angeles when he was growing up, I can't recall what he said their name was.

When we got back to the Piggotts', Bob had arrived home and he and I went out in the Willys; he directed me up into the hills on some fire roads, pointing out the strength of the engine, and I was falling in love. I'd had an older friend, when I was in school, who'd had a truck like this one and who lived in the foothills of the Berkshires, beyond Albany, New York. My first long-distance bicycling trip had been the thirty or so miles out, from Albany, to visit him and his wife—the last couple of miles to the house itself, though, were unpaved and he'd arrived at the church parsonage from which I'd phoned to ferry me over that final stretch. It was near sunset and I recall the way the truck looked as it crested a hill in the near distance and came down toward me; they're extremely high vehicles—there was all that *space* above Doug's head as he approached. We loaded the bike into the back and bounced out to the house on Horseheaven Road and Judith and a steak dinner. Their house had had a lot of shadow and corners in which huge dogs—Newfoundlands—lounged: we drank beer with our steak and laughed and talked into the night, all this in West Stephentown, New York, in November 1971. Twenty-three Novembers later, up on the hill above Beaver, I made a three-point turn on a muddy ridge and came back down a steep straightaway, letting us fall toward 101 in second with the clutch out and my foot off the gas, waiting to feel it pop out of gear. But it didn't, it ran wonderfully all the way, and Kathryn and Jim and I spent the night in Port Angeles and the next day took it over to the Pepsi mechanic, who owned one, and he said it was OK, so I bought it and left it there and caught the afternoon ferry across the Strait of Juan de Fuca to Victoria—I had engagements, in the following days, up in B.C. You can *see* prim Victoria from gritty Port Angeles, it's not that far; all those cities cluster around the same water. After the ferry ride I stood in line to enter B.C. in the blocky terminal building downtown; my Customs officer, a young chunky blond woman, politely asked me if I was packing a pistol. I said I wasn't and she looked off into the air vacantly and gave me leave to come into the province. I went to the places where I was supposed to go and then, a week later, I was on the Empire Builder myself, heading back to Bloomington.

Katharine and Madeline arrived in Seattle on New Year's Day and I was there to meet them at the King Street Station, where, when I was two years old, my mother and I had greeted my father when he returned by ship and train from the war in Korea; I have only the vaguest and most suspect memories of that time and none of Seattle. Madeline was very excited about "the green car" but Katharine was reserved—I'd described the Willys to her, of course, when I'd returned from my reading tour (and Kathryn MacDonald had sent a photo), but here we were loading luggage into the cavernous cargo area and then easing out into Seattle traffic and riding in it was different: all the bumps and draftiness and the engine noise, all these things were facts now. She was willing to put some of her concern aside but she discussed with me—as we tooled around the waterfront looking for a place to have lunch—the prospect of driving six hundred miles north, into the heart of winter, in such a machine. Then, in the parking lot in front of

Ivar's Acres of Clams, we burned out the ignition wire: it was nothing really—the key clicked uselessly in its switch and a little plume of electric smoke drifted out from under the dashboard, but when I popped the hood to investigate I discovered that I could start the truck by jiggling the charred wire itself. It would be easy to fix, I announced cheerfully, not a big deal at all.

We ate at one of Ivar's good tables, one of the ones facing Elliott Bay, and talked about Madeline's school, the train trip out from Illinois, my convention in San Diego. We didn't talk about going north in the green car, but that issue hung in the air over our chowder and razor clams; it was difficult, really—even for me (or especially for me)—, not to see the gone-to-glory ignition wire as a thin line of warning, as a gentle predictor of future difficulties, of a spate of little things waiting to happen to us up in the snow. In truth, Katharine had never been thrilled with the prospect of spending the winter in Prince George, and when I'd received my award letter from the Fulbright people in April, her heart—she told me later that spring—sank. She'd been there, to Prince George, one time: when we lived in Vancouver (three years before this) we'd driven up for a couple of November days in a rented Chevrolet—we drove through a blizzard and had had to go around a couple of car wrecks and the city itself was winter-grey when we finally got to it and fairly desolate. It's not one of the fabulous eastern Canadian cities that celebrate winter with ice-skating downtown and imaginative Christmas window displays in the big department stores. And neither is it tropical, sophisticated, green-all-winter Vancouver: the six months we lived there is probably the closest to paradise that we're ever going to come. Prince George isn't lovely or graceful—it's a lumber town and it reeks of its pulp mill. We talked about it through that summer, though, and into the fall and Katharine got to the point where she began to see it as an adventure—both of us have that weakness for adventure—and consented to go and began making plans for a photo documentary project, something that would be hers. We'd have enough money to live someplace decent, there'd be things to do and see, it would be OK. And Madeline was looking forward to all of it: a long train trip, a new funky green car, and very deep snow to sled through. It would be OK.

But now here we were in the new funky green car at the first edge of things, on the Seattle waterfront in the line of very ordinary cars waiting for the Bainbridge Island ferry to transport us across to Kathryn and Jim's. We clunked on and then went upstairs to the lounge and sat by one of the giant windows and Seattle's lights fell away behind us and the huge motor throbbed and I began to realize that it had been a bad idea. We went back down to the car deck early—a few minutes before docking—so I could wiggle the ignition wire without holding up the people behind us and that evening and the next morning we talked it out and came up with a plan: Katharine and Madeline would take the British Columbia Railway on to Prince George (the house near the Nechako was, by this time, rented and waiting for us) and I'd fly back to Bloomington, get "the good car"—the Volvo—, and drive out to join them. A friend of Jim and Kathryn's said he'd house and occasionally drive the Willys until I could decide what to do with it, either sell it or bring it back to Illinois.

But first we all three had to go to Vancouver. I was the person who'd been given money and permission to enter Canada for several months and so I had to escort my dependents across the border. We went up on the Greyhound, figuring that that would be the easiest and most reliable way over; we left in the afternoon but almost as soon as we got out of Seattle it was dark, so we could have been traveling through any landscape. The border too was undifferentiated: I mean it was the typical remote location, the place in the northern fringes that looks the same, no matter where you are: a truck stop, someplace to eat, maybe a fireworks dealer, the duty-free shop, all clustered together someplace out in the middle of nowhere, far from anything. The Canadians have shown no particular interest either in building down to their border with us. (Detroit/Windsor and Niagara Falls/Niagara Falls are exceptions, as are the two Sault Ste. Maries and Calais, Maine/St. Stephen, New Brunswick; but in all those places, even the last, there's a formidable water separation, a natural boundary. Officially the border's unguarded—we boast about its being the longest demilitarized frontier in the world or some such thing—but to slip across you'd have to walk for miles. Or have a four-wheel drive.)

The Fulbright people had assured me that my name would be in the computer and that crossing would be a breeze. Of course, that's not the way it went—there were forms to fill out, computer screens to be puzzled over, inquiring phone calls to be made to Ottawa, and a student visa to purchase for Madeline; and the bus—having to get the rest of the way to Vancouver by a certain time—left without us. We killed a couple of the hours before the next one eating a leisurely dinner at a restaurant in a strip club across the highway from Customs/Douanes—the restaurant wasn't really in the club itself but in an area in the basement of the building. A door connected them; we could hear the music swell on the other side of the wall and men hooting but no one ever came through the door. It turned out to be a Ukrainian place and I had my first ever pierogi. Our waitress was young and pretty and Katharine and I wondered if she worked in the club on alternate nights. We paid for dinner with the Visa card; I don't know what side of the border the restaurant was on. The food was very good; we were the only customers.

We spent the night with friends in Vancouver and the next day we went downtown and bought good boots for Katharine and Madeline. Then I caught the Greyhound back to Seattle and the next morning at five I got on the city bus for the long ride out to Sea-Tac to catch the 7 a.m. cheap flight to O'Hare. The bus was packed with people going to work—it was jolly, everyone knew each other, most of the passengers were black. Some ways into the trip a friendly man sat down next to me and we talked about this and that for a while and he asked if I was on my way to a job. I replied that I was on my way to Illinois to get my car and then to drive it back here and then on into Canada. "It's a ridiculous story," I said, feeling oddly apologetic as I imagined—maybe there on the bus for the first time—the many huge states I'd soon be driving across for days. We were near my companion's stop and as he gathered himself into his coat and rose he reminded me that I had to do what I had to do and that, throughout it, I should hang tough. "And we'll see you when you get back," he said as he got off the bus, blessing me and my ridiculous story.

Seattle had been, as usual, warm and humid; Chicago was harsh—a slate sky and that wind. Out some distance from the main terminals at O'Hare is the interface with various types of more public transit—the subway, the buses. You have to walk outside, into the wind, to get there. I was headed for the subway and asked directions of a black man in a uniform of some sort—he was standing out at the end of a concrete pier over parking lots and bus stops, over a basin of vehicular activity. Many of the men and women I'd been with on the city bus in

Seattle had been wearing uniforms similar to his, generic uniforms, the kind likely to have your name sewn in above the breast pocket. Frederick Douglass once described the poor fabric of his own clothes as "negro cloth." Nearby a group of black boys, eleven- and twelve-year-olds, was running for a bus— "Hold the goddamn motherfucka," the fat boy called to his friends who were closer to it, "*hold* that motherfucka!" His voice hadn't changed yet, it was shrill and loud, the shriek of a child. Everyone on the pier turned and looked. "You *know* that's the projects bus," the man in the uniform said, classing us off, separating himself and me from the boys.

I went down to Union Station and got the Texas Eagle back to Bloomington. My friend Ron Strickland met me at the Amtrak depot in Normal—Bloomington's twin city, the municipality across Division Street—and helped me, the next day, get through some errands. I bought the Swede an oil change and a new Sony radio; I tried to buy a block warmer but Süd's, the local dealership, didn't carry them—"There's been no call for 'em around here," the service manager said, and assured me I could get one "up there where you're going." By three o'clock I'd done all the car stuff and was almost ready to be on my way again.

There was the typical confusion about drugs—Katharine was going to need prescriptions refilled and soon—so I spent my last moments in Bloomington at the Osco pharmacy counter reviewing the rules for the international shipment of medications. The pharmacist and I divided the pills up into several little bottles and I put some of those into a FedEx envelope and, on the way out of town, dropped it in the collection box near Stahly's Truck City. It would get to Fort George before I did. I swung out onto Veterans then and took it across town: I'm usually out there on its eastern route but it loops west too, around the southern edge of Bloomington and out to the interchanges on the far side of things. The sun was beginning to set when I got on I-74 and headed north and west across the prairie, crossing the Illinois River at Peoria and getting through that town's hills and back up onto the flats before it got totally dark. The landscape would change again at the Mississippi River and Iowa was on the other side of that. Fort George was days and plains and mountains away, almost unimaginable. Still in Illinois, in the dark, I pulled in an NPR or Pacifica talk show from out ahead in Iowa City—there was a long segment on a group of women, nurses, I think, who ministered to homeless men who were dying of AIDS in some city, somewhere in this country. Guys different from me, guys who had nothing. Some were reticent, some were very needy. Some could be courted—out of their reticence, out of their embarrassment at their situation. One woman, speaking haltingly, said she felt a strange kind of honor or privilege—a feeling she'd not expected to encounter in herself when she'd begun this work—to be out there at the hour of someone's death with that person, to be able to walk the guy out to whatever was out there, she said, to walk with him right up to the gape of the edge.

January 1995, a little teary-eyed, alone in the car, on my way to Canada.

Ways Over

I was always going to Canada, the next country.

Years before, when we lived in Ithaca, New York, I'd phoned my parents in Dayton to say I was bicycling up to North Bay, Ontario, in a few days and my father asked whether I knew that that was where his father's brother had lived. Yes, I said, way *up* in Canada. He countered that it wasn't all that far and told me that we'd once almost driven there, impulsively, when we'd been in Sault Ste. Marie and he'd seen a road sign for the place that said it was ninety miles away but my mother, he said, had nixed the trip. I hadn't known any of that but I remembered the day—1959, when I was eight and my parents, my sister, and I had been staying in a cottage we'd rented near Mackinaw City in Michigan. The drive to Sault Ste. Marie had been a day outing from the cottage, across that strip of the Upper Peninsula and on into Canada—my first ever trip to Canada—over a drawbridge which I recall with almost perfect clarity: we'd had to wait for a boat to get itself past the bridge and two or three bicyclists had glided by our stopped car, stopping themselves farther up in the line of traffic where lowered gates blocked entrance to the part of the roadway that had actually risen. An hour later we were picnicking at a roadside park in Ontario and on a track on a ridge next to us a steam locomotive sans train raced by (the last one, aside from tourist excursion items, I ever saw or remember seeing), this also a memory of incredible clarity.

My mother got on the extension and reminded my father that my grandfather had never had anything good to say about his brother. And she reminded me about her considered opinion that long-lost relatives should *stay* lost—"If you run into any Giscombes up there," she said, "just don't give them this address." Her tone was jocular but then she was silent, waiting for me to agree to that.

This was in September of 1988. The day before I was due to leave I was on my bike, blasting down the hill from my job at Cornell: I was in a hurry and I was thinking about North Bay more than the Fiat Spider that had stopped abruptly in front of me, its driver desiring to let a pretty woman walk across the street in front of him. When I did realize the car wasn't moving it was too late to do anything but slam on the just-adjusted-for-the-trip-to-Canada brakes, skid into his bumper, fly over his trunk, hit Campus Drive, and bounce into the far curb. I was on my feet in a second, though, yelling at him about not having brake lights and the pretty woman was yelling at him too, though I suppose the accident was really my fault, whether he had brake lights or not. My shoulder hurt rather badly and I was scraped up and bleeding but was able to ride the rest of the way home, even with the nasty wobble the front wheel had acquired.

By the time I got to our house, though, the ache in my shoulder was getting worse and starting to worry me: the year before, when we'd been living in Britain, I'd broken my clavicle in another cycling accident and though the break had healed quickly—three weeks later I was back, if uncomfortably, on the bike—having it had not been a pleasant experience. I'd known it was broken before I got to the hospital: the pain was intense and, when I'd felt the bone with my fingers, there was an obtuse angle where before it had been straight. This didn't hurt as badly and the clavicle's angle was the same as I'd got used to it being; but the injury was in the same general area and the X-ray technician at the British hospital had told me that broken clavicles were the most common of the serious cycling mishaps, that that was, in fact, how she had broken hers. So I was afraid I might have a hairline fracture or one of those hideously subtle things like torn ligaments, things I knew little about. Katharine drove me up to the hospital at the edge of Ithaca, where they poured hydrogen peroxide in the cuts and X-rayed my shoulder.

When I was ten I'd fallen from a grape arbor playing Tarzan, an irony that I didn't see then, and broken both my arms, the left one terribly. Gangrene set in, as they say, and I lost the arm to that above my elbow, all this the week before Easter, 1961. Thirty-something years now of prosthetic devices, a 1-Y deferment (though I was in college during Vietnam and no one I knew or even knew of in college was ever called), and an inability to play the guitar. And odd, contradictory ideas about mortality, since, for a while, the smart money had been on me dying: on one hand I knew that it wasn't how things were on TV, that anyone could in fact cash in at any time, any place. I mean I'd found out: I was in Miami Valley Hospital for some months back then and other kids I knew in the hospital died there. But on the other hand—the one I no longer had—I felt immortal, bulletproof, for years because of it, because of having gotten closer than most up into the obvious face of death; and I figured that coming back maimed by the experience was enough and that I didn't have to pay any more. My sister, the psychology Ph.D., would say that this is because I've never known anything about probability.

The doctor in Ithaca was young and eager to please, he laughed at my jokes. The X rays had showed that all was right except—and here he gently manipulated the shoulder, staring off into space, feeling the thing for himself—that it moved with surprising ease, perhaps because of the amputation and the weight of the prosthesis, he said, into and out of dislocation. He shrugged his own shoulders and gave me leave to start for Canada whenever I felt ready.

I rested for the better part of a week and then got on the road. The first day out was unpleasant and all through it I kept hearing the doctor's words and worrying over them. The second day was awful, a forced march, but the third was better and by the time I ferried across the mouth of the St. Lawrence that evening I had stopped looking back.

2 (May 1970)

I was sitting with a woman on a hillside overlooking a stream excavated into a canal: we were drinking a dollar bottle of sweet wine and discussing whether we were in New York, where I was old enough, or Vermont, where I wasn't. Where we were was at a country intersection in a lush system of valleys and rises, the southern foothills of the Adirondacks and the Green Mountains: the one road came in, from someplace called Comstock, on a one-lane bridge over the stream and

T'd into U.S. 4, the two-lane we'd been traveling on. She was two years older than I was—old enough anywhere—and white, both of which were, for me, off-putting. But there was much about her, certainly, to counteract those or at least challenge them. She was complicated—she probably still is—and I'm sorry we never got beyond a point where all or most settings were, simply, difficult.

To the west, from the south, a train was coming, we heard the diesel horn a mile or so off but clear and sudden over our shoulders: there was something wild too in the sound and we jogged across Route 4 to where a gravel road went up—through a wide break in the trees—to the lip of a set of railroad tracks. The horn went again, much closer this time, and a moment later the train eased into view and stopped: a huge, long-snouted blue-and-yellow diesel locomotive, three or four blue-and-yellow passenger cars behind it. There was no station house, but a pink-faced conductor stepped down from the first coach and placed a footstool on the gravel so that two Hispanic ladies could step daintily, with his hand at their elbows, off the train: they were dressed in beautifully colored dresses, great dashes and flowers of color, open-toe high heels, and summer hats. It was a wild moment there in the middle of nowhere: the train taking off, resuming its trip, myself in my Levi's, desert boots, and raggedy shirt along with a white woman dressed more or less the same way, and the two Spanish women *them*selves up here in what did turn out to be New York, dusty upstate with the sun beating down on all of us. They asked if we knew where they could get a bus, or maybe they said *the* bus, but we didn't and so they commenced hiking off into the distance, their heels clicking across the bridge, on out of sight.

We were hitchhiking, which I did then with a certain passion, and got eventually that long, long weekend to Montreal, my first trip there. We went to an all-day music thing at some stadium on the edge of the city, smoked a lot of hashish, talked very little, and had great difficulty getting out of town on the arterials, the hash making it seem less "interesting" than interminable, but by then enough time and adventures had passed so that I was no longer enamored of her or of being on the road and that may have helped too. By dawn, though, the high had worn off completely and we were still within sight of the Jacques-Cartier Bridge: we were perched, or collapsed, on a guardrail at the edge of some four-lane and there was no traffic, it being Sunday morning. Finally a provincial cop stopped and buzzed us out to near the border, where another, better traveled, road merged with the one we were on. The ride hadn't been an offer. He'd said "Get in" unambiguously and then turned ambiguous in that way cops *have* when I'd asked where he might be taking us: he said, "I'll give you a good ride," but I was too worn out to press him and gladly did I accept the real offer which came a second later—his right hand poised over his shoulder holding the opened wide-mouth Canadian pack—of a cigarette.

It's a young person's habit, smoking, a thing for those whose bodies can take abuse without flinching, a thing for people who live more casually than I can now that I'm past forty, that age taking the edge off immortality. But that morning I'd been out for hours and to this moment I remember the taste of the one the cop gave me, how I smoked it in my nineteen-year-old life in the clean backseat of that car that had no door or window handles, no way out. (It was a Player's straight, *sans filtre*: creamy and crisp and bitter at once.)

My second trip to Canada, my first to Montreal. I don't remember the border crossing either way.

(That's not true. An interracial couple picked us up after the cop dropped us off and we all stopped someplace for coffee, Joan complaining when she came back from the ladies' that no one—meaning, I suppose, me—had told her that her nose was sunburned red, that she looked like a clown, she said. The man was in the Air Force, at the base in Plattsburgh, bigger and somewhat darker than me; the woman was smaller and older than Joan, she looked haggard. They looked an exaggeration of us in some way, some circumstance I figured was less difficult, but there's no real reason for me to think that. I remember that they said something in low voices to one another once and then kissed as he was driving and I recall wondering if the man's uniform would get us back in, would get us effortlessly through Customs, given the racial makeup of the car, but it or something absolutely did, which is probably why my memory of the crossing itself is so hazy. We must have stopped after that, since I bought a pack of cigarettes from the machine at the diner and I remember that they were L&Ms, a U.S. brand. We all smoked through our coffee and I remember feeling quite comfortable, the first time I'd felt that way in days, but don't recall what we talked about. He got the check for all of us.)

3

By the time I was twenty-eight I'd been off cigarettes for a year and was feeling good enough to become interested in my bicycle, the orange Gitane I'd bought years before on impulse during my first week in graduate school at Cornell. In Ithaca riding means riding over very steep hills and soon I was able to do it, to make it all around town without stopping, taking a pleasure in my body I'd not had in the almost twenty years since I'd lost my arm. I think I'd rediscovered, or simply discovered, the possibility of physical grace and in the spring of my twenty-ninth year I figured it was time to try bicycle touring, since it combined that new grace with camping—which I'd always loved—and that uncertainty (*where will we be tenting tonight?*) which I've always needed. So my day trips got longer in the name of practice, I spent some money on a set of bottom-of-the-line panniers, and early in the fall of 1980 I took off one morning for Montreal, three hundred some odd miles away.

The third day out was the best, as I came to realize in later trips that it always was or is, and in midafternoon I had my first view of Canada and the wide St. Lawrence. A couple of hours later I got to the big bridge at Ogdensburg, New York—a hundred miles upriver from Montreal—, one of those two-lane steel-deck monsters that rises and then falls precipitously. There was a toll house at the start-up but the man waved me past, calling out that I should just be careful when I got up on top. Border talk. I was and cruised down the far side into Canada feeling good in that breeze that came off the river and feeling good too to be leaving the U.S.A. behind me for a little while. This was more than adventure, it was the *unlikely* adventure of bicycling alone to another country, and more, it was the promise I'd made myself when I'd stopped smoking— this was sport, this was an athletic prowess hitherto beyond myself, this was *grace*. The man at Customs/Douanes came out, looked at me knowingly, and asked, "Ever been in trouble with the law?"

3.5

Most Canadians live within a hundred miles of the U.S., sandwiched between us (us?) and that Canadian *space* above them. "Border towns," someone said in an Orson Welles movie from the fifties, "bring out the worst in both cultures"; the line stuck with me because it seemed patently false, so *much* of a lie, and yet was delivered with the ring of truth or at least the spirit of wise inquiry. I only understood it years later when someone pointed the obvious out to me: that the film—*Touch of Evil*—was about miscegenation.

3.7

Seven falls later—October 1987—and I did the trip to Montreal again. This time, though, I went the hard way, through the Adirondacks, and approached downtown from the south—over the car-and-bus-choked Pont Jacques-Cartier—during rush hour. (At the border they'd been suspicious and wanted to know how much money I had: they'd been satisfied when I showed my Visa card.) I checked into the guesthouse where Katharine and I always stayed at the east end of downtown, napped for an hour and then went out and wandered some, feeling unusually lonely, lost in spirit as I ranged that night down Rue Ste.-Catherine. I was trying to snap out of my funk by walking at a quick, city pace when I passed a short white man my age whose look I recognized and, since I was by then close to forty, who I was glad to have left behind me. He caught up, though, at the next corner and when the light changed we walked across together, both of us looking over at an ambulance screaming by down the middle of one-way Ste.-Catherine. "Everybody gets to ride in one of those sooner or later," he said. It was then, when he turned to speak, that I caught the wildness of his eye—before, it had been the way he was walking, I think, that had clued me to his being a certain crazed garrulous type, a type that finds me attractive. But an apocryphal story on Abe Lincoln has him, during one of his visits across the Potomac, tipping his stovepipe to a slave who had tipped his straw hat to the President, and explaining his behavior to a white companion with "I'd not want him to think he was more of a gentleman than me"; I responded to my companion that I was going to try to put off the ambulance ride for as long as possible and he agreed that that was a good idea. He didn't like the East much, he volunteered then, all these laid-back businesspeople. I liked the mix of cultures, I said, the sense of possibility and adventure that a big city brought. He owned that he was in the import/export field out of Vancouver and was used to "dealing with Chinese," in whose language "there ain't no *word* for mañana." Perhaps he thought I was Hispanic. We walked on like that to the end of the block, where he turned south, calling over his shoulder, "Good luck in your travels, m'sieur!"

It's a version of the blessing I'd get years later from a black man on the Seattle airport bus: other side of the border, other side of the continent. I'd been right, of course, about whatever it was I'd recognized when first I'd passed my little white man this night in Montreal: something crazed on his part with a soft racial edge to it—the Chinese, the Latinos, and where am I in all that? But he spoke so casually about mortality, and what was it he understood that allowed him to sing out such a parting blessing—*Good luck*—even if it was, arguably, mixed?

3.9

We were always going to Montreal. By car, by train. We'd rent a room at the cheap, clean Armour Tourist Hotel on East Sherbrooke and go Christmas shopping there back in the eighties when we had a little money—the Bay, Eaton's, the funky shops down by the river—in those years we lived in upstate New York. We were always going to Montreal but alone I was always going to Canada, the slow fade across the border, over the St. Lawrence by bridge or ferry, going on across into that deep geography: forms of land and water against which the national must, I'd think, define itself. And define itself also against the U.S. and what passes here for municipal culture or New World Order or whatever this country is selling now. Whatever's being broadcast. George Bowering talked about "the antenna grope for Buffalo TV," that in a poem written before cable. The gaze across water at the islands of another place.

4

The second time I went to Burlington, Vermont, I came in at dusk on the ferry across Lake Champlain from Port Kent, New York—the lake forms that part of the borders of New York, Vermont, and Quebec. This was summer 1971, I was with Chase Sebor, a white man my age, a friend from school, and when the boat touched shore we commenced a walking tour of downtown, looking at the locals and letting them see us, the way of twenty-year-olds everywhere. Another young man—I still recall clearly his thick blond hair and mustache, his wild eye—approached us in a park and welcomed us to the venue, turning his head to assure *me* that "people treat each other decent in this town."

An article about Vermont in a 1991 or 1992 *Ebony* refers to it as "the whitest state in the country," demographics proving that true. Though I had understood that the blond man's speech was rooted in his idea of race, I'd not been aware of how anomalous I most likely was when we walked that evening through Burlington. Nor had I been, of course, when I'd landed there the first time, more or less on account of a sudden, drenching rainstorm that had come up out of nowhere when I was traveling alone earlier that summer. I'd actually spent precious little time in Burlington proper then: I'd been planning to camp in my own company on the Ottauquechee River out in eastern Vermont but instead I found myself huddled for two hours in a diner downtown drinking coffee and talking about movies with some New York City people I'd met earlier on the road and then we'd all caught a little bus out into the country north of town. The rain had stopped sometime during the bus trip and when we got off we walked for a long time in sunshine out a dirt road that wound way into the hills, eating oranges and apples that the woman named Ciska had had in her pack, until we got to someone's cabin by a railroad track where we spent a long night of various improvisations. Lots of pleasant impromptu.

But out of that trip I wrote rather much, mostly out of a kind of twenty-year-old desolation that greets its lonely self everywhere, that finds reference in all settings. In one poem, though, I had been able to see myself clearly, myself with my friends from that trip together with them and separate at once in the way of the world, that poem titled "A Nigger and a Hippie."

4.5

Years later I sailed from Port Kent into Burlington again, this time right ahead of Hurricane Gloria. This was in 1985, the year before Madeline's birth, and that city was the pivot point in a several days' cycling trip: I'd intended from Burlington to go either on over into New Hampshire or up into the townships east of Montreal, which I'd never seen. And since I'd been on the road for almost a week, it was time to do a general repair—laundry, shower, dinner in a decent restaurant.

I set up my tent at a park on Lake Champlain at the northern edge of town. It was late afternoon then and the weather was getting weirder: the sky was bright but hazy and the wind was gusting in any number of directions. On the lake, people in wet suits were trying to ride their windsurf boards among the whitecaps. I showered at the park's bathhouse and went back into town to see a man I'd met and liked a year earlier, an English professor at the University of Vermont. It was cordial but a little tense, as I suppose I'd expected it would be: I'm not the good visitor I might have been able to pass for once, I don't have an easy way of being able to drop into somewhere where there's no agenda, and so I'd begun to get nervous on the ferry, which probably guaranteed that the visit would be awkward. I think my man is the same way, which is probably why I found myself attracted to him to begin with—but then there are the two of us being like that in the same difficult space, that awkward setting.

The next morning it was drizzling and the park owners were walking around warning everyone of the coming hurricane. They'd put me on a bluff with another biker, a blond man with a Swedish name from Madison, Wisconsin, so we could split the $6 campsite fee, and as they explained to us which trees could conceivably—though not likely—fall when the wind got to the predicted speed, my bunkmate was getting visibly nervous. While I sat in my tent and wrote in my journal he went off to make phone calls, coming back to announce that he was going to ride this one out in a cheap motel he'd found by letting his fingers do the walking and did I want to join him? I thanked him for the offer but declined and he broke camp to head out to wherever it was. I left my tent up and headed into town with a load of laundry in one of my panniers and the three-prong plan of Laundromat, food, and a movie.

I spent that rainy afternoon watching *Kiss of the Spider Woman* and then *The Ploughman's Lunch*. The theater was staffed by an attractive group of people in their twenties and thirties and—when I hung out in the lobby in between shows—I watched as they cavorted around through their own intrigues, their own gossipings. My friend, the professor I'd seen the night before, and his family had gone off across the lake to some land they owned in the Adirondacks. Later, after the second film ended, I had dinner at the counter in a diner downtown—grey rainy centerless light outside—wondering if it was the same place where I'd hunched over in a booth fourteen years earlier and held forth about Robert Altman's movies, which were new then. The waitress was my age and harried, distracted by something I didn't know anything about. Outside, an old black man with a silver conk and a neat mustache had been sitting under an awning on the pedestrian mall and had stared at me as I wheeled my bike by, declining to return my nod, but when I'd finished my dinner and come out it was a late, drizzly twilight and he was gone.

In the morning I realized I was sick of the infinity of outward and headed south—back toward home instead of farther on. I pushed it hard all day, crossing into New York at Fair Haven in late afternoon, and, by the time darkness came, I was in the middle of nowhere, scruffy upstate with the moon beating down on me. The map said I was twelve miles or so away from Hudson Falls, where I figured I could either camp or crash at a cheap motel, so I pressed on into the night. I came down a hill, though, and suddenly all was awash with light and I realized that I was cruising through huge Great Meadows State Prison, Comstock, New York. Medium-security, razor-wired Honor Block was on the north side of the road, the immense sprawl of the rest of the prison was on the other—it stretched up a hill under guard towers, immense, well lit, and absolutely terrifying. I'd realized years before—I don't remember exactly when—that the prison was where the two Hispanic ladies I'd seen get off a train in 1970 were most likely heading, but this was the first time I'd ever seen *it*, the first time I'd ever been on the road they'd disappeared down. I realized that night, though, in among all the instinctual terror, that soon I'd come to the old girder bridge they'd crossed and pass then the weedy country inter-section where I'd shared a bottle of Richard's Wild Irish Rose with a woman I'd liked very much once: a squirt of nostalgia for a former more innocent self, a little burst to get me past the slammer, past the vision of the prison house. But the road had been rebuilt: it crossed the Champlain Canal *and* the railroad tracks on a high curvy arch and met the relocated and widened Route 4 in a flurry of turn lanes and streetlights. I swung south and headed on back into the dark, quick and disappointed, feeling a touch more than casually tragic.

4.7

But the touch of the local on one—on myself—is what I'm always wanting when I travel, something specific, an order not with myself at some "still center" but getting—as we say—*over* and getting the physical self—*my ass*, as we say—over something in the way, both. Plus there's the solitude I need, my own restlessness—or rootlessness—, the way my sister and I were raised, the incredible self-consciousness we both have which I trace back in myself at least as far as kindergarten, the self-consciousness that cut me off—as my arm was severed and yet I am alive, escaped alone to tell thee—from many, many assumptions, from much. The need then to make a knowing cultural statement out of the weight of many things, like jazz is made—a made thing—out of what else but other things and in the specificity of place, or *against* that. Katharine says the important thing is "being portable." When I travel I need to go far enough to see the country change before I turn around and come back. (To see it bend, as if to my will?) "People remember you," my mother said once, more than once, meaning it as praise for what she understood to be my *presence* and as a warning that I should watch myself, both. When a black friend—a Cornell professor—had gone to one of the state prisons near Ithaca to talk about books and writing with the convicts there, the white guard who let him in looked at him knowingly and remarked, "We got a lotta guys in here look just like you."

4.8

Actually my trip to Montreal with Joan Schoonmaker was my third time in Canada—not the second, as I claim somewhere in the story before this. Memory rights itself again and again. The second time was with other kids from Camp Kern in Dayton. I was old enough in the summer of 1964 to go on the camp's week-long trips and one of these was to a park on Lake Erie in Ontario. We went up in two or three vans and set up a tent city at a campground; we were noisy enough once for the police to come, not the park cops but the actual Ontario Provincial Police in a white-and-black cruiser with "O.P.P." on the door. One of my fellows, a kid named Al Johnson, suggested that they be called the Ontario Party Poopers and I've never been able to think of anything but that whenever I'm in the province and am passed by one of their cars. The O.P.P. out making their rounds.

Al was black and he tented with a Jewish kid named Brad Donoff; Jews were at least as rare at Y camp as black people were but they—Al and Brad—were the most popular of any of us. They were older, fifteen, I think, and seemed wise and aloof—even beyond their proficiency at various athletics—, different. They inhabited an apparently effortless grace. I don't know where I was in all that, I don't know how or if my camp-mates remember me.

We'd gone up Interstate 75 to Detroit and then taken a bridge over into Windsor. I *really* don't recall Customs and I don't know, either, what side of the river we were on when we saw the woman. She was on a sidewalk by a wall near the bridge with children a little younger than us—or she was *near* the children anyway, perhaps proximity supplied a relationship for us. And she was *sexy* in ways that we all—out of our experiences with *Playboy* or even television—recognized. She was big-boned and out in public in a tight dress, a light-skinned black woman with straight brown hair; the children were significantly darker than she was. One of us called "Those your kids?" but not nearly loud enough for her to hear—it was a joke for us and there were giggles and loud smirks but then someone else hissed "Shut up!" I think, looking back on it, that this call to silence was a liberal sentiment produced for my benefit—our counselor was outside doing something and Al was in another van—but I didn't feel it as racial until later. The call to silence was followed by actual silence, the mark of shame (or at least embarrassment) that sexual joking among teenage boys *never* produces. Racial joking does—I've witnessed the silence enough over the years to recognize it now. But I'd not thought about that then, race: it was just puzzling to me, the comment, as the sex talk of older boys often was. I don't know what they were thinking: I wondered, much later, if they'd not realized she was black but I don't think she was light enough; perhaps I underestimate their abilities and sophistication—maybe they understood the hierarchy that U.S. black people have placed on skin tone and saw the "fact" of her darker-than-her children as a funny statement in that welter of assigned values, something having to do with the concentration of white folks in her past that was apparent, maybe even to them. But I don't know—I don't know, even now, what white people say to their children about miscegenation. I do know the old phrase "Bright, light, and damn near white," one of the rhymes we still use, a funny gesture at a hokey emblem of privilege among us.

Which is related, of course, to another thing we joke about, our ability to spot one another, no matter how pale the skin or "good" the hair—"Blood will tell," we say. We'll laugh but there's truth there; because black is such a big category, because such a wide range of people's bodies count as black, we're used to looking at people in a fairly discerning way. We're used to tricking the shade of an identity out of the mass of European features, to coming upon the African trace there in the countenance. To seeing the "creole" or the "Spanish" or the "Gypsy" for what it is. It's a meeting we search for. Whiteness is different, is defined by the absence of non-whiteness among the forebears; it's a celebration, as far as I've ever been able to tell, of not mixing. Or a *claim* of not having mixed.

Strikingly, on our trip to Ontario in 1964, we encountered no Canadians (except for the O.P.P. cop); we kept to ourselves and there were enough of us for that to be easy. It's a trip full of disembodied parts, strange icons. When I think about going to Canada that time seeing the woman on the bridge is one of the events I recall—but my memory of the trip itself's always a sudden memory, it's one that's not in the front of my mind, one that's easy not to remember as a-trip-to-Canada.

(So this was a journey out of the Midwest to the next country that took place thirty years prior to my arrival at Fort George. But it's no seed, even if the plains of northern Ohio resemble the Illinois prairie I crossed in our Volvo on my solitary way north and west, even though Canada's still the other country it was then. There's no leading metaphor here even though the reason I'd chosen that particular week at Camp Kern was *because* that was the week of the camp's trip to Canada. Border crossings are always sexy. And racial. This I did understand, on some level, even as a child. You leave *something* behind when you wade out into that water. But those are things to elucidate about later, when you're past forty and back from England and Jamaica and Fort George. Canada to me at thirteen? Once we got there we dodged mosquitoes and swam every day in the lake. One afternoon we played an incredible hours-long game of Capture the Flag. Our bodies were changing; I pined for a lovely, irreverent girl named Brenda Marie Bailey with whom I'd just completed seventh grade. Bears had been seen in the park and Marvin Applegate claimed that one had chased him when he was walking alone to the concession stand. Some of us left half of our dinners out one night and sat up with flashlights until 2 a.m. but they never came.)

5

In June of 1990 we drove from Bloomington back east where I was to teach summer school at Cornell. Since I'd be working hard most of the summer we decided to make a bit of a holiday of the trip itself and we planned a long route up through Wisconsin and the Upper Peninsula of Michigan, over into Canada at Sault Ste. Marie and through North Bay and Kaladar, and back into the States via the Wolfe Island ferries.

Halfway through the second day we stopped in Gladstone, on the Upper Peninsula, to indulge Madeline's wish for a playground: swings, a teeter-totter, monkey bars, etc., all in a pretty little city park fronting on Lake Michigan. As she was climbing up the ladder to the slide a group of seven- or eight-year-old boys was playing nearby on the swings—painted metal horses suspended from a set of pivots on a bar above them—and one of them began to declaim about how his pal, because his horse was painted black, was "riding a nigger horse." He found this amusing enough to repeat a couple of times though his friends had nothing to say in response and the two teenaged girls lounging nearby put on blank faces or perhaps they'd been wearing them all along.

I thought about what I should do. I think Madeline, who was four then, was concentrating too much on her own playing for the voices of kids across a playground to have made any impression on her. And I don't know if the boy—a wiry little blond—was aware of the word as anything other than something having to do with the color black that older kids or, as likely, his parents made jokes about. But neither do I know that it wasn't our presence in his playground that had inspired him to begin his nigger horse joke: I mean, though he seemed to be ignoring us, not as a message in itself but as children in a group will typically be unaware of the people surrounding them, I don't *know* that his talking so wasn't a bold, sly way of seeing what he could say and get away with in front of a black adult; I've seen children do this sort of thing, and seem to remember having done things like it myself as I'd dangle from the monkey bars.

I watched his acrobatics, his hideous grace, and was conscious of myself then *as* an adult, a person with the advantages of that status, just as white people have the advantages— whether they understand that or not—of their status in this old world. I watched him being energetic: now on the horses, now at the jungle gym: he was Tarzan-like in his flips, always catching himself, the way Johnny Weissmuller had managed to keep sleekly ahead of that squad of dusky extras, leaving us in his dust as he'd bop through the Hollywood-built jungles. What status does irony have in this old world? Anyway, I resolved to do nothing until he said or did something that I could construe as an affront directed at us. I let Madeline play a *long* time so as to give him the opportunity, but it never happened. I mean, I'd intended, had he referred to us as niggers, even to his friends, or something like that, to squat down next to him and talk to him and send him home crying with a message for his parents about what the *next* black person who even heard him say "nigger" about a metal horse would likely do to his little blond ass.

But such a warning presented to him as a public service message would have been a white lie. In his famous and much-anthologized "Letter to My Nephew," James Baldwin said: "You must accept them and accept them with love. For these innocent people have no other hope." I love Baldwin but I'm sick of that word smeared loud or soft across the mouths of white people and I'm past the point of trying to love them or feeling obligated to love them and therefore trying to save their asses or their souls or the Republic either. I was wanting instead to do something to him and to his parents—who probably loved him in their stupid way—that none of them would ever forget. The evil in me would have enjoyed that.

Back in the car leaving Gladstone, Katharine, who'd stayed in hearing distance but otherwise on the edge of things while I'd squired Madeline around, sighed over the place. The little park with its swimming beach, its vista, and its playground had, initially anyway, pleased her: it had seemed to indicate that the community of Gladstone was directed toward something positive, a statement about the prominence of the local geography, about the conjunction of land and water. In this way, she said, it had seemed different from our city, Bloomington, which is largely focused on shopping. She looked off disdainfully at the houses, at the little business district, her idea of the town was gone.

I looked way down the road toward the bridge to Canada. This was the summer I'd just finished reading Margaret Atwood's novel *The Handmaid's Tale*, the *1984*-esque book about how the

U.S. gets taken over by the religious right. Ms. Atwood's book really isn't about black folks, so we're just mentioned once or twice: people of color are referred to as "Children of Ham," that old chestnut, and sent off (off-camera) to Detroit to be resettled there on, presumably, some sort of urban reservation. The hand-maid of the title steals away (probably, or her Memorex'd tome does anyway) to Canada in one of the book's penultimate moments. It was a teachable, as we say, literary book: unambi-tious, full of the right gestures, and oddly smug in its holier-than-thou Canadianness; the last time I was in Montreal the huge graffiti on Rue St.-Denis reminded BANQUE DE MONTREAL $=APARTHEID/CANADA COMPLICE. But it had an almost nauseating resonance to real life, since that summer was also the summer of the flag-burning amendment, the summer of the Hon. Jesse Helms's continuing attack on the National Endowment for the Arts, the summer of Justice Brennan's resignation from the Court.

And we *had* been talking, I'll confess, for months before I read it—pillow talk, talk over nightcaps—about driving casu-ally into Canada and just never coming back, as the handmaid and her husband and *their* baby daughter had tried, unsuccess-fully, to do before the main action of the novel commenced. Stopped at the border, the wife arrested, the husband shot, the baby carried off by her fellow Americans. And with that in mind it felt almost good, coming down off the bridge later that day from Sault Ste. Marie, Michigan, into Sault Ste. Marie, Ontario, and being waved through Customs. We had all our stuff for the summer jammed into the back of the car and Madeline's tricycle was bungee-corded to the top. She'd been staring out the window during the entire trip through Wis-consin and the U.P. and Ontario, watching the tricycle's shadow—she confessed to me later—to make sure it didn't fall off the top of the station wagon. The trike had been making people laugh good-naturedly all the way through the trip and there were no questions for us at the frontier.

Once over, we stopped at the tourist information center and Katharine went in to gather maps and brochures while Madeline and I explored the perimeter of the building, looking out toward the Soo Locks, toward the Algoma Central yards. She'd been to Europe and had had her first birthday there but this was the first time we'd taken her across into Canada. Sault Ste. Marie had, of course, also been the site of my first moments in Canada and I tried to explain that we were in a different country now, remembering my own excitement over that thirty-one years before. But I'd been twice as old then as she was now and the idea of "country" was puzzling to her. So I told her that the last time I'd been in Sault Ste. Marie I'd seen a steam locomotive and she was polite about that but not terribly interested.

It was midafternoon by then and we were planning to shoot over to North Bay and spend the night—I'd been there before, of course, but I'd never got to it from this direction, from the Michigan border, and I was looking forward to the ride through country that was new to me. I figured we could do it in a couple of hours and see the town leisurely before getting dinner and a motel. But when we rendezvoused back at the car Katharine looked at me ruefully and reminded me that I'd told her North Bay was ninety miles or so into Ontario. She'd told the tourist lady that and had been met by a politely incredulous stare followed by headshaking and the woman pulling out a map and suggesting we could make the 250 miles in about six hours, barring incident.

Family, family, family, the primacy of that in all contexts, at all edges. So the way was much longer than my father'd presented it as being and, doubtless, this had something to do with my mother's nixing this trip three decades earlier. She looks at maps and understands them. I don't think they'd meant to set us up before when I'd been on the phone with them about North Bay but they had, oh they *had*, and Katharine and I laughed and laughed there in the parking lot, finally getting the punch line—being told the punch line by the lady at the border like she'd been waiting there—to a very old story.

Winter in Fort George

The country changed a great deal in the days it took me to get across. It was dark by the time I made it over the Iowa border but during the next day—the drive from Des Moines to Sidney, Nebraska—the landscape grew more and more desolate and, after Lincoln, the traffic thinned. From Sidney I kept west and crossed the mountainous bottom of Wyoming all in one bright cold day; I-80 follows the Amtrak route and I chased the Pioneer for an hour or so, losing it when I stopped for gas. I went inside to pay and use the facilities but the john was closed, the attendant said, the pipes having frozen, and I should just go out back. Out back was a tumbledown three-sided cowshed attached to the tumbledown gas station and I peed into the straw; it was bright and very cold but out of the wind. Around me were several nests of shit and toilet paper but there was no stink because of the temperature. I was heading toward winter's homeplace, Fort George, but it was winter everywhere. Later, just past Green River, I got off the highway and went a mile out into the actual purple sage on U.S. 30 before losing my nerve—taking the two-lane would have cut some distance off the trip but it was near dark and this was the winter and the road was utterly deserted. There'd be enough of that coming up in B.C., I figured. I got back on 80 and made it through an unpleasant, icy canyon into Ogden, Utah, and the next day drove across a corner of Idaho and on into eastern Oregon, stopping at Pendleton. I'd kept pace, through Nebraska, with a tiny woman in a huge, new Dodge truck from Pennsylvania; in Oregon I kept passing and being passed by a woman in a rattly Subaru with those green Vermont plates. Out-of-state license plates are rare in Bloomington—I don't know that I've ever seen a car from Vermont there. From Pendleton I went up into Washington and crossed the Cascades on I-90—Snoqualmie Pass—and got to Seattle at rush hour. I was coming in, though, from over the mountains, and everyone else was heading out toward the eastern suburbs: it was raining, a bright grey day, and I sailed smoothly past the stalled traffic in the oncoming lanes. (I saw one Willys-Overland wagon during the trip, in the Yakima valley just over the Washington line; I saw a few Volvos in Des Moines and Ogden but not a single one on the interstates between Bloomington and Seattle. In Wyoming the road signs had said WATCH FOR GAME, but no animals had crossed the road there or anywhere else during the trip. I ate in Chinese restaurants every night except in Sidney, where I had to settle for Pizza Hut—in Ogden I flirted a little with my waitress at the China Pearl, a young woman with two kids, returning to school; she was the first black person I'd seen for days.)

The next day I rested up at Jim and Kathryn's. She and I went out to lunch and then antiquing over in nearby Poulsbo, where I surprised a shop owner with my knowledge of her mission furniture. We have a collection and I recognized her sideboard and her rocker as second- or third-string products; the sideboard, the more interesting of the two, had likely been an industrial arts project. I spoke kindly to the owner about the pieces, though; in truth, I'd been surprised myself to find them there—I associate the furniture with the East, with its obvious makers in snowy upstate New York and bland Michigan, and it felt suddenly odd to be seeing mission here, out on the coast. Of course, I should have expected to meet it—four years earlier I'd located John Robert Giscome's obituary in the Victoria paper and there, on the same page, was a large ad for "The New Furniture": drawings of tables and chairs and desks very much like the ones that Katharine and I have made a point of procuring to sit in and write on. He died in 1907, during the short period when mission was at the first height of its popularity; I'd not put those stray facts together before I leaned into a microfilm reader at the University of British Columbia's library and found them both staring up at me from the same page's projection.

I set out again for Fort George the next day: back to Seattle on the noon ferry and then north on I-5. At Bellingham I got off the highway and went northeast on a two-lane toward the border crossing at Huntingdon, B.C., from which it's a hop, skip, and jump to the Trans-Canada. I'd stay in Hope that night, I figured, and do the rest of the way in daylight the next day. Hope's where the mountains start, where the Fraser River turns north, and where the road divides into three strands, like a braid coming undone—one strand zigzags east, another (the new toll highway) goes northeast, but I wanted the one that heads straight up into the Fraser Canyon, the Gold Rush Trail highway, Route 1. This was the turn inland: the road would go over the mountains and through the desert and up into the forest of the Cariboo, where Fort George sits—it's in the heart of the forest, it's deep inland. A drizzle had started in

Bellingham and it was still drizzling when I arrived at the border. The fellows in the Customs house were friendly as they shrugged over my documents and wished me well and a few minutes later I was on the Trans-Canada and at six o'clock I pulled into Hope. It was dark then, and still raining, but I didn't feel like I'd put in a good day of traveling—I'd started late and hadn't covered much ground. And, as I poked around Hope, halfheartedly looking for a place to stay, I began to think about the incredible Chinese restaurant I'd discovered three years earlier in Boston Bar, this on my first trip to Giscome and Fort George; I was on my bicycle and had arrived there in the dark at the end of a long day and the restaurant had been an unexpected reward—it was called the Charles Motel Coffee Shop and it was in an eccentrically rambling building that also housed a tavern and the rooms of the Charles Motel itself. I'd bought a room in the Charles Motel and gone into the Coffee Shop anticipating some sort of basic mountain fare, meat and potatoes, and had been surprised to find a menu that featured a number of Chinese dishes—my soup had been exquisite, my main course delicious. I realized that I could do it again—stay in the Charles Motel and eat good food. I drove out of town and got on Route 1, figuring I could make it to Boston Bar, forty miles north, in an hour.

Twenty or so minutes later—at Yale, B.C.—the road narrowed and a few miles after that I began to encounter patches of snow and an icy, ambiguous fog came up from somewhere. The road is gated in a few places—sometimes winter closes it—but the gates were all up, so I went on, still thinking about wonton soup and a peculiar halibut and vegetables dish that I'd seen on the menu and wanted to try. The Fraser River had become a presence—the road began to follow the river's curves and about ten miles later, at Spuzzum, I crossed it on a high steel-deck bridge. By this time snow and slush were real presences on the road and soon after the bridge the road surface itself disappeared. The fog got thicker. It wasn't fun, but then a couple of trucks came up behind me fast and sat on my bumper—the one in front flashed its lights at me and I could hear the bellow of its engine brakes. I was being urged to more speed, I suppose, or to pull off to let them by; but the road was too curvy and slick and the rocky side of a cliff was hard on my right, just across the shoulder which had seemed so generous when I was cycling here. There were temporary signs up, AVALANCHE DANGER DO NOT STOP, but there was no place to stop. The road curved and I curved with it, tapping the brakes for the man behind me but letting the transmission govern my speed, cursing not having stayed in Hope; finally a rest area appeared and I skidded off into it and the two trucks barreled past in a big cloud of white and headlights. I sat there in the turnout until a couple of others went by and then ventured back onto the road, hoping I could make it to Boston Bar before someone else in a hurry appeared in my rearview mirror. The Volvo's good in snow: it has that low center of gravity and it's fairly heavy and I can take it through anything as long as I can go as slowly as I need to go. Back on the road I found myself alone; a few trucks went past in the southbound lane— the one that's right above a fatal drop into the river itself—but I got to the long China Bar tunnel without anyone rushing me and then there were the lights of Boston Bar. I pulled into the slush of the Charles Motel parking lot, got out of the car, and discovered my knees were shaking.

The Coffee Shop was still open when I staggered into the building. It had been three years, though, and things had happened: the restaurant was under new management, the Chinese menu was gone, and the best I could do was order the steak and the french fries. The potatoes were greasy and meat was tough and tasteless. Mountain fare. A bottle of A.1. sauce helped.

Next morning, though, the breakfast they served was better and indeed the whole day went smoothly: the highway was clear and there wasn't much traffic and I made good time. At Lytton I left the Fraser and followed the Thompson River along northeast through the desert, slowing down when I went over the pass where I'd ridden through the aftermath of a truck accident back in 1991, on the cycling trip. That trip had been my introduction to this country and, this time through in the Volvo, it was still very much in my mind as a series of overlays and comparisons. (I'd driven this road once since that—the snowy November trip in the rented Chevrolet I mentioned— but I was with Katharine and Madeline then; this was the first time I'd been up here alone since biking it and alone's an important designation for me: it's not better, necessarily, but it's different, profoundly itself—there's alone and then there's everything else.) I left the Thompson just before Cache Creek and drove up the hill to Clinton and on through 100 Mile House and when I got to Lac la Hache at two o'clock I was conscious of the end of this trip looming before me and felt the pangs of that. Just north of Lac la Hache is where I'd met another solo biker—he was very young, in his twenties, and he was coming south from Alaska, heading for San Francisco, chasing the good weather; I, of course, had been finding the climate just fine—this had been a beautiful fall day, bright and about fifty degrees. "Why'd you wait so late in the year," he'd asked me, "to start your trip?" I'd not been looking for the spot where he'd swooped across the road to speak to me, it just came up—a sudden memory—when I got to it. But on the short steep hill out of Williams Lake I did look, without success, for the Sasquatch carving I'd seen out in front of a taxi-dermist's shop. Stories of the Sasquatch—the Woods Man, Dzonoqua, "Bigfoot"—get told all through British Columbia and have been told there for a very long time; John R. must have heard them. The tracks tend to be the palpable thing: the creature itself—if there *is* a creature, if the creature is something other than us or our imaginations of it—is glimpsed very rarely and most often, it seems, at a distance. If there's a creature out there in those woods it's beyond us somehow: inaccessible, unfindable, mute. The carving I remembered having seen had been chainsaw art, but it was unusual—the being that had emerged from the block of wood had been star-tlingly lithe and had had more human features then we usually fancy Bigfoot as possessing and I was disappointed when it wasn't at the place where it had been before.

At Quesnel I picked up a CBC show called *Definitely Not the Opera*, a hip Saturday afternoon event from Winnipeg, and listened to a breathless woman named Cathy Bond talk about "bad girl" movies. Quesnel had been the place from which John R. and McDame left for their 1862–63 expedition to the Peace; and Quesnel had been the place where, on my first trip, I'd put up my tent in the courtyard of a motel and then gone downtown to see *Point Break*, Kathryn Bigelow's film about surfing, loyalty, Southern California life, and bank robbery. (The film had been insistently picaresque and overlong and, finally, Brechtian; kids in the theater had thrown spitballs at each other during its expository stretches and screamed "Fuck you!" to their friends. It had been an overwhelming movie and I'd had a brief but profound shock when I stepped out of the theater and got hit with the wet stench of Quesnel's huge paper mill. This was not California, this was the North, this was the stink of inland.) From Quesnel it's seventy miles to

Prince George and I covered those easily and found 137 South Lyon Street and was greeted by Katharine and Madeline. The last day had been such a slack and easy trip—I'd ambled along listening to a pleasurable radio show and the weather had been mild enough, even though there was snow on the ground, for me to idly wish that I was on my bicycle—that I had little sense of having come across the continent.

But here I was, finally, sitting at the kitchen table in Fort George with my wife, sipping on a whiskey sour. It had been cold, she said, and she and Madeline had walked in that to the bank, the grocery store, to Madeline's school, around the neighborhood. It'd been cold but the boots they'd bought in Vancouver were good, their jackets and hats were good—it was pleasurable, Katharine said, to be out walking in the snow on those afternoons and mornings. People had been nice, especially John Harris and Barry McKinnon. This was the fifteenth of January, this would be OK, the rest of winter stretched out before us. And Fort George lay all around us and around Fort George were the woods and the mountains. And those rivers.

We had dinner—Katharine made it, normally that's my job—but I can't recall what we ate. Afterward it was time for Madeline and my after-dark ritual, Night Patrol. She and I had started it during the fall we lived in Vancouver, a simple evening walk around wherever we are, wherever we happen to be. It's a trip out "to see what's what"; we don't do it every night. Sometimes it lasts twenty minutes, occasionally it goes for an hour and a half. We've gone out on Night Patrol here in Bloomington and in the Jamaican countryside at the edge of Mandeville, once in the industrial wasteland around a Motel 6 in Columbus, Ohio, on Saltspring Island, in the Maine woods, and in Moose Jaw, Saskatchewan. We've been barked at, had headlights flashed at us, and been observed suspiciously by screech owls; we've seen people undressing in front of open windows and we've smelled the warm, ubiquitous and oddly comforting smell of laundry in the winter evening air.

This night we walked the two blocks to the snowy end of Lyon Street, to the place where there's a little bluff overlooking the CN track and the Nechako River—this was the edge of town or an edge of town and there, on the railroad below us, was a black fox. "*Vulpes africanus*," I said aloud, but of course it was really old *Vulpes fulva* in the black phase, a color variation common around Fort George. The fox trotted down the track and out of our range of sight. There was a path down to all that but it was icy and a little mysterious and forbidding, so we agreed to save it for later, to do it first in the daylight.

Giscome, B.C.

Three and a half years earlier, July 1991. I was having coffee with my old friend Rajani Sudan on the sun-drenched deck outside Willard Straight Hall at Cornell. She's one of the few people I met in Ithaca—during the long years I lived in that town—who were actually born there. Her parents had come to the U.S., to Ithaca, from India when her father, a plasma expert, accepted an academic position at Cornell University, which is where we met: she was a Cornell undergraduate when I arrived there from Albany to go to graduate school in the seventies and she was a graduate student herself during the eighties, the years that I worked as editor of the Cornell magazine *Epoch* and taught part-time in the English Department. When I'd decided to leave all that for good I walked around New Orleans with her during a Modern Language Association convention, this in 1988, the year we were both looking and interviewing. I'd wanted to have a straight academic job—I'd finally had it with being on the academic fringes—and at the convention I got my tenure-line contract at Illinois State. Rajani found a three-year position at Bowdoin, in Brunswick, Maine.

But people drift back, on various pretexts, to beautiful Ithaca in the summers and early that afternoon, after we'd both been at our respective institutions for a couple of years, there we were, sitting on the deck outside Willard Straight: from there both the curve of Cayuga Lake to the north and the forested Inlet Valley to the south are visible, a hundred-mile view if you're willing to rotate your head. By then I'd been at Illinois State long enough to begin to understand how it could be *so* other from Cornell; and I'd also come to understand that my work in such a large and public institution was important and different from ways in which it might be important or might have been important once at an exclusive place like Cornell. And yet again there was much about the situation of actually *living* in Illinois that I found to be a trouble. I was a bundle of ambivalences and Rajani thought there might be a job for me opening at Bowdoin and we were talking about all that and some other things too. Maine, she was saying, was kind of a trip for people of color and she talked about how she was dealing with that as she approached the termination of her contract and asked how I thought I would.

I surprised her some by saying that I'd been there a lot. My parents had rented the same cottage on the same lake—Pleasant Pond—for the same two weeks in August for the better part of thirty years, the first time having been in 1960 when I was nine. The couple from whom they'd rented were black Maine people their own age who owned that "camp," as they're called in Maine, and another one, both on a point at the end of a dirt road off long Pond Road in Litchfield township near Gardiner; the other camp was always rented to other black people, professional men and their families, from one or another of the eastern cities, so it was that many years of passing acquaintances there in Maine. And a long friendship with the Redds, the people we rented from. My view of Maine, I said to Rajani, is "an intensely black view."

We went inside then because of her allergy to insect stings—the deck, being a popular food area, was swarming with yellow jackets—and talked some more and, before we parted, I gave her a big intra-campus envelope full of writing samples, vitae, and a statement about what I was planning to do in British Columbia.

Here, if this were a movie, the scene would shift suddenly to an air shot of an endless forest and perhaps THE CARIBOO, in white letters, would be superimposed on the bottom right corner of the screen. That, in conjunction with the scene before—in which I'd passed Rajani Sudan a folder of papers as we sat in the shadows just off such an obviously wealthy, well-appointed verandah—, might suggest that this was a big-budget spy film. Our dark skins would make us right for what I was predicting then to be the American near future's popular international intrigue genre, one in which the interminable conflict would be Northern Hemisphere vs. Southern—these were days I could see coming.

But it was the more immediate future that was looming up before me that afternoon at Cornell. The Cariboo loomed. This was July 1991; at the end of August we were going to go to Vancouver for six months, my whole little family and me, we were going to B.C. for the first time—we were going to get on the train, the Pioneer, and head west through Iowa, Nebraska, Wyoming, etc., the route I'd retrace alone three and a half years later in the Volvo. We were all looking forward to it, to our coming sojourn down on the coast, as they say in B.C. I'd won some fellowships that year and those had been enough for me to finagle a semester away from my job at Illinois State and go out there and begin work on the poetry book *Giscome Road*, which I finally finished in Fort George, four years after I started it. (I'd intended the book to be about John R. but poetry doesn't go that way and the *Giscome Road* book's about the way landscape is described, the language and landscape of jazz, and the gods of Dahomey. It's about Miles Davis's playing and about some of the stuff that gets talked over in "Heart of Darkness" and *Invisible Man*. The book names and charts a lot but it doesn't explain much.) In Vancouver we rented a small basement apartment in the Mount Pleasant neighborhood, from which I commuted to the UBC library, where I read descriptions of the Cariboo and Cassiar districts and histories of the province. I went to the Provincial Archives in Victoria, where I found two articles about John R.—one in *B.C. Outdoors* and the other in *British Columbia Historical News*; at the archives I also read the correspondence of Peter Dunlevy, the trader whom Father Morice credits with having named the Giscome Portage, and the balance sheets of the men who built the Giscome Portage "waggon road." I read about James Douglas, the first governor of the province, and his "creole" origins in Guyana. We traveled on ferries to Saltspring Island, which had been settled in the 1850s by black Californians. I sat at my desk for four hours every morning and wrote poetry out of all that.

The Tour de Cariboo

And toward the end of September I set out to bicycle the five hundred miles up into the Cariboo, up to Giscome itself, up to the site in the far North that named John R. Giscome's arrival there. I was writing more and more about geography, so I wanted to experience—in as profoundly physical a way as I could—the country changing as I went north; plus, approaches are important in that one does, often, choose how to make them. It's not that there would have been a "wrong" way to get, for the first time, to the country where John R. had flourished, but if one has—as I did—several choices at one's disposal then the act of choosing one way to start (over others) has obvious value, obvious significance. The choices that come after that first one come out of other exigencies, other—unforeseen—obligations: such is as good a definition as any for "adventure." I was forty years old then and continuing to do this, to take these long bike tours I'd started after kicking cigarettes so many years before.

The village—Giscome, B.C.—was named that by the Grand Trunk Pacific in 1913 or 1914. The Giscome Portage was still famous then and this was as close as the railroad was going to come to it—both the village and Giscome Portage appear on the 1914 railroad map I found in an antique store in Ithaca, and both are spelled Giscombe. The track still comes in from the east—from Jasper, Tête Jaune Cache, and McBride—along the south shore of long Eaglet Lake, and what's left of Giscome is still there at the west end; the daily passenger train, the Skeena, would stop there, if "on signal," until 1985 or so; now the train's triweekly and you can flag it in Willow River, to the west of Giscome, or Aleza Lake, which is a few miles to the east. Taking away the Giscome stop was a business decision, made in the VIA Rail Canada offices, just as naming the town had been a business decision of the Grand Trunk. By the time Giscome, B.C., was laid out, John R. had been in his grave for six years; the town wasn't named for him, there was never a statue of him there or plaque commemorating his exploits. Giscome got to be famous for being the site of the largest sawmill north of Vancouver and the mill employed great numbers of people; it was a company town, a town quite literally owned by the company, and when the company began to lose money in the 1970s the town was auctioned off and then bulldozed—the houses in which mill workers had lived, the buildings in which they'd watched movies and bought food, the mill itself. People bid for and bought and carted away radiators, porches, furnaces, and the like, anything reusable that would fit on the back of a truck. The population—575 in 1962 according to my Rand McNally—was transient and it relocated, it scattered. Now about 30 people live there; there's still an elementary school, Giscome School, and there's St. Frederick's Catholic Church. The caretaker lives in the house next to the church; the priest comes in from elsewhere.

As I'd done final things to the bicycle and my gear prior to leaving Vancouver for Giscome I was suffering from the typical pre-trip mortality fears and premonitions, the ones I've always been prey to. They disappeared, as they tend to, before the end of the first day—after I'd gotten used to the weight of the panniers, after I'd made it out of the city and its traffic, after I'd stopped a couple of times for apple juice and Mars bars, after nothing had gone wrong with the bicycle for that first several hours—but this time out I was forty and I recall how the empty fact of that age weighed on me that afternoon even though I was feeling good and strong. I'd just been approved for a decent life insurance policy, which meant that if tomorrow an RV did smack me, Katharine and Madeline would get a hundred thousand U.S. dollars, that that was what my life was worth, all and exactly, and the finiteness was disconcerting. As I made camp that night in a strange and deserted campground on the lower Fraser I was thinking about the policy and it did not make me feel peaceful and secure and happy as the advertisements suggest. I lay in my sleeping bag and listened to the freights—coal trains, so many that night—go by along the river: there was a little steel trestle over a feeder creek I couldn't see in the dark and the trains coming back with empties from the coast made a different noise on it than the full hoppers did on their way out to the docks in Vancouver. Export, commerce, money—a blues in the night indeed. The next day I turned north and went along the road built on ledges through the Fraser Canyon—this was the Gold Rush Trail highway, Route 1, and the road was marked with blue-and-white signs showing a prospector leading his mule. I'd gotten a late start that second day and had taken a long lunch break as well, so I was significantly behind my schedule and hurrying to make up some time through the afternoon. *I don't want to get caught in the canyon*, I said to myself, *after dark*, but I did—as I would again some years later—and made the last hour to Boston Bar that night in the glow that two Duracell C batteries cast on the road ahead. The shoulder was wide and I was grateful for that, but I still had long curving tunnels to contend with, and double-trailer trucks and ambiguous recreational vehicles, and I figured, when I did arrive safely in Boston Bar, that I'd earned a night in a bed and bought myself one at the Charles Motel and then went downstairs and discovered that fine restaurant and was quite happy.

Two days later, exigencies had made me decide to abort the trip and I was in Clinton, B.C., waiting for the Cariboo Dayliner, the southbound train on the British Columbia Railway back to Vancouver. That morning I'd discovered, as they say, blood in my urine which I'd not been pleased at, especially since there's a little history of bladder cancer among the Giscombes—I'd found a local doctor, though, and had decided, on his advice and because of his professional shrug at the symptoms, to get it checked out once I got back to Vancouver but not to become distraught over it, to carry on northward. "We see that sort of thing a lot around here," he'd said, "because of all the fellows riding horses"; I'd had to climb, I'd pointed out, about 3,000 feet to get to Clinton from my previous night's campground at Spences Bridge, near Cache Creek, and the doctor had agreed that that could very well do it. So, resolving to be cautious but not insane-with-fear, I girded up and commenced rolling out of town; but I was rolling unhappily, resolute or not, and on the way I couldn't resist stopping at a roadside phone to call Katharine and lean on her just a little bit, have her tell me all'd be OK: when I got through to her, though, she turned out to be beginning her annual diverticulitis attack and that changed the stakes some—the attacks are nasty (they can put you in the hospital) and their duration's unpredictable. It's not a good sickness to be alone for and, besides even that, Madeline was five then, and demanding. So I looked once at the bicycle just beyond the phone booth, braced there against a utility pole all loaded up and facing north and, though Katharine made a point of telling me she could take care of herself, I said I'd get back to Vancouver that day.

Clinton's a flag stop, there's just a green piece of metal to hang, as a signal, from a post next to the track and after I'd deployed that, I took my journal and settled down against one of the bulkheads of an empty lumber car that was spotted on a siding. What to write? Across the track itself was the town dump and I watched the crows soaring and swooping over the trash, the ever-changing dump being full of images. But instead I wrote, "Here B.C. feels like Maine: the conifers, the cool breeze, the low forested hills, the sound of a chain saw working." This was the familiar, I suppose, my child-self creeping in in its own images to thwart the bloody piss, the inflamed gut of middle age. But the Cariboo *does* look like Maine, the central Maine of my memory: the long roads hump up over the hills, small signs point the way to towns hidden off beyond the woods, lakes occur with frequency. From the dump came occasional whiffs of burning as the wind would shift.

The Augusts I was twelve and thirteen and fourteen I'd go out fishing with my father and Mr. Redd—I was, I see now, a fifth wheel, the child tolerated among men on this, my father's vacation, the two weeks of his not being on call, of not being the physician he was for the other fifty weeks in Dayton, Ohio. I'd grown up in Dayton, in the big black middle class we had there, and Maine was quite different from all that I'd got used to: it was interestingly wild but extremely white and lower-class (and different from the lower-class white areas I knew in and around Dayton) and within that Mr. Redd knew the way to hidden lakes and who owned what property on them and how one lake connected to another. He'd insulted Jack Paar once, when he'd been fishing on a lake that touched that man's property at Poland Spring, he picked up hitchhikers on the Maine Turnpike, he'd encountered moose. He'd retired from the Air Force when he was still a young man and so was living on the pension and dabbling in a few other things: he ran for some state office once (as a Republican!) and lost, he went to law school for a while, he worked on and off for the State Racing Commission. I don't know if it was a good life or not. We caught bass and pickerel in those lakes and, when we'd return, he and my father would sit on the porch by Pleasant Pond or sit in the kitchen by the woodstove and drink and talk and tell stories. Benjamin Redd, but everyone called him Cherry. He was decorous and courtly and had the sweet voice and accent that I've always associated with black politicians.

But Madeline Redd's voice had nothing in it that I can identify as African-American, nothing from that range of voices I'd got used to when I was growing up—the voices, that is, of people who'd come from the South or whose parents had. She'd been born in Maine, her mother had come south to there from New Brunswick, I don't recall where her father was from—I'd met them when I was a child and they died shortly after that. Madeline's brother, Reynold Burch, had gone to Bowdoin and then left Maine and become a doctor, had a practice in New Jersey where Cherry Redd had come from—I imagine them passing each other on the Massachusetts Turnpike, going opposite directions—and often, when we'd be in Maine, he and his wife, Mary, would be in the other cottage. Buster—as Dr. Burch was known—had a patrician, if booming, New England voice with the faintest black edge to it, owing, I suppose, to his years in Jersey or to his years with Mary. I don't know where she was born, but when she talked there in Maine, she sounded to me like home. All these voices in two cottages and laughter in that accent and this accent too, drifting out across Pleasant Pond. This is what's stayed with me, this sound of that place.

But the morning was passing slowly in Clinton, B.C., and the train wasn't due until 1:30. I noted in the journal that the crows were "majestic," a word I don't usually use, and that "two did a *pas de deux* down toward the ground, unbelievably graceful free fall with them coming almost together, almost touching 3 times before veering off at the lip of the ground." The morning before, a ways north of Spences Bridge, I'd come across that bad accident in a high desert place above the Thompson River where the road had been blasted out of some rocks. The ambulances and cops had already gone by the time I got there and had left it to the fellows who'd come out with their tow truck to clear wreckage off the road. It was a lumber truck on its side, the cab half sheared off, half crumbled, lots of lumber scattered down the pavement. Impossible to surmise whether or not anyone had been injured or killed or had survived. The stretch of road where the wreck was had some sudden twists to it, and the rocks towered on both sides. I'd made it through, past the tow truck men standing in the road conferring, and over the top of the rise at the end of the rocks when I had a flat tire. I pulled off to fix it and a couple of minutes later the men closed the road so they could clear it unimpeded. Traffic piled up quickly and a young man driving a tractor-trailer got down off his rig to ask if I'd seen the wreck, and when I described it to him he asked what kind of lumber it was. I said it looked like 1×4s and he nodded. "That'd be cedar," he said, "that shit *slides*."

He'd suggested, though, a place to eat in Clinton—the Cariboo Lodge—where I had a splendid dinner when I arrived in town that night; the restaurant has corridors leading to remote dining rooms and up on these are blown-up photographs of the old days of travel on the Cariboo Road: stagecoaches, etc. One group of men standing by a wing dam looked black but up close turned out to be Chinese. The great road started in Lillooet, at the end of navigation on Seton and Anderson lakes, and twisted up through the desert—this would have been the other option for John R., going out along those lakes (as opposed to the route I'd taken up through the Fraser Canyon) and starting off on foot or on horseback at Lillooet. The routes—the one I was taking and the old Cariboo Road—meet near Clinton, which is in the forest, and go on as one to the goldfields near Barkerville, near Prince George. Years before, at the Cornell Cinema, I'd seen Charlie Chaplin's *Gold Rush* film—men lined up on the snowy ledges on the way to their fortunes, on the way to their doom. There had been a picture of the new Cariboo Road in my seventh-grade geography book, an air shot that showed how modern Canada had become and so quickly. Photographs abound but there are none I've found (and I've looked in Fort George and in Vancouver and in Victoria) of John R., and as I sat on the lumber car in Clinton I thought of him, tried to picture him, and came up with a memory of my grandfather, the *ur*-Giscombe of my family's adventure in America, the first Dr. Giscombe. The year before he died he'd taken my sister and me out driving in the country around Birmingham one afternoon, looking for trains. He knew I liked them and had found us one to look at, a short freight pulled by two switch engines going by on a ridge next to the road. Him gesturing at that freight train and pressing himself back in the seat so I could see it past his upper body is the last memory I have of him.

A week later I was back on the BC Rail heading north to Clinton to resume my trip at the place where I'd bailed out. Katharine had gotten better very quickly, to everyone's surprise, and I'd found a urologist who'd arranged for a cystoscopy to be done in a couple of weeks; as the train crept out through moneyed North Vancouver I was thinking of that coming up, waiting for me on my return from Giscome. Most of my fellow passengers that morning were single men close to my age and here and there were a few older couples; but one young woman was traveling with her small children—a boy and a girl—and when I heard her speak to them I was not surprised that she said whatever she said in French: her face was broad and delicate at once and, for a Caucasian, she had a pleasantly dark complexion and thick straight black hair; a beautiful woman. A Caucasian? Napoleon's said to have said something to the effect that "Africa begins at the Pyrenees" but when I ran that quote past a very worldly graduate student at Illinois State, intending to impress him, he'd countered by telling me that Churchill had said that "the wogs start at Calais."

And how we've all spread. In 1964 I went with my family and the Redds to see Lyndon Johnson speak in Lewiston, Maine, a town with a large Acadian population. He was running for president then and I recall nothing of whatever he said. Yet I recall with great clarity the scene in Lewiston itself: a street downtown was closed off and sawhorses kept the crowd on the sidewalk while cynical-looking cops sauntered back and forth on the surface of the street pausing now and then to speak to friends in the crowd, sometimes in English, but usually in French. My mother had been quite taken with the beauty of the French women in the throng but Madeline Redd said that it was a beauty that didn't last, that by the time they were forty they'd look "hard." Ten years after that she died, Madeline Redd did, when she was in her fifties, maybe sixty, much too young to be dead in any case. Lung cancer. "She was a *good* person," my mother said, "and she never even *smoked*." Bitter, disgusted, incredibly sad. My daughter, Madeline Giscombe, is not named *after* her but the name Madeline struck me as possible for my child because of her. It's a name from that time in my life among those people there in that countryside. And Madeline Redd also was a beautiful woman, an intense woman, and her blackness, which she wore consciously and yet, I think, effortlessly, became her; her incorporation, her embodiment, of race was of a sort that was or had been unfamiliar to me and because of that was profound. We've spread widely.

By the time the train was nearing Lillooet an older couple had got friendly with the French woman. Perhaps they were Americans: they were speaking English to her loudly and precisely in that way Americans have while she smiled and spoke English tentatively in response. The talk was about children and marriage—the woman was on her way to meet her husband in Prince George. This happens—these comradeships springing up on public transportation—with a certain predictability and that made the scene familiar, meaning that it seemed both remarkable and clichéd at once. I looked around the coach then and thought of all of us there, heading into the North randomly together, each with secret passions and fears hidden as our bodies were beneath our clothes. This is, of course, exactly the stuff of which thousands of B movies and bad novels are made, this is the formula. But those books and films and their evocations of some unforeseen situation forcing passengers to reveal themselves (heroically, as capable of cowardice, passionately) to one another are popular for a reason. I think it's beyond cliché, though, I think it's its own archetype or, as my students would say, Everyone can relate to it.

In my early days as an editor at Cornell my magazine's office was across the corridor from the largest seminar room in Goldwin Smith Hall and that room was the one, because of its size, in which the English faculty met. The meetings were typically at 3 on Friday afternoons and by 2:45 or 2:50 the faculty would be milling around in the hall outside the room waiting for an actual seminar to end so that they could go in and start. They were and are a fairly distinguished group but the conversations that would come wafting into the *Epoch* office were more often than not about things like the squirrels in someone's side yard or the first signs of spring or fall, about vacations. I had a couple of friends on the faculty then, and when I complained to one about the trivial nature of the pre-meeting talk, he said that his colleagues were not social people and dealt with one another nervously, that that's what I was hearing in the voices, people talking nervously without form and, therefore, insistently about nothing. But now I'm a faculty member and I go to the meetings and I see the jockeying for position and the dead seriousness, I see the self-importance and I think now that what I was hearing in those afternoons when I was in my twenties was people older than me—people who could see the ends of their lives coming—trying to be human for a few minutes, trying to establish *some* commonality with one another before the business set in: I suspect the squirrels in the yard were important to whoever was talking about them—this was life and its aimless value, a value that isn't affirmed much in the language, outside of places like the Disney industry, places we don't go. But I think what I was seeing or hearing take place in the hall was the fact that the allied and consuming demands of ego and the business of being professors left no space for much more than such little and awkwardly stated demonstrations—the closest it was possible to come to being casually human with other people. (Squirrels? "Rats with furry tails," someone said once, but then there was my old boy the Mariner, who looked down at those slimy sea snakes, "blessed them unaware," and that dead bird fell *off* him.)

The conductor on the northbound remembered me from the trip down to Vancouver a few days before and understood, without my having to explain it, why it was necessary for me to resume my tour at the place where I'd aborted it. All my travel seems to have a train component built into it one way or another, they're a central metaphor. I helped the conductor off-load my bike and panniers at Clinton and off I cycled, into the northern landscape and its towns. I recently found, in a journal entry, the account of another moment at Lac la

Hache, aside from my meeting another biker near there, an odd little jolt from my late-in-the-year trip:

Riding all day up from 100 Mile House and had got warm enough to strip off my sweater—old blue wool sweater vest—earlier. At Lac la Hache I stopped to buy something or another—candy bar, apple juice—at the gen'l store there & dawdled inside, in the warm store, over that. When I came out a woman in a rusty Suburban was getting out of the truck and hurried for the door. "Isn't it cold to be riding?" she askt. I sd some nothing reply but it did feel cold, outside, after having been inside—gooseflesh, etc. She was my age, a bit stocky, lovely face. Red cheeked, short sandy-grey hair, glasses. She was wearing a shirt just like mine—old red Duofold long underwear style—& her nipples were poking right through it, stretching the red fabric of the shirt even though she was wearing a bra. Looked down & saw my own nipples poking through the same shirt. Hers were big & blunt on her ever so slightly stocky self, her rusty truck—oh cold weather, northern sexiness.

Four days later, late in the afternoon, I came into Fort George for the first time ever and bought a room in the Downtown Motel. Barry McKinnon—whose poetry I'd read and liked when I was at Cornell and with whom I'd corresponded—came by early that evening and we went to his house and sat in the kitchen and drank beer and talked, letting it get dark slowly all around us, finally going out to eat around ten o'clock. The next day I rose early, breakfasted at the Simon Fraser Inn and cycled the thirty miles up to Giscome. There's little there: a few houses and recently built Giscome School, the central metaphor of a railroad crossing, old St. Frederick's. I looked in through the school windows and saw the children's gym shoes stashed in little cubicles stacked in a main corridor and a handmade banner stretching over the shoes that said WELCOME TO GISCOME. The Rockies are visible if you look east, over Eaglet Lake. Barry and I had agreed the evening before that it could be a place, Giscome, even if there was *nothing* there, liking that unification, opening another beer in its honor. I was rereading Margaret Atwood's novel *Surfacing* that fall and had it with me when I got to Giscome—I mean it was the only paper I had along and I wanted to write something about being there and on one of the blank pages at the end of the book I scribbled, "This feels to me like the empty center of the continent to-day."

Wreck Beach

The next day I was back on the train riding all day back to Vancouver and a week after that I was at University Hospital waiting to be scoped out. I'd planned to rise early on that day and go swimming at Wreck Beach, the naked beach at UBC, and then walk over to the hospital—which is at another edge of the campus—smelling like the ocean, all elemental, etc., but I'd had trouble getting to sleep the night before—typical anxiety—and then finally slept too long that morning, so I just barely made it in in time on the city bus. I was unhappy as I lay on the gurney in that interminable waiting mode at having blown the chance and intention to go to Wreck that morning, since it was a beautiful day and since the beach was a comfortable and comforting place in that the people who swam there tended to be my age—thirties, forties, fifties—and wear their bodies well. And *such* bodies, which bespoke much, evidences of both pleasure and suffering: I have some very good scars to show for my having lived some but so do many others, and the scars there are on display and all complete instead of diving into even the scant cover of bathing suits. There are, certainly, some conventionally beautiful young people frolicking about but it's the bodies of those my age and older that I recall: stretch marks, the occasional missing limb, the one man who had a colostomy bag. Much had befallen all of us and yet there we all still were, nude near the place where the Fraser River entered the Strait of Georgia, striding across the sand and into the waves.

But it went off all right and when I woke up the urologist was there to knowledgeably shrug—probably the climb out of the desert, he said. I paid for the procedure with my Visa card and the next day we rented a car and drove down to America to pick up our computer. My old friend Robert Thacker was teaching for the year at Western Washington in Bellingham and we'd arranged to have our Macintosh UPS'd to him instead of us and thus avoid the special permits and charges involved with shipping it across the border. He and I had been in high school together in Dayton—we used to go out and drink beer along the Stillwater River, north of town, and here we were twenty-five years later doing the same thing. We sat outside the house he'd rented on Lummi island and looked across the water at Mount Baker while I spoke about Illinois. One of the things that Katharine and I both found troublesome about it, I said, was the flatness beyond town: we found that much more oppressive and much less interesting than we'd hoped it would be. But he'd just published his book *The Great Prairie Fact and the Literary Imagination*, in which he argues that beauty is a culturally constructed idea even when it pertains to landscape. He takes Lewis and Clark to task, for example, for not noticing "the uniqueness of the prairie in favor of the conventional 'sublime' of a waterfall . . ." It's that old European standard he means by "conventional" and his idea's hard to disagree with, even with Mount Baker moving in and out of clouds before us. Robert usually teaches at St. Lawrence University in Canton, New York—where the state is truly Appalachian, both in culture and scenery—but he'd gone to undergraduate school at Bowling Green State in northern Ohio, which resembles the Illinois I live in now. I'd visited him several times during those years—years I was living in upstate New York—and once we drove out under a green sky looking for the tornado that had been reported, twisting the radio dial in my International for updates. We were twenty-one and twenty-two and immortal and I recall how impressed I'd been then at what I later described as the prairie's "stark spirituality," at the vastness and changeability of the sky. How odd these days, then, to be in the same boat with Thacker's Europeans: I mean the thrill's gone now that we *live* there—the sky, even the brilliant sky looming up over Veterans Parkway, is not enough. He'd noted, in his book's first chapter, that when Coronado had crossed the prairie the members of that expedition had marked their path across the then-tracklessness with piles of cowshit (they'd brought livestock along with them) that towered above the grasses and I mentioned this to my friend Curtis White when we were cycling one afternoon after I'd returned from my semester in Vancouver. We were headed for Danvers, Illinois, because there's a hilly, twisting, treed road that goes there, one of the few such conventionally European roads in the county. Even so, even with the roll of the road, there's a point, just east of the village, where you realize you've made it to the top of a tiny ridge and from there you're faced with the great fact itself that to the north, east, and west the flatness stretches indeed to the horizon. I don't know how many miles you can see by rotating your head, maybe thirty. It seems that that day we were able to see the water tower back at Normal but I may be embroidering.

(We had a club back then in the early nineties, Hell's English, and we'd go out riding forty, fifty, sixty miles on Sundays, four or five of us, all English professors in our forties. It was fun, it was a good thing to do on Sundays. We'd turn on the Weather Channel to see which way the wind was blowing, head into it, and then turn around and let it blow us back to town, let it augment our pedaling. In Ithaca I'd go off riding into the hills above the lake, above Inlet Valley, and then come back down out of them, back to that town, back home. Riding out of the wind isn't the same: you can get going pretty fast, you can stroke it up to about thirty-five and if you're strong, if your legs are good, you can maintain that for a little while, but it's not the same. When you're coming down a steep, smoothly paved hill, even one that's only a mile long, you're *falling*, you're accelerating some as objects do, you feel like you're almost in free fall—it's inevitable, getting to and then right on past 40 mph, the digits appearing on the handlebar computer, and pedaling won't make you go any faster.)

Victoria Again

A woman named Linda Eversole had written the article about John Robert Giscome for *British Columbia Historical News*. She'd found, and quoted in her piece, the lengthy newspaper account of his year-long prospecting trip into the Peace River country, the trip on which he'd made that first "non-Indian" crossing of the Giscome Portage. Her work had been a major help to me in my project and I wanted to thank her for that, see what else she knew, and just spend some time talking with her.

So in November 1991, toward the end of our stay in Vancouver, I phoned around and got her number and called one day and we met the next afternoon in the Provincial Archives in Victoria, where she, it turns out, is well known. We went over to the Provincial Museum tea shop and she spread papers out before me, including a Xerox of the original newspaper account, which I had, by that time, already seen, having been alerted to it by her article. But she contended two things about it that I hadn't thought of: one, that John R. had written it himself (even though it appeared in print in the third person), and, two, that the detail of the account had convinced her that "he was in it for more than the gold." He was an explorer, she said, he was *interested* in what he was seeing—and she pointed to places where the account told how he and Henry McDame had named a tributary of the Peace River and had brought back—all the way down to Victoria—samples of volcanic rock. A few years before, I'd found a copy of one of the Victoria city directories—the one from 1892—in the library at Cornell: John R. Giscome lived on Fort Street then and had listed his occupation as "miner and explorer." I told Linda about that and she nodded.

But he had done OK in terms of the gold. He spent the last decade of the nineteenth century and the first decade of the twentieth in Victoria, buying and selling real estate. He lived in rooming houses, though, and when he died in 1907 he left his money to his last landlady, Ella Cooness. The estate was valued at $21,000, maybe half a million in 1997 dollars—significantly more than the combined worth of my decent insurance policy and our property holdings (including the redoubtable mission oak collection). We confessed to one another, though, Linda Eversole and I did, that we'd both been shaken when we read the account of his death in the *Colonist*; I was in the Government Documents & Microfilm Room at the UBC Library, I don't know where she was when she found it. John R. himself is quite elusive—no spouse, no photographs, no diary that has surfaced. Perhaps Linda and I both felt his death so hard because neither of us knew a great deal about his life aside from what we could piece together from a handful of newspaper articles that were, in form anyway, about other things. The articles that reported his last illness, on the other hand, were—though brief—very much about him and very, very final. Close parentheses. The *Colonist* had praised him as a man "worthy of honour and respect" and had speculated shamelessly on what was then the rumor of his money.

And Linda suspected that there'd been an interesting duplicity on the part of Mrs. Cooness. John Robert Giscome's will had described her as "a widow, absolute," but in fact, Linda said, she was married to a much older man named Stacey who did indeed live right there at the same address (and died there too, a year or so after John R. did). Her— Linda's—reading of the situation was that she'd *told* John R. that her husband was dead and that this old man for whom she cared was her father or father-in-law and that way produced the sexy aura of her own availability. That she was, in some measure, a gold digger. But John R. Giscome was himself dying at the time of his will; Linda described the shaky quality of the signature on it and, years later, I found a copy myself—he messed his signature on the first attempt at signing it and spilled the ink but the second try was passable. If very shaky. He'd made the thing out in fact—or dictated it or agreed to it—only a few weeks before he did die, before he did cross that line, and I imagine him looking over out of his own death at Bro. Stacey and deliberately calling Ella *widow* in that grim way we sometimes have about us.

The Fiji Islands

By then, though, it *was* November and as I ferried back from Victoria I was aware that the end of my semester away was actually coming. November's my birth month and I was nearing my forty-first birthday and there were no good academic jobs for a person of my qualifications and needs in the new MLA list. I'd heard nothing in all this time, though, from Bowdoin. So I called Rajani Sudan, way over in Brunswick, Maine, and she sighed deeply about the old boys' network and told me it wasn't going to happen. It's OK, I said, but of course it really wasn't and what I wanted was to go out with her then, as we'd gone out three winters earlier, and eat oysters and drink Dixie beer, but she was nearly three thousand miles away and New Orleans—where it was warm in December and where it had seemed to me that my life bristled with possibility—was very far away from either one of us. We'd been in the same boat then, in that city, we'd been comrades and spoken out loudly in bars in the Quarter. I hung up the phone realizing that I was looking at at least one more year at Illinois State, but as I sank back into our rented couch it was all the years at Cornell that came back to be present with me. I'd taken a lot there but I'd deflected a lot too and built myself finally into a singularity, an anomaly, the thing that Giscombes, if I understand my family, tend to become as we age. Cornell had not loved me—this was clear—but had tolerated me and my excesses, I suppose because of that singularity, which is what made me feel free, finally, to leave Cornell. (It was my predecessor at *Epoch*, Tom Merwin, who came up with Goldwin Smith's disease as the name for what he described as the "laid-back hopelessness" that so many people felt in that building; I based my Illinois workplace affliction, Adlai Stevenson's disease, on his example. My pet disease, though, is a little less laid back and a little more hopeless: the first sign may be talking to yourself in the men's room, but there is no second symptom.) Singular, anomalous, craggy in those and a little cancer and some hypertension among the Giscombes, but we're suspicious and tend to live a long time, and tend to be or get a little grim too (even for the grim peoples) as we age.

But in December I was invited to a *party*.

I'd been out looking one afternoon for what might come closest to being a black historical society and got referred, finally, to a lady named Michelle Williams who ran something called the New West Black Theatre. More or less single-handedly she puts out a newsletter—apparently the only one—that's about history as well as being a calendar of black events in Vancouver and its suburbs. It's a small population and one that's diverse in its origins—West Indians, Africans, Americans, even some Canadians—and spread out over a wide geographical area. She rejected my offer to have coffee sometime—"too busy"—but she invited me to the Christmas season Open House that she and her husband, Rico, have every year. Everyone in town was invited, she said, which I understood to mean everybody of African descent as well as the friends and lovers of those certain people.

By December I'd lived in the library and at my desk for a long time and so it was with trepidation that I set out that evening to meet all these *people* in this wide-flung and very foreign-to-me community at Rico and Michelle's house. Katharine and I are not particularly social and she declined to accompany me out to this gathering. We had no car and busing would have taken forever, so I rolled up my khaki pants and bicycled the six miles east in a fine, almost dry sleet, locked my bike and helmet to a streetlight, unrolled my pants, and, feeling both self-conscious about having arrived by such transportation and foolish for feeling self-conscious, went on up to the door.

Rico waved me on in, saying, "You must be the guy from Chicago," before I could introduce myself, showed me the buffet table, and took me downstairs where everyone was. There were twenty or thirty people, all of whom knew one another, but over the years I have learned how to mingle. Even so, I spent most of the evening talking to a Jamaican woman a bit younger than me, a freelance journalist: we talked about books and about George Bush and she told me about color and caste in Jamaica. She was worldly and thoughtful and Jamaican like John R. Giscome was—whatever that means—and like this, my own name, is and she had a beautiful voice even though she didn't sound much like home.

So I had a pleasant time talking with her and, indeed, a pleasant time for the couple or three hours I spent at the party. But as I was thanking my hosts and heading back up the stairs a short plump man was coming in and, when people expressed surprise to see him because everyone thought he was still up in Prince George, I slowed my exit, intending to ask him what he knew about the Giscome Portage. But he'd launched right into a story about the provincial office for which he'd been working up there: in short, two of his co-workers had been razzing him for a long time about being from "the city" and he'd succeeded, casually, one day in sending them scurrying out of the office like fools to shoot the moose he told them he'd seen grazing on the building's lawn. Gullible boys full of adrenaline; they shuffled back in, embarrassed, a few minutes later.

Everyone laughed, myself included, but I also recognized it as a Trickster story, rather much like the ones I try to teach in African-American Literature. And it was a story the like of which I remember hearing myself, hearing men and older boys tell, when I was a child, hearing less often, it seems, in my adulthood. I suppose it's always been rare, though, to hear good stories. I let someone else point out to the storyteller that my last name was the same, more or less, as the name of a town near P.G. and he was politely impressed. I took my leave then and brushed the snow off my seat and headed back across town. The precipitation had stopped, it was a crisp clear night I had to bike through, no traffic. It was as if the whole town was gone with just these buildings and streets left behind.

Rico and Michelle's had been not noisy but joyous: a fine story had been told, I'd heard the sound of black people talking in differing voices in a northern house—this was the audible edge of my landscape, the laughter drifting out across Lillooet Street, into the low hills of Rico and Michelle's quiet neighborhood.

Some bad days were coming—here I don't mean my predicted days of international apocalypse and intrigue but a series of family crises. I had an inkling, during our last month down on the coast, that some things were about to happen though I didn't know then how bad they, the coming days, were actually going to be and they turned out to be pretty bad; nothing fatal but they spanned the distance between our leaving Vancouver in January of 1992 and our arrival, exactly three years later, in Fort George—things were pretty bad for a long time. My mother has gone on record as not ever wanting to know the future—"We'd all commit suicide," she's said, "if we could see what was coming." Instead we roll with it, we deal with it, we survive the future. We live long. If grimly. Bad days were coming but that night I'd been told a good story, one that was Canadian (from that countryside way up there, specific to that country, the Cariboo, and its animals) and yet recognizable as a black archetype as well. A familiar story. I followed the elevated Skytrain line north for a while and then crossed Commercial Avenue, where a lot of the Third World immigrants to Vancouver had settled. I'd had my hair cut on Commercial Avenue recently, at the Fiji Islands Barber Shop, it being the only ostentatiously non-white establishment I could find in the Yellow Pages. Still, I'd never even *met* anyone from the Fiji Islands and had approached the shop gingerly, not knowing what reception was in store for me. But the barber, an older man, had been kind: as I walked in he'd greeted me by calling out, "Hello, my brother."

Winter in Fort George

Our northernmost house, the one we'd rented in Fort George—John Harris's and Vivien Lougheed's house—, was at 137 South Lyon Street, in the Quinson section of town. The neighborhood's a grid of square or almost square blocks on a wide rise that ends at the cliff above the Nechako; Lyon Street itself is flat but many of the adjacent streets drift over some undulations. A few houses have tallish evergreens out front or in back but it's not a lush area by any means. The house in which we lived was built in the 1960s and is considered to be old; it's a small ranch-style affair with three levels—the bedrooms are up a couple of steps from the living room and kitchen and downstairs is a family room and two studies. Vivien writes about travel, John writes short stories; while we were in Fort George she was walking across Africa and he, not liking to stay on Lyon Street when she's off on a long adventure, was south of town in the house in the woods he'd built for himself some years before. The oldest house in Quinson was around the corner from us—it's essentially a large and rather graceful cabin and when Kent Sedgwick, the local historian who'd written the article about John Robert Giscome for *B.C. Outdoors*, pointed the place out to me and told me that it had been built around the time of the First World War I saw it had some Prairie-style features. Kent's piece—titled "The Missing Link"—was about the portage trail, John R.'s route over the continental divide, but it was also about the settlement, the Huble Farm, that had sprung up in the early days of this century at the foot of the portage, about thirty miles north of Prince George. In 1904 (or possibly 1905 or 1906) Albert Huble and Ed Seebach opened a trading post there and later they ran freight wagons over the portage up to Summit Lake. Huble built a house on the site in 1912, and in 1915 (when John R. had been dead for eight years) he and Seebach established a post office called Giscome Portage. The place thrived—river steamers routinely called at the trading post and the freighting business was good. But the province was growing and the inevitable highways came—the road from Prince George to Summit Lake was built in 1919 and that was the end of the Giscome Portage route. The trading post closed that same year and the property became part of a big operation, the WM Ranch, and then a common grazing area for some nearby farms. Al Huble's house fell into disrepair—it's a hollow-eyed sagging elephant in the photos that accompany Kent's 1979 article—but in the mid-1980s the Huble Homestead, as it came to be known, was made into a regional park and the buildings were restored and period furniture was brought in (though none of it's mission); young women in long dresses show you around. The whole place is under the administration of the Giscome Portage Historical Society and John R. Giscome and Henry McDame are mentioned on a couple of the signs, and even identified as black men from the West Indies; but the focus of history in northern B.C. is white penetration and settlement, the narrative that started with Mackenzie in 1793 and that continues rolling on down the Hart Highway in the recreational vehicles an increasing number of modern British Columbians call home. The old joke about how you can live in your car but you can't drive your house no longer applies.

At the Giscome Portage Regional Park the trail between the watersheds is marked (and maintained) but the park's focus is the story of Al Huble's family's life in that house. Photographs of the family are prominent, the structure itself's an icon of white B.C. history—built in 1906, it's the oldest house in the region. But it is a beautiful house—it's arguably a vernacular example of Gothic Revival and the roof features triangular drops and high peaks; the planed-log walls are smooth and substantial and notched tightly together. I recall bouncing down to the park for the first time, down the gravel road from the Hart Highway in a rented car in the summer of 1992, and coming to it in the unruly wilderness; it was a hot, bright day and the house sat in its clearing catching the light, the cool Fraser a hundred yards downhill from the porch. I was struck instantly by how wonderful it would be to wake up here every morning. Oh for this to be mine. It's public, though, and people do come in their Winnebagos and Bounders and Tiogas to be shown through Huble's house in the woods; the woods are a presence—a bear, I've been told, frequents the big parking lot. The woods, unruly or not, are its only neighborhood and the river is wide and beautiful here.

At the one end of our street in Fort George, Lyon Street, was the Nechako River but at the other end was the Spruceland Shopping Plaza, anchored by the huge grocery store, the unfortunately named Overwaitea. Overwaitea's a family name, probably a border corruption from some original European spelling, and the supermarkets are a B.C. chain. I walked over there for the first time on Sunday and wandered the aisles, poking around for something for dinner and seeing what they had. I love grocery shopping, and the mom-and-pop corner stores and the extensive twenty-four hour supermarkets are all connected to the same welter of associations. I love the specificity, the range of smells, and the amateurishness of the former but I love the plenty of the latter. In Bloomington, when my friend Soncia Salter talks of taking the two-hour grand tour of Schnucks, heads nod—in a city such as Bloomington, Schnucks is our alpha and omega, our horn of visible plenty, our Left Bank. I make a point of pronouncing it "schnooks"; no one notices. But everyone, I think, needs to surrender now and again, to give in—we need to lose ourselves in something bigger and Schnucks will do; it's the self-described "Friendliest Store in Town" and all the employees speak to you. It's pleasant, if a little Fellini-esque. But Overwaitea—out there at the rough-and-tumble end of civilization—had even more variety than our wealthy, suburban Schnucks with its acres of parking, its proximity to Veterans Parkway, its nighthawks. Overwaitea featured twenty chrome tables stacked high with fresh vegetables and fruit, even mangoes, a big book area with real books, kits for making beer and wine, many, many, many bins of spices, and five or six brands of balsamic vinegar (to the Schnucks store's one). My fellow shoppers were the Prince George citizenry I'd rubbed shoulders with in previous visits: white Canadians, muscular, unpretentious folks of the North—the parking lot was full of 4×4 pickups with cracked windshields in whose front seats lounged grizzly dogs. I saw one black man working in produce that first day and a "mixed race" child spoke to me in the Bulk Foods aisle; otherwise it was white, patrons, clerks, and managers alike. (Excepting the few Chinese and one couple from the First Nations, as they're called in Canada now, at least in the newspapers. Soncia Salter is both black and Jewish.) I don't recall what I found us for dinner but I do remember being well received, joked with in one of the little bouts of flirtation that are common in commerce, that are finite and a kind of friendly nothingness, in line by the checkout girl, a young woman with a Russian name.

The next day was Monday and I walked Madeline to Quinson School, which was right around the corner, and came back and sat down at Vivien's Macintosh. So here I was, in town and ready to document John R.'s long sojourn in this country—I typed the date, 17 January 1995, and then I typed "John Robert Giscome." I looked around at the walls covered with Vivien's books in homemade bookcases—I thumbed through *Moby-Dick*, a collection of bawdy ballads, and *How to Shit in the Woods*. I went upstairs to the kitchen and got more coffee and looked out the big picture window in the living room: the land of ice and snow and there were those big bluffs too, across town, looming over the pulp mill. Katharine was reading. I came back downstairs and stared at the screen.

I'd brought a big shopping bag full of papers and books with me and I rummaged in it and came to my Xerox from the 1863 *Colonist*. I read through the article again and got to the statement of John R.'s arrival here: "Mr. Giscome left the Mouth of Quesnelle in November 1862 in company with his partner, Henry McDame, and proceeded up the Fraser in a canoe. Endeavoring to reach Fort St. James but failing to do so in consequence of the ice they made Fort George on the 24 of November. At this Fort Mr. Charles, the company's chief trader, received them kindly. Giscome and his partner here built a cabin and wintered . . ."

I typed "Winter in Fort George" at the top of the document and saved it that way on Vivien's hard drive. Then I wrote,

I am, as usual, on an edge of town—drawn here—or at a place in town from which the edge is palpable, reachable. Visible looming through, as it were, the trees & against the enormous distance beyond here. I'm at a loose end, I am a loose end & static, blunted. The edge however is soft & ambiguous: at the curve of Lyon St.'s a precipice, at the bottom of which are the Canadian National tracks &, just past those, the Nechako River covered partially—almost completely—with ice. Madeline Giscombe & I saw a black fox below us on the railroad on our first trip out walking at night.

I typed further—some observations about the big ravens I'd seen flying over the house (and how their voices sounded disarmingly like human speech) and then some lines from one of my poems: "This is no story, / " I'd written, about the way out of the South, the way north across the Ohio River, "this is the way in & further in." And I found myself thinking then about Dayton, Ohio, where I'd grown up on the West Side—the black side—of town: on the West Side there were, of course, several different neighborhoods (Westwood, Residence Park, Crown Point, etc.) but they were all lumped together under that banner—the West Side—, that area that began at Infirmary Road and stopped at Wolf Creek to the north and the Miami River to the east; water marked the edges. (Across Wolf Creek were white Catholics and beyond the Catholics were the Jews, who, I discovered when I went to the Society of Mary's high school, loomed almost as large as black people in the Catholic imagination. Downtown lay across the Miami.) I have a theory that, at least in border states like Ohio, black communities formed along the principal route

of ingress *from* the South—the West Side was really the south-
west quadrant of Dayton, the streets along Route 4, the road in
from Cincinnati, the "Gateway City to the South." My parents still live in the house on Liscum Drive in which I grew up;
it's remarkable to me how little the neighborhood, Crown
Point, has changed since the days I was a child there—it's still
the farthest-out neighborhood on the West Side, it's the place
where the city ends, and our house was the very last house in
the city. In the fifties a rim of black suburbs was built beyond
Crown Point, to the southwest, over the edge, but expansion
in that direction halted in the sixties, maybe because of the
advent of integration, maybe because of economic collapse.
When I visit nowadays I bring my bicycle and it's possible to
leave my parents' house, get through the 'burbs, and be riding
in the country in under ten minutes. It's Ohio, it's no wilderness, but there are a few patches of woods and some creeks and
I've seen deer pitching through the fields off Liberty Road, the
long road that intersects Liscum Drive just past the edge of
Crown Point. Crown Point itself is poor but the poverty's
southern rather than urban: when I went to elementary school
my black schoolmates were from the deep South, or their parents were, and my white schoolmates were from Kentucky.
The streets are as rutted now as they were then and still have
no sidewalks; the houses are small bungalows, statements in a
vernacular. In the forties, my parents bought the corner of
what had been a prosperous farm, including the big old
white house that's anomalous in Crown Point if, in part,
because of its age. "This house is a landmark," my mother told
me when I was a child. So I grew up in a landmark: now it's
been the Giscombes' house for fifty years and Giscombes still
live in it.

But here I was in Vivien and John's house in front of a

humming computer screen. "Winter in Fort George" was, thus far, a quite measly document. What in the world was I supposed to be doing here? I dug into the shopping bag again and came up with a box of diskettes: I found the one marked "Fulbright," popped it into the drive, and opened the essay from my application. I'd written, "I want to begin a book—a prose meditation on John Robert Giscome's exploration of northern B.C., a book that will obligate me to trace and travel as much as I can of his routes in the Cariboo and Cassiar Districts and in the Peace River country, a book that will integrate maps, interviews, a few photographs, found documents, etc. with my own language." This sounded good but it wasn't helping. I scrolled down and read further, about the figure of my interest: "Indeed, the public space in which he has best survived is the area of geographical description."

So here I was in Fort George looking to celebrate some Giscombe or Giscome thing more geographical than these houses and less palpably edgy than the Nechako River or the Fraser. Way up here in Canada the most public legacy of John R. was the trail connecting the watersheds. It was not the edge but the way between edges: a bridge over a river connects two static, locatable shores, but John R.'s way connected two river systems themselves, the farthest inland reaches of two oceans. His way's a reversal of the assumptions and emphases of bridge. And here I was to look for images or language or anything that might have *something* to do with his presence. My previous experiences in the unpeopled North had suggested to me that the jungle takes back whatever relics you leave, that its density prevails. I'd described Katharine in a poem as "the density at all edges," by which I'd meant to imply an intricacy that was beautiful and other from me; perhaps I meant "human." This was winter in Fort George, though, and the density, the jungle, was snow; and here I was a black Marlow going into that seeking black Mistah Kurtz. And for whom?

From the Fulbright application: "I see this book as connected to my interest in B.C. literature as I see John Giscome's own situation as being that of a self-aware outsider"—I could have been describing myself here. But Fort George was not literature, it was not some parable or system of symbols, and I was not the first stranger in the village. There's a black obstetrician in Prince George (a brother, it turns out, of Maurice Bishop, the late prime minister of Grenada) and Lance Morgan, the minister of the large Baptist Church, is black. There's a handful of others. When I'd come through in November I'd met a fellow from Chicago named Granville Johnson and had asked him about how things were for us here—"It's OK," he'd said, "but you're always the only one." Before I left Bloomington I'd been talking with Becky Hawkins, a white woman who owned my favorite local restaurant, Bec's Texas Thai Grill. She was from the Northwest, from Oregon, and knew people who'd gone to Prince George. I asked her why anyone would go up there and she'd looked at me knowingly and said, "To be alone."

The first days passed in John and Vivien's house on Lyon Street, but we weren't that lonely. People—friends and friends of friends—invited us to some dinner parties and we went walking in the snow in Cottonwood Park with Barry and Joy McKinnon. Later, when Katharine and Madeline and I walked alone in Wilson Park, which was near our rented house, we were surprised to come to the same sign, bolted permanently to a tree, that we'd seen a few days earlier when we were with Barry and Joy: "Bears have recently been seen in this park," an illustration of a bear, and a number to call "if you see a bear." My friend Alan Broughton said he'd run toward the one he saw in a tree in the Adirondacks, arms outstretched. And Katharine had a club when she worked at the Ross Park Zoo, Bears for Baudelaire—all you had to do to join was to say, at their cage, "Mon semblable—mon frère." The bear on the sign's illustration was a black bear, Ursus americanus. (Grizzlies were an hour away in Vanderhoof, where they're "a problem.") Winter meant that the black bears were in "semi-hibernation," unseen, a hidden presence of black fur. Clarence Major's Dictionary of African-American Slang mentions the phrase "Nothing to the bear but his curly hair" as a taunt to express some lack of courage.

My second or third evening in town, as I was putting her to bed, Madeline asked if Bigfoot could look in her window; it was the question she'd been saving for my arrival in Fort George, since I was the family Bigfoot expert. The reports vary—six feet to eleven feet tall. Supposedly one was captured in the Fraser Canyon at Yale in 1897 and became—goes one variation on the story—Jocko the Dog-Faced Boy for Ringling Brothers. If the individual was ten or eleven feet tall and stood on John's snow-covered motorcycle, which was parked underneath the window in question, then he or she *could* look in— but the motorcycle, a Honda 250, would be untrustworthy as far as balance went and I pointed that out to Madeline, which relieved her some. The statue I remembered from the road just north of Williams Lake was the size, I think, of a tall human, about six and a half feet. Perhaps that's part of what made it so startling.

Many Bigfoot reports are rather obviously sightings of bears. Booze, I suspect, is a big factor; but I think there's also the desire to see something distorted and familiar both, some avatar, in some sort of primordial place. But even bears are metaphors for us, being the same shape, roughly: a shocking description of us, a wrong exaggerated depiction. "Old man in the fur coat," said Gary Snyder in a poem, and "grandfather blackfood."

But as I trudged through that first week in Fort George I was thinking of family ties more than Bigfoot or bears. More than houses. It had occurred to me that I was here looking for John R.'s trace on behalf of the family, that that was for whom I was pursuing this, that that was the *us* I was Marlow for. It was less a deep realization than a way I understood I *could* look at things; it was a tradition of looking—the lens of family—with which I was familiar, one that was available to me. And the semester before, I'd received a come-on from a business in northern Ohio offering for sale something called "The World Book of Giscombes": the outfit targets people with unusual names and two of my fellow professors at Illinois State have their advertisements—one for "The World Book of Parrys," the other for "The World Book of Van der Laans"—posted on their office doors among the announcements of conferences and cartoons from *The New Yorker*. These "World Books" themselves are an obvious effort to cash in on the *Roots* phenomenon, on the consciousness of family ties that came into big numbers after the success of Alex Haley's TV saga—they're gatherings of quite generic information (about names in general and about places to begin researching your family history) but they also include a list of addresses and phone numbers of people with your surname in the States and Canada and Britain, and that legwork, that research and computer time, that's what I sent in my thirty dollars for. (This being before I had access to the Internet.) In that first week in Fort George I typed up and printed many copies of a broad letter to all those Giscombes asking if they'd ever heard of John Robert Giscome, asking about the spelling of the name, asking whether the name Giscombe accurately reflects "your ethnic, racial, or national background or identity." I addressed them all by hand one long afternoon, bundled them up, and drove them through the snow to the mailbox by the bicycle shop. All those names—Giscombe after Giscombe after Giscombe, the black ink of my handwriting on the white paper—went into the Canada Post and I came home then feeling a little relief—here, I'd finally *accomplished* something—as I stopped at Overwaitea to pick up dinner.

But I kept being unhappy in Vivien's study and after a couple of more days I backed off a little and stopped trying to aggressively write my "prose meditation"; I began reading Wallace Stegner's *Wolf Willow*, a book I'd been meaning to get to for years. I wrote open-endedly in my journal. And I went back to work on the almost-completed poetry manuscript, the *Giscome Road* book. That book isn't really about John R., as I mentioned earlier, but he appears now and again. One night in Bloomington, a couple of years before we got to Fort George, I'd dreamed a long, involved dream of the Giscome Portage— waking, I wrote it down in my journal and it stayed with me and became, more easily than is usual for such things, a longish poem, a part of *Giscome Road*. John R. was a short, dark-skinned man with a neat white goatee and a missing leg and in the poem (as in the dream) he "got around the site with a single cane, in shorts // which showed the muscle of the one 'good' leg, // which flapped empty from the other . . ."; and, later: "He spotted me & called 'We have some things in common' . . ." I say now that it was John R. with the gone leg and the goatee but in the dream this was never clear: it was a final knowledge or identification that was, curiously, held back. It was a static uncertainty, one that I accepted without question, satisfied with the surface, with what I called, in the poem, "the countenance // of the man's woods." In the dream, in spite of the man's never having been identified as John R. Giscome, I knew that the swath of land I was traversing was certainly the Giscome Portage. It was a walking dream and in it I'd pressed on on foot, the poem (and the dream) ending this way:

>   . . . the named road I wanted
> turned off the apparent continuation of itself
>
> the name continuing way on into the uplands even further, past
> the pavement's end—
>
> so I took it, climbing over the rocks, a jumble
> of rocks until I got finally to some stairs
>   (wch the rocks had become
>
> up to a door in the side of a red wooden house perched
> at the top, in the rocks at the top
> of the hill.

It was the first week of my residency in Fort George. I went out on Night Patrol with Madeline several more times and we saw the taillights and headlights of trucks on the Hart Highway across the Nechako River, the road that curves up the hill toward the Giscome Portage, toward Alaska. At least once during each walk we'd peer over the embankment at the railroad tracks but the fox we'd seen that first night was never there. We threw snowballs at each other among the dark houses.

Ontario Towns

Up early in my room in the Kaladar Hotel and important to stop departure preparations for however long it took to note in my journal that "I feel the landscape making subtle demands on me." I'd broken down in a misty rain in Kaladar the day before—a flange had cracked on the hub of the bicycle's rear wheel, a thing not supposed to happen—and had had to thumb sixty miles to the nearest cycle shop and then sixty miles back with a new wheel, arriving finally again in Kaladar in deep fog: it was by then six and I couldn't see where I was going anyway, so I bought a room for $12 Canadian. I'd left the bike in one of the unused service bays at Neueport Services, a combination lunch counter–gas station–cheese shop run by a large and articulated family from India: husband and wife, brothers-in-law, pregnant young women, teenage children. They'd been sweet to me, letting me leave my stuff there, saying that if I returned late and found the station closed I should knock on the door of their house up the road, walking me out into the mist so I could see it and know it when I came back, pointing at it. Kaladar is a crossroads and little else: Neueport

Services and the hotel across the street from it together are the business district. The patriarch of the family was a man in his mid-forties, a bit older than I was then, and he walked and walked around, he was always in motion: checking, worrying. He insisted on helping me put the bike back together upon my return (meaning it took twice as long as it should have) and politely inquired, after I'd got off his pay phone with Katharine, if everything was OK at home, sounding nervously pleased when I said yes, relieved almost. For me? I'd come out of nowhere on a bicycle: I don't know what he thought was at stake.

This was the trip to North Bay, that's where I was heading, my journey to *see* the very far-off Ontario place that my family had extended to. The family at Neueport Services then was like mine: people of color from near the equator here among the great outcroppings of rock, mosses, ripple-less still lakes choked with lily pads, coniferous trees looming through the pale, pale mist, all the *northern* things, all their "subtle demands." Across Route 41 the Kaladar Hotel was a ram-shackle building, it smelled bad—musty and something worse than musty as well—and so seemed appropriately *of* the place. It had a harshly lit little dining room on the first floor, and I ordered a roast beef sandwich, tough and jagged little strips of meat on quartered white toast. Back upstairs I drew some water to take my nightly anti-asthma pill, gulped it, and then spat out as much as I could, it was so awful, fetid tasting. "This is nowhere but I'm alive at the bone," I scribbled that night, appropriating *alive at the bone* from Michael Ondaatje's Billy the Kid book, "in this perfect little room," and then went to sleep for seven hours, leaving Kaladar at 8 a.m. in bright sun-shine, waving to the people at Neueport, pleased to be back in the saddle, glad to be going on.

At stake? Later that day the odometer I'd been using all summer turned over onto 1,000 miles, which pleased me further because I couldn't remember what all the instructions-for-use had said and hadn't known if the little machine *would* flip over onto 1000.0 and not simply and suddenly read 000.0. It was a fine day to be out banging across the Canadian Shield: the atypical early start, shining sun, good lunch—by the time 1,000 miles was drawing nigh—at a hoity-toity Swiss restaurant I'd found in the crotch of an otherwise nondescript fork in the road, and the easy, continual thrill of traveling through at that moment the kind of country I like best: rolling hills to muscle over without dropping down more than one or two sprockets. Singing "John Henry," singing the "Rally 'round the flag, boys" verses from George Root's old "Battle Cry of Freedom" song (which is—if one can forget this moment's popular stupidity about how bad it is to burn a flag—actually quite moving, the lines in particular "And although they may be poor, / Not a man shall be a slave"), singing "Erie Canal," and "Hesitation Blues," singing "Midnight Special" about going to North Bay and how, once there, you better walk right. Old songs are the best. This was long day five and it came in, at sunset, at 90.08 miles.

(At stake? I'd started in front of my house in Ithaca, N.Y., milepost 0, intending to bicycle to North Bay but then go farther from there and make it into the Arctic watershed—I'd intended to traverse some regions, to get from the Finger Lakes across the Canadian Shield to where the rivers flow north into Hudson Bay. I'd catch the train home from one of the weird towns of the north, Iroquois Falls, say, or even fabled Cochrane, where the Ontario Northland crosses the CNR. It was a typical desire—I wanted to press out over an edge and keep going. When Madeline turns fourteen we'll start in

Vancouver—or so the plan is now—and bicycle to Alaska, though I'll be almost fifty. John R. Giscome at fifty—or early in his fifties—was a miner still, living and working at McDame Creek in the very isolated Cassiar District. We'll pass through it on Route 37, the less-traveled road to Alaska, and arrive at Anchorage ten days or so later and get the boat back to Prince Rupert or Bellingham. Then what'll I do?)

I camped that night at Lake Doré, in a pay place, and got the more typical late start the next day, cruising into Pembroke at 11:30: industrial, long, low shank of a town on the Ottawa River. I crossed Route 17, the next road I'd planned to follow, on the approach, the outskirts, and was dismayed to find its shoulders made of sand and the two-lane itself choked with fast traffic. Sand's quite impossible to bike in (the wheels sink) and the degree of traffic suggested that even if I stayed at the most extreme edge of the pavement I'd still have a fair chance of getting smacked within the first hour. That far north in Ontario the number of roads declines dramatically: this one was the only way out of Pembroke in the direction I wanted to go. Bad news, too much to deal with, so I drifted into Pembroke proper, where suddenly it was noon: a lot of women who looked like secretaries were in the streets with bag lunches, walking up the hill from river-level downtown—going where?—still in their summer dresses (it was September, so only the nights were cold), one very dark black man among them walking stiffly in a three-piece suit. West Indian? No, African, I thought as he didn't meet my eyes, looking through me instead, haughty. I realized there at high noon in Pembroke that I should have taken the other road, the one that cuts west through Algonquin Provincial Park, I'd passed it many miles previous: backtracking then, taking the extra day, was how it would have to be. But right then I was hungry and my every piece of clothing—except a pair of long khaki pants—reeked of sweat and road, so I did a laundry and ate some lunch and, while my clothes were in the dryer, on an impulse, I found a phone and called VIA and there was indeed a train to North Bay and it left Pembroke in thirty-five minutes. I got there, though my socks were still damp, and the conductor lifted the bike into the baggage car. I dropped down into a coach seat and the big extravagantly tattooed pink-faced young man sitting across the aisle tossed me a can of warm Budweiser from an apparently bottomless stash. Leaving Pembroke.

The train went out along the Ottawa and crossed Route 17 now and again, the sandy shoulder visibly continuing. Ugly little towns but the deciduous trees were just starting to go over to colors. What route would my grandfather's brother—whose name I didn't even know as I was sitting there in the coach trying to think about him, we're that kind of shut-mouthed family—have taken to get to North Bay? This one, from Montreal or Ottawa, or, more likely, the Ontario Northland Railway, the straight shot north from Toronto? My grandfather had also wanted to go to Canada, to B.C., as I said before this, but I really don't know why. It's my imagination that John R.'s legacy in the province had something to do with it but maybe that man's life in the North and in Victoria and my grandfather's inquiry to the Medical Board (fourteen years after John R.'s death) are just part of the stack of coincidental non sequiturs; I can certainly imagine good reasons for any black person to want to leave the American South of the first half of this century. But then my grandfather was a black doctor, and living in a place with a large black population sounds like both a good career strategy and a way itself into a life rich with meaning: the obituary made note of his "deep and active interest in

Negro health in Jefferson County." How will my interlocutors sum me up when I've shuffled off to Buffalo for the last time? Anyway, I know neither why my grandfather thought of going to B.C. nor why he didn't go, it was never discussed, and he's been dead now almost forty years. A certain impenetrability lies at the heart of things, the ball of what? family tendencies I can see in my father, the aloneness centralized, the deliberate silent space around the human part of it. I can see it in myself. The train lurched and squeaked past a beaver lake: ferns, marsh grasses, larches. The tattooed man across the aisle was from Nova Scotia and was going out to work the forests up in northern B.C. "Fucking fourteen dollars an hour," he said, "and that's just to start, eh?" I saw a porcupine moving along beside us in that slow-motion way they have and then fell asleep in my seat. An hour later we came to North Bay.

Which I'd always heard described as a hole, a ragged frontier slum town, the heart of nowhere, or its *edge*. It *wasn't* lovely—too much traffic for the narrow streets and particularly devoid of trees—but it was no particular slum and the people I met were, on the surface anyway, more conscious, more alert (meaning alive) than people one tends to butt up against in towns in, say, upstate New York or downstate Illinois. Maybe the landscape demanded it of them. No Giscombes, though, in the phone book there in the station waiting room, not that I would have called. At stake? What would I have said? I didn't know where I could camp thereabouts and neither did the station agent, so she directed me instead to the Ontario Provincial Police station, the inevitable O.P.P., she and I joking companionably over her directions so much that I got lost in the process itself and found myself on a street full of blank-faced postwar houses. I hailed a girl who was walking by—about twelve, the breasts bouncing free under her tunic having more to do with fat than with adolescence—asking her if she knew the way to the police station, and she stared at me then finally exhaled Holy shit! and called another girl slightly older who came running from a house and didn't know either but who called a third girl, assuring me that she—the third girl, Joyce, I think— knew where *everything* in town was. Joyce came bopping across the street in her high-tops, one blue and one pink, and deck pants pulled tight over her wiry self. She was pale as the other two girls but her skin's definition was different, supple where theirs was rough and with a deep glow to it: that and her hair and especially the line of her jaw told me—though it didn't consciously (or *verbally*) register till hours later when I was describing her in my journal—that she had a few African ancestors. Her pals told her how I wanted to go to the O.P.P. station and so she directed me, with elaborate gestures and succinct qualifications (first explaining to the others, e.g., that she would direct me, though, in a stage whisper, "we do not know *why* he wishes to see the police, nor shall we inquire") and gave me advice for cycling through North Bay. She was casually encyclopedic about the layout of her town and her words and phrasings were measured: descriptions of the unimportant tossed off, *ways* of proceeding through certain intersections stressed. Fourteen and held in esteem by her friends, a leader of those white girls, the power of language singing within her, singing out from her. "Hey," she'd called after I'd thanked her and was pedaling down toward the end of her street, "it was good meeting you," the salute to the social, to the incident itself, from a very mature child. More? I wondered the next day, did she know she was black? And I wondered later still, two days and a hundred miles up the road it stopped me, at the chance of her being a relative.

In the morning I headed out of town, stopping first at a sewing supply shop to buy a needle and thread to sew the button back onto one of my two pairs of shorts. The lady insisted on not charging me and gave me the official Transportation and Communications Ministry map of northern Ontario. "We'd not want you to think," she said, "that the only thing going on in Ontario is Toronto." She opened it up to help me find the road I'd be taking and there was the great colorless blankness of the map: vast, vast, vast Ontario with rivers running through it, symbols for O.P.P. outposts and tiny airports, lakes, hardly any roads anywhere, more rivers, a huge profoundly, blankly white map—it covered the counter and draped over, North Bay at its bottom—of largely unbroken space.

And it was that space I made for, leaving North Bay that morning in weak sunlight that faded into hours of drizzle and more mist, heading farther and farther north, sharing the less traveled of the two roads north with, mostly, little convoys of lumber trucks, cruising for two days along the Ottawa, crossing into Quebec—at a strange lumber town with Italian antique fountains at every intersection, the town, I think, that Margaret Atwood describes at the beginning of *Surfacing*— and drifting up alongside the east shore of Lake Timiskaming, seeing Ontario (the lake's the border) through breaks in the fog and rain. The subtle demands of traveling in rain. To be moving through that—through bear, wolf, and moose country, though I saw none of those animals—was what I'd come for, to be alive and taking myself farther north, farther away from landscape I knew. I'd wanted to be moving and, at the same time, up close against the big space—rocks, exotic mosses, big skeins of wires coming down in cuts through the trees from remote hydro projects, animals, trees and more trees beyond those—stretching away from the edge of my body all the way to the coast of Labrador.

But early the next day it began raining again and I realized I wasn't going to make it into the watershed—I was missing Katharine and Madeline and I was tired, I'd gotten five hundred miles out from Ithaca (not counting the little skip on the train) much of which was in rain and had had it—so I cut west, up over the top of the lake back into Ontario, and came to New Liskeard a bit before sunset. I'd picked up a schedule in North Bay—the southbound train came through here at midnight. Here? New Liskeard's a lovely town, I discovered, built on terraces up from Lake Timiskaming or up rather from an estuary of that lake. Coming in, cruising through downtown, I was glad to pass a movie theater showing a film I'd not seen and figured I could stand seeing, A Fish Called Wanda, a comedy that featured some of the Monty Python players. I found the Ontario Northland station and left my panniers there, put on the pair of long khaki pants, and came back to the theater for my night out: it was strange to be suddenly sitting back at a movie eating popcorn and drinking a Coke alone among strangers laughing together with them at John Cleese and Jamie Lee Curtis. And it was strange being entertained in public at an entertainment palace after nights of sleeping out (and one night in a gnomish hotel), strange to pay to be distracted, the distraction oddly more pleasant for my seeing it for what it was.

After the movie I had a surprisingly decent Chinese dinner, then wandered back to the station. It was a cool night, cloudy as it had been all day, a breeze blowing in off Lake Timiskaming; seventy or eighty miles, I guess, short of the Arctic watershed. Years later, in Fort George, the edge of that same watershed would be easy to reach and cross and return from on a day ride and I did take that ride several times. What was at stake, though, here in Ontario? It's a wonderful name— the Arctic watershed, redolent of houses and ice and exotic coldwater fish—but it's really just a fact of drainage; perhaps there would have been a sign. But it was—or would have been—an extremity, a new physical state to muscle *knowingly* into: body, mind, geography. (But here I was only as far as New Liskeard instead, having had a good dinner, having enjoyed myself at a film, having coincided with an artistic black child in surprising North Bay, having cycled seventy, eighty, and ninety miles a day for day after day, and now waiting for the southbound feeling OK. I was thirty-seven and alive and, more, corporeal—feeling strong and it was good to be even this far north—and consciously deferring the big gratification. A long freight train came by—incredibly bright constellation of three headlights on the first engine, two of which were down low at either end of the base of the triangle, *the better to see you with*—picking up speed, and the stationmaster and I were standing there in the wind it made on the platform watching it, car after car after car until the shapes blurred: I don't know what was in his mind but I was thinking of living a long life of this.) At stake? Why was I always running to Canada when I had some time, crossing that border to touch the big otherness? Why does it feel so good to be alive at the moment when, alone and far away, you turn around and start heading back home?

I woke up once during the longish stop in North Bay and then slept all the way until we slowed for the Toronto 'burbs: Saabs and BMWs were jammed into the commuter station parking lots, it being midmorning, so all the lawyers and bankers and what-have-you had already been at their desks a good two hours. And more or less suddenly the city itself was visible, one of the major ones of the Western world: publishing, theater, commerce, immigrants from all over the world, a thousand posh things to do at night. But still, above the tracks where it would be visible to the commuters on their trains that also used this route in, was a huge billboard advertising hiking boots, good old-fashioned Vibram-soled waffle stompers to live in all day whilst tromping across the muskeg, through exotic mosses, along the marges of those still lakes, *that* sense of the world saluted at the marge of sophisticated Toronto. All that space behind me, I thought, that I'd gone off into and come back out of and I'd not even got to the place where the rivers flow north or the place beyond there where the roads stop (or the place beyond even that where the Ontario Northland tracks stop). This, I thought—though I recognized the presumption a few days later—, living *with* all that space, this was what it meant to be Canadian.

June 1989

I glided down the hill into Kaladar and there was Neueport Services, doing a brisk trade in the heat, cars lined up at the pumps for that Shell gasoline. This time it was only the end of my second day—I'd gotten a lift from Ithaca to near Watertown, New York—and it being only six and one of the longest days of the year I was thinking of going farther, pressing on to the provincial park twelve miles up the road. But it was hot and I was tired and they remembered me when I went in to buy a bottle of apple juice. The man I remembered as being the patriarch was absent and one of the younger guys— who perhaps had always really been in charge? the other having been only patriarch*al?*—took me around to show me how they'd expanded the business since I'd been there the previous September: the under-one-roof complex now included a package store and a novelty shop, the sort of place where one buys funny bumper stickers. I was pleased that they were doing well and said so as I felt my body beginning to acknowledge road-weariness, as the miles caught up with me, as they say, as the Kaladar Hotel squatting—again—across Route 41 started to look good.

This was a different kind of trip, a bit more frantic, that much more directed. I'd broken one of my rules for bike traveling—*all trips* must *start at home*—and taken the car ride for the first 150 miles with my friend David Warren to Lake Bonaparte, at the northwestern edge of the Adirondacks: this meant I could head straight west and actually be—via two ferries—in Canada, the big otherness, by the end of Day One. What was at stake: After living twenty years in upstate New York I'd had a pre-middle-age surge of ambition and taken that faculty job at Illinois State University, in the Corn Belt, far from everywhere in the world I'd got familiar with. This was— as I explained to two cyclists from Toronto who I met on the first of the two ferries to Kingston, Ontario—my farewell tour of the East. *It was good of you,* said the woman as we cycled across Wolfe Island to the second ferry, *to take your farewell tour in Canada.* I camped with them that night in Kingston; her name was Jackie and she was tough and arrogant and smart and awkwardly sweet. I don't recall the man's name: there was tension between them, their end probably as lovers (or the awkward *beginnings* of them being lovers). At stake? I wanted to get back to North Bay and spend a day or so checking out the Giscombes there—what public history or notation I could find—and then get myself quickly back to Ithaca to recommence packing for the move west. North Bay's a long, long way from central Illinois: this was just about the last chance to get up there, even this casually.

Leaving Kingston the next morning, Sunday, in hot hazy sunlight and pressing on north through Napanee and then up into the woods and lakes, I got to Kaladar, the end of Day Two. I steeled myself and went on into the Kaladar Hotel, finding the lobby different: it didn't smell bad, the moldy stacks of magazines were gone, and there was a large etching propped on one of the couches (which were new) of a black man playing a flute. No one around, though, except in the dining room, which had also been refurbished. The waiter took me back through hallways and there, in a tiny office, was one of the new owners. The hotel itself, she said, wasn't ready yet, they were still fixing up the place, having just bought it in April. But I persisted until she agreed to let me have my old room, with its spray-painted #1 on the door, just for the evening, "since you stayed here before and know what the rooms are like"; she filled out a lodging card for me, taking care to cross out the name of the former proprietor, Beulah Tricky. In the dining room her husband, the cook, shook my hand and told me to sit anywhere. She was white, he was black, both somewhere past fifty and from a town nearby. Their names—Donna and Andy Anderson—were listed in the hotel's ad on the Chamber of Commerce paper place mat in among the car dealerships and fishing camps, "Open Under New Management." I ordered a bottle of Labatt's and the day's special, liver and onions, using the beer glass to prop open my copy of Eugene Genovese's book about the slaves, *Roll, Jordan, Roll*: I'd be teaching African-American Lit for the first time ever in a few weeks and I wanted to know as much as I could about context. A fellow at the next table inquired as to what I was read-

ing and we began talking about *recent* history, about Salman
Rushdie's troubles and what few options the British had in
dealing with matters of his protection. Soon we were talking
about nations and the nature of power, politics, things that
related rather much to Brother Genovese's themes in *Roll,
Jordan, Roll*. It was a conversation I'd not expected to be having in the Kaladar Hotel. He was, it turned out, a white (or
apparently white) Trinidadian, a bit older than me, who'd just
given up on finishing *The Satanic Verses*, having found it tiresome. A young man sitting nearby commenced about how the
Rushdie thing was nothing but another insult to the West by
the A-rabs and that the Brits ought to just nuke Iran, but the
man from Trinidad and I agreed in gestures and in a couple of
words exchanged over the younger man's head that the world
is what it is.

The dinner Andy Anderson brought me that evening was
one of the best dinners I've ever had and I didn't even know I
was very hungry. Simple food exquisitely prepared: the liver
was more tender than I'd imagined it ever could be, more deli-
cately breaded, more beautifully garnished with asparagus and
cauliflower and broccoli. Afterward there was pie and easy talk
with him and Donna. They bought up dilapidated places like
the Kaladar Hotel, had been for years, and would run them
until the places got successful and they—Donna and Andy—
were bored, at which point they'd move on down the road.
They were both older than they looked. Looking at him, listening to him talk in that Canadian lilt (with no recognizable
black inflection), I thought, naturally, of my grandfather's
brother: I mentioned then how I was going to North Bay to
look for family things, seeing if he'd have anything to say
about that, but didn't press the point when he didn't. Now, of
course, I see it as being a constellation of points: I mean my

ignorance of black life in the Ontario bush and frontier towns, my ignorance of the context within the context. I didn't—and still don't—know what's at stake in the bigger pictures: I'd been thinking of my great-uncle's blackness making him anomalous in North Bay, but that's the way my family has always thought of itself: *whatever* the context, we are separate from it. I'd had my hiking boot epiphany on the train the year before about Canadian identity, but that was myself being knee-jerk literary, meaning detached from anything specific as well as presumptuous. I'd not been prepared to meet a native black man in Upper Canada who served me an incredible dinner while wearing penny loafers. And besides, in my house at home I'm the cook, for company and the weekdays both, and have been for years—I'm intimate with that whole production including some of the metaphors. John R., according to Father Morice's book, had worked at some point as a cook for Peter Dunlevy. Otherness? How are we different, exactly, and how are we similar (exactly)?

Halfway through the next day I made the turn I should have made the year before and pressed on northwest over the hill roads. One stretch of ten miles was all uphill and under construction: great stretches of the road were loose gravel and dump trucks were plentiful (meaning layers and layers of dust in the air). The lads had all the other big yellow machines at play as well (more dust) while bored flag girls sat on coolers smoking cigarettes, 90 degrees or so: it took an hour and a half to get that ten miles but then I came to the hamlet of Palmer Rapids on the Madawaska River and turned there onto a beautifully paved wide-shouldered road that went alongside the river for ten more, straight and flat, the river hidden beyond a thick line of trees but its coolness touching the road. I camped that night at Carson Lake Provincial Park, eating cold beans for dinner and then dozing off still dressed. Waking at midnight, I stripped and swam out into Carson Lake itself until I got a chill and the fact of swimming alone at night in a strange lake suddenly struck me as being a bad idea. I'd come that day eighty-five miles.

Two days later I arrived in North Bay, again by train. I'd intended to cycle all the way this time but a terrible and persistent headwind—on the day I left Carson Lake—had held me to 7 and 8 mph all across big Algonquin Provincial Park and that skewed my schedule just enough to matter, so I spent the last fifty miles of the trip set up in the dining car drinking coffee and watching the landscape slip by. I'd come in from the east before, on VIA, but this time I was approaching from the south on the Ontario Northland. Certainly this was the way my father's uncle had got to North Bay, and on this train ride I knew his name—Charles Giscome. The spelling's different, of course, from my name and the difference is due—at least in part—to a mysterious argument that Charles and my grandfather had. Before I'd gone this time I'd asked my father some specific questions about that part of the family—names, jobs, etc.—and he went on to talk about how they, the brothers, "fell out over something or, more likely, a lot of somethings" early in the century and that his uncle had changed the spelling to spite my grandfather, to publicly distance himself, and then—to make or as if to make the distance real—had moved out to the farthest edge of beyond. Years of high dudgeon in North Bay. Or two solitudes—one in North Bay and the other in Birmingham.

I set up camp where I'd camped before in North Bay and the next morning went out to the regional museum at the edge of town. It was cramped and ugly but not a bad place at all and the intense young man in charge found a J. Giscombe—

spelled like that—on the list of local men who'd come back alive out of WW II. Johnny, whose name I'd heard before, my father's old pen pal: the obvious—that they'd stopped writing because of Johnny going off to the war—hadn't occurred to me and I was relieved to discover that he'd not been killed there, that I wasn't present at the site of some fifty-year-old tragedy. By the time I quit the museum and was cruising back downtown it was noon, and the construction crews were breaking for lunch: lots of building was going on, a new subdivision to fight the woods back some—a couple of the fellows were black, we nodded to each other in the sunshine. (Two years before, when I was cycling through Wales, I met another black man walking toward me on the road out of Penrhyndeudraeth. We both slowed, making eye contact, realizing that some sort of exchange, some sort of salute, was called for, Wales being what it is. But all either of us could think to do was discuss the distance from the point where we *did* stop to speak to one another and the town I'd recently passed through: he asked how far it was, I told him. We wished each other well then and continued on our ways. He had a strange accent, a soft and lovely voice, neither West Indian nor one of the sets of intonations I recognize as African. Perhaps he was Welsh.)

I took my lunch at a crowded greasy spoon back downtown on the main drag, sitting at the counter near the window so I could watch the city parade by: not *many* black people, but more of us than I'd figured from my first trip there. That afternoon I settled down in the library with the big stack of city directories. The earliest one was 1914 and there he was with his name spelled G-I-S-C-O-M-E. Charles Giscome was a chef then, living on Front Street in what seemed to be a largely Italian neighborhood, immigrants like him. Later there was a wife and later still there were children. I made pages and pages of notes on the family's progress, jobs, addresses, then lost the notebook when we moved to Illinois. Typical. But I remember that Charles Giscome's kids took jobs, moved away from home, apparently lost the jobs, and moved back. One—Sybil, I think—eventually became a teacher, another ran a realty company. The old man himself, in the thirties, was listed for a while as a "labourer" and then for a year had a tourist camp. And then in 1940 both he and John had been porters, the *classic* middle-class job for U.S. black men for so many years, porters on the Temiskaming & Northern Ontario Railway. But the next year they were all gone, all of them: I stared at the book at the place between the two other names, Giscard, I think, and Givens; and they were gone for the year after that as well and then there were no more directories until the fifties and they weren't in any of those either. Suddenly then I was back in the library basement and it was past three o'clock, too late really to start checking out anywhere else—city hall, the schools, etc. (When I came across the porter job I'd called the railroad archive and got nowhere.) I felt tired and hot, as though I'd walked across town several times, and began to think about how I'd spend the rest of the day, the suddenly immense blank time before the 3 a.m. train south.

I fumbled through the library some, reading bits in *Certain People*, white Stephen Birmingham's book about the U.S. black middle class and, from the same shelf, some social science essays on the black Canadian community, an entity "prone to fragmentation," or something like that. Leaving the library, I cycled around until I found Front Street but the numbers were all wrong. Still, I realized that I was in the same neighborhood I'd been in the year before where the black girl had talked so beautifully to me: it made, of course, *sociological* sense but it pleased me as well on the other levels. But the fragmentation was setting in, the feeling of breathlessness, of a profound and generalized *fade*, meaning severance, meaning the coming invisibility: no name in the street in this town or in Ithaca. I must have looked lost: a teenager wearing a Simple Minds T-shirt asked if he could help me find something. I gave him a number, an address, on Front Street beyond the point where the street teed into another, asking if Front recommenced somewhere later on, across the RR tracks, say. No, he said, this is it, man, and asked the name of the people I was looking for. I told him, warning that it had been a long time since they'd lived there, let him shake his head no. It felt something like good, though, pronouncing the name aloud into the North Bay streets, into the woods and lakes past the gates to the city. In a spate of the directories from the mid-thirties, the name was spelled, oddly, *with* the "b," and I imagined as I sat in the basement of the North Bay library that during those years my great-uncle had been aiming at a reconciliation with my grandfather, the name spelling being *emblematic* of that; or maybe whoever put the city book together "corrected" the spelling, based on hearing the name or based on *-combe* being a common feature of British names.

In my imagination there in North Bay I felt G-I-S-C-O-M-E taking root as "the Canadian spelling." I'd been asserting casually for years, in conversation, that John R.'s name was an "arguable phonetic spelling" of my own, forging a tie that way between myself and John Robert, between myself and *out there*. But as I'd stared at Charles Giscome's name in the city directories I'd begun thinking that maybe this was something beyond the phonetic, a blood connection, a real family *thing* in the insistence on particular spellings (and whatever loyalties that might imply) at the heart or *alongside* however the long heart of a family is figured or construed. I don't care much for mysteries, they make me irritable. But I do have—and always have had—this thing for the North. This has been the family's progress, of course, the movement from South up this way; indeed, it's an African-American archetype—culture occurs in landscape—and here I am, the first generation born across the Ohio River (and born, admittedly, bourgeois), still having the impulse, *north!*, though it's metaphorized into something other than the sane set of reasons-for-migration that belonged to those who went earlier. But the part of North Bay where I was looking for my great-uncle's addresses does look strikingly like the west end of Bloomington, the side of town where the poorer people live, the side split and split again by those rail-road tracks. The difference, of course, is that North Bay *is* Canadian, so there's no one big empty street, as there is here, in Bloomington, as there is in every U.S. city, no one big empty street named for Dr. King.

The station agent in North Bay remembered me from my having been there before but I embarrassed and surprised myself by failing to recognize *her* when I trailed into the depot that night: I'd thought *about* her, recalling that I'd liked her and had wondered, hopefully, whether or not she'd still be there working for them, this last as I sat through the new and dull *Batman* movie at a theater downtown, killing time, two of the many hours before the train. But if she was offended she didn't show it and why should she be? It's not as though we'd been lovers or even friends. But she is, I realized at some point, the person I know best in that town, which is one of the farthest known edges of this my ragged family.

Three o'clock came and the depot was filled with people waiting for both the southbound and the northbound, which were due to pass each other at North Bay. Four o'clock came and still neither train had showed. Many of us were out on the platform by then watching for them and telling stories. The station agent came out and joined us after a while: we had all seen the headlight appear but the train itself had stopped half a mile or so down the track, so we got the light mixed up with other lights down there, streetlights, God knows what else. Soon the sky itself began to lighten and only then, slowly, did the train ease in. The agent went inside and came out again, with a sleepy crowd behind her, saying *This is the northbound*. I looked up and saw the red-light-marked tail end of another train backing silently in behind on the same track, a conductor with a walkie-talkie riding the vestibule. When it stopped, ten feet from the northbound, I got on the coach looking over my shoulder at the woman working both trains with the baggage cart, wondering how long she'd remember me from this time.

But then the train started with a soft jerk forward. "Now *he's* gonna have to back out," the conductor said to another passenger, pointing back at the northbound. The sun was almost in the sky, my last long night in Canada spent where else but in a train station. One needs songs to sing on the road, of the road—music should have come up, some sort of as yet unimagined straining *northern* jazz, an *insistent* strain, say, of straying muted horns, fragmented, breaking. Leaving North Bay.

November 1989

Midterm exam in my African-American Lit course, English 165-01, Illinois State University, Fall 1989. I'd assigned three essay questions about the books I'd had the students read and, for many, these were the first three essays they'd been called upon to write since they'd left the university's one required Freshman English course. I hadn't known, at the time, that this was the case. But all that's to say that lots of distraught kids called the night before the morning the paper was due telling me that they had no idea what the questions were about and could I please tell them "what you want." They were thrown, in part, by my using terms like "discuss" and "evaluate," which they'd, apparently, not encountered much before.

Most of my students in that course were black like me but from, for the greatest part, Chicago, a city I didn't know then, and from lives I don't know—I was their age twenty years before this and in college in upstate New York, living, more or less by default, with white people and described accurately by those people as a loner: walking all over town by myself, reading books, trying to write. "We're not a reading people," suggested another new black professor here, though he is and I am. And I think that his comment, made over lunch in the quiet, spacious week after our first year at Illinois State had ended, made us both uncomfortable or, more to the point, brought home to us the strain between ourselves and our students. My white ISU students didn't read either but that was a different problem. Yet I suppose that the black students at ISU are really rather much like the white students, the ones who've come from the Wasp suburbs west of Chicago: I mean they've come, like those white students, without a tradition of scholarly achievement (or cut off from that tradition which I saw so much of when I was coming up in the black middle class) and with a sense—almost invisible—of self-defeat that, in the white students, isn't as important because the white system that produced them will take care of them, reabsorb them after they graduate by giving them jobs and allowing them to grow jowly and comatose in those jobs until they retire and die. (It'll also take care of the black students but I mean "take care of" in a different way here in this sentence.)

But that night there I was on the phone with the kids— one-on-one—after speaking so much from my spot in the rough circle I'd had them pull the desks into three mornings a week and from which I'd suggested Genovese's Marxism to them and tried to get them to speak about Frederick Douglass or Zora Neale Hurston, about Langston Hughes. I'd suggested to them the presumption I saw in white authors like William Styron and Eudora Welty when those authors dealt in fiction with black characters. But only rarely would one of them come to see me during office hours. Though my white creative- writing students often came: I think I was, in most cases, the first black teacher they—the white students—had ever had, and likely the last they'd ever have. Or even more than that: I suspect I was the first black adult they'd ever had to deal with or the first one who'd ever addressed them unflinchingly and consistently (and without bothering to be arrogant with them) from a status that was higher than their own. Of course, my white students were, for the greatest part, in creative writing and writing students are themselves a little arrogant and arro- gance allows for curiosity. But the black students at ISU were, as a group, very different from the black students I'd had in the years I'd taught part-time at Cornell: a percentage, oddly (or predictably) enough, of those Cornell students were the chil- dren of West Indians who'd gone to New York City instead of Toronto or London or, God knows, North Bay. Immigrants' kids. But on the phone that one night with the kids from Chicago I began to realize how much of what I'd been asking of them—meaning *expecting* of them—they hadn't understood in spite of all the years I'd spent teaching and studying and talking about the act of language, the years spent achieving some success with my own written work. "But all value is assigned, / is brought in," I said in a poem. Once, when I was in Britain for a few weeks with Katharine, I'd cycled (while she was at a conference) from London up to Edinburgh, and when we got back to the States, back to Ithaca, a black friend, Ken McClane, had suggested that I was "probably the first black person ever to do that," seeing metaphoric implications, I think, regarding England's colonial power, not to mention it being the place where our language—he's also an English professor—came partly from. Assigned value. So I came to realize, during my evening of talk on the telephone, that other things were at stake for my students now, their expectations were other than mine or even what mine had been. But *how* are we different, exactly?

One woman was close, I think, to tears over the question concerning the character development of Janie Crawford in Hurston's *Their Eyes Were Watching God*. I asked her about other novels she'd read, thinking that if we had some book in common I might be able to get her considering the function of character in *Their Eyes* by talking at some length with her about the characters—how minor ones complement major ones—in that book from long ago. But she hadn't read a novel since sophomore year in high school and couldn't remember what it was she'd read then. I figured I'd better try a different angle.

"How 'bout movies?" I said. Films, books, what the hell's the difference between made things? "You like movies? What movies have you been to recently?"

She paused, then laughed ambiguously and said, "*Batman*."

And there I was again, out of my kitchen in Bloomington, Illinois, a million miles away from my office at Illinois State, from meetings of the faculty and of the handful of interested students who make up the Black Writers' Forum, off the lone prairie and back in a sweaty line outside a theater in Canada and then inside with the loud crowd, slack-faced and noisy— every fool in North Bay had been there. And I'd *liked* North Bay, I'd felt comfortable and curious both in that raggedy-ass narrow-street town at the edge of deep and romantic space where that beautiful black child had spoken so brilliantly to me. (She must have known she was black, I think, as I reconstruct her now in Illinois, in memory, her gestures had that *thing*, or edges of it anyway—maybe she her-supple-self and her language of easy reference, point casually fragmented into inventive variations, vocal dances for a stranger, the *semblance*—the half rhyme—of relation, maybe this was the northern jazz I'd longed for when I was leaving North Bay.) But there in the movie theater that night had been nothing but 42 million dollars of U.S. junk culture shrunk into a two-hour format, seven or eight hundred white Canadians who were lapping it up, and myself the only black person in the house. Of course, even sweet and smart Jackie, the lady with whom I'd sailed into Kingston, had warned me, as we'd loitered at the ferry slip, that I'd be "in the minority in Ontario," waiting a beat to smile broadly and explain that I'd be in said predicament because I wasn't wearing a *Batman* T-shirt. Change the joke please, I'd thought, try for a different double entendre, save yourself. *Batman.* Poor Billy Dee Williams had had to walk around looking baffled through the whole flick, jive-ass in Gotham, and this the final evening of my farewell tour of the East. *Is this my life?* I'd thought unhappily in the theater, my characteristic thought when I realize I'm wasting time, just killing time as though time wasn't committing suicide on its own fast enough. But the landscape changes and the changes make their demands, revise the experience.

"OK," I said, "we had, say, four characters: there was Batman himself, Jack Nicholson as the Joker, Kim Basinger as the love interest, and, say, Police Commissioner Gordon."

Winter in Fort George

Saturday afternoon, my sixth day in Fort George, and Madeline and I made it down the snowy slope at the end of Lyon Street and walked a little ways west on the CN tracks. We found a lot of animal prints and when Katharine joined us on a subsequent trip she brought her Olaus Murie guide and we identified the trail of *Ursus americanus*. Barry McKinnon said his friend Charlie Russell, who knows bears, claims that they come out of semihibernation once every week or so, step out to pee, and go back in. We stood there next to the railroad staring down at the snow, at the prints that quite perfectly matched Murie's drawings—this was one of those moments, for Katharine and me anyway, that were unambiguous and relatively irreducible, the casual fact of bears within a half mile of our house. The railroad quickly became a favorite place for us to walk, both in daylight and as a Night Patrol tour—it skirts the northwest edge of town and yet, being at the bottom of a wooded slope, it feels remote. The woods go up the hill on one side and the Nechako's on the other. (Charlie Russell knows about all sorts of bears but he's written about the Kermode bear, the white-colored black bear, *Ursus americanus kermodei*, which lives way out on the B.C. coast, the bear created, according to a Kitasoo story, when Raven went out and turned every tenth black bear white to remind the world of the time of glaciers. The population's named *kermodei* after Frank Kermode, a past director of the Royal British Columbia Museum; it's produced by a recessive gene. The metaphoric baggage here is various yet obvious—trying to be clever about it would be tiresome, so I'll gesture at it, identify it as a site with metaphoric baggage, and leave it alone.)

We borrowed a sled from Barry and Joy and took Madeline sledding on a slope popular with kids. Katharine swam at a pool downtown; I went to an aerobics class at the University of Northern British Columbia. We walked a lot and read. I marched further into *Wolf Willow* but also revisited an old favorite, one I'd impulsively brought from Bloomington— *Eyelids of Morning*, Alistair Graham and Peter Beard's huge tome about "the mingled destinies of crocodiles and men." In the preface Graham reveals the announced purpose of his study of the Lake Rudolf crocodiles: "to discover why the population distributed itself around the lake the way it did . . ."

I waited for replies to the letters I'd sent out to all those Giscombes.

I visited a couple of classes at the College of New Caledonia, my official host in Prince George, and spent some time there talking with faculty members. I went out with Katharine on her photography trips—she'd been studying landscape and documentary and would balance the camera on the roof of the car or shoot through the windshield for various effects.

(*Eyelids of Morning* is a mingled photo and words text: the pictures mostly illustrate the story and a few of them are rather grisly. One of these is a large picture of a human leg protruding awkwardly from a cardboard box—the caption identifies it as having belonged to "William K. Olsen, Cornell graduate ['65] and Peace Corpsman." He'd been wading in a river in Ethiopia when the crocodile pulled him down under the water; Lake Rudolf, the site of Graham and Beard's project, is mostly in Kenya but an arm wanders over the border into Ethiopia. Perhaps we were foolish to walk at night along the CNR tracks, along the Nechako River—the prints we'd found were those of black bears, not grizzlies, but there are some black bear horror stories. Anyway, we never saw a bear there.)

Some evenings we watched movies. John and Vivien had left us a TV set and a VCR but no cable—all television in Fort George came in via cable or satellite dish, so there was nothing we could actually watch on TV. It was just as well—the O. J. Simpson "trial of the century" was on CNN every day and I would have had to have tried hard not to get sucked in by it; all the metaphors were present—race, money, death, class, sex. Barry McKinnon saw bits and pieces of it and kept me informed of new developments. Katharine and I rented films up the street at Wilderness Video, popular stuff—we saw *The Professional, Mother's Boys* (a "bad girl" movie with Jamie Lee Curtis), *Natural Born Killers*, some others. One evening, feeling daring, we rented two porn films from Adults Only Video, which was next to the Tim Horton doughnut shop. One was the typical story of a young woman who visits a household full of randy characters but the other was an "amateur" tape, the first one of those either of us had ever seen. A fairly attractive couple engaged in a variety of sexual activities, for the better part of an hour, in a California roof garden. The man was short and wiry but his penis was very large; the woman was a little taller than he was and she was tanned and healthy-looking and her face was pleasant and open. She had two or three orgasms, apparently real ones. The man came too—twice, as I recall—but that's what you always see in porno. They'd both look, now and again, up or over at the camera and smile nervously, like children being filmed at a birthday party.

The Film Version

A year after we came back from Fort George I mentioned to the poet Alvin Aubert that I was working on a prose book about John Robert Giscome and, after I explained who John R. was, he said the thing that poets say, that the project sounds like it would make a great movie. Film rights. Money. I was excited about this for a few days until I realized that there's little popular film potential that I can see to what I know of John R. Giscome's life and travel in British Columbia. There are no daring escapes or rescues mentioned in any of the literature, no principled stands for human rights, no assassinations, no sex scandals. The national crises that might reasonably be connected to him—slavery in Jamaica, the Civil War in the States, Louis Riel's Métis rebellion—occurred before his lifetime or in places far from where he lived and worked. He was in the gold rush, or one of the gold rushes—when Katharine, Madeline, and I took the boat to Skagway we sang on deck the theme song from *North to Alaska* but our singing, at least for Katharine and me, had a profoundly goofy antique feel to it. And even when I remember my own favorite films I see little I could apply to his life in the north—I'm thinking right now of the two Bergman efforts I like so much, *Shame* and *Persona*, and I'm thinking too of *The Maltese Falcon* and *Casablanca*, Orson Welles's *Touch of Evil*, some of the westerns (*High Noon* comes easily to mind, as does *Stagecoach*), and, among more recent movies, Spike Lee's *Do the Right Thing* and *She's Gotta Have It* (which I saw in England, the only black person and probably the only American in the theater), a couple of Robert Altman's films, *Eraserhead*, *Night of the Living Dead*, *The Mother and the Whore*, some others—popular films, "art" films. Amazing how many are in black-and-white. Erotic films are especially rare—the original versions of *The Postman Always Rings Twice* and *Cat People* (neither one's in color and there's no skin in either), some of Bertolucci's work or Bertrand Blier's. Porno, though, translates sexuality and all its baggage to an odd, arguably comic series of camera angles and besides that it's a very strange genre—sex becomes a kind of edgeless documentary (even in the amateur film we rented); metaphor has no place in it.

The articles these days, though, are about pornography as *work*, as a group of jobs held by people. This seems appropriate, I suppose. Life rolls over and plods forward, time clocks get punched. One can emphasize, surely, and one can omit but the sort of life that's most possible to trace in most instances is the life of work. The B.C. provincial directories always listed occupation—it defines us now as it did then in fairly profound ways. The shape of a life may elude the researcher or the descendant but what we did for money—to "make a living," as we still say—is a handy tag to attach to the toe. I'm a ———, I was in charge of ———, I worked at ———. When the cops finally caught up with her and, in the business of the arrest, gave her some forms to fill out, Patty Hearst listed "urban guerrilla" for occupation. Even Batman had a job—he was a crime fighter. Work was done, money got made and invested and put aside, and then John R. died and his worldly goods were dispersed. We go to country auctions sometimes here in Illinois: a widowed person hangs on alone for a long time and then dies at home or after a short "final illness" in hospital and then, if there are no heirs or after the heirs take what they want, all the stuff gets put out in the yard, under a tent if it's raining or going to rain, and the auctioneer walks through the accumulation with a portable mike, the crowd clustering around his call. The house usually goes on the day before the contents. John R. owned a lot of property—real estate—toward the end of his life but he lived as a lodger in rooming houses run by women.

And in those years at the end of his life he'd list his occupation as "miner." But sometimes he'd list himself as "miner and explorer." Once he listed only "explorer." It was work, exploring, a process to be engaged in—I imagine him at sixty thinking about what was and had been important to him and defining work that way, listing it as that. I parted some things out, pieced them together, and came up with an incomplete chronology, a fabric—it's below, a voice-over text, an edge for a documentary (as opposed to the infinitely more popular docudrama genre). I concentrated on work's defining graces and, a little bit, on money. And on the fact of representation: when you ask for the corporate rate at motels they ask, Who are you representing? (I usually say Illinois State University, a true enough story.) Simon Fraser and the Knight—as Alexander Mackenzie is still known in B.C.—represented Western culture, they were extending it farther west into the West that was beyond the metaphorical West; they were part, that way, of a public, discernible tradition. Their trips into this country were staked by interests back in civilization. John R.

Giscome and Henry McDame, however, were up here representing no one but themselves, no moneyed tradition existed to either back them or easily scoop them up and incorporate their adventures. O Canada! There'd be an African-American tradition—public, historical, unmoneyed, but shriving—for them if they'd been escaped slaves taking the boat trip across Lake Ontario and a black Canadian tradition if they'd been born a century later and come to Toronto from the Islands: the annual festival, Caribana, grows bigger each year. I've never been but imagine the festival, effortlessly enough, as *Black Orpheus*. But this was the inland West, the land of ice and snowy mountains (as Madeline Giscombe called them), the place of rivers: they were black but they were beyond the very real black metaphors of Canada.

Here's a chronology, an essay at something filmable.

The title at the bottom right of the screen would announce, in white letters—

PANAMA, 1855
—and then the letters would fade out.

Full shot: A railroad track in construction beneath a bright sun, in a lush, tropical area. Black men and Asian men swing hammers, spiking rails to the ties. Taj Mahal singing, faintly, "John Henry," repeating the lines "It's gon' be the death o' me (Lord, Lord) / Gon' be the death o' me."

In the 1850s, the stories go, John R. and his brother Peter left their home in Jamaica to work on the railroad line across the isthmus in Panama. This route was the shortest—meaning here "most economical"—way for the Americans to get from East Coast U.S. to West, which is where the gold was in those days, and back again. It was Colonel George Totten's railroad and the colonel built it along with his partner, John Trautwine, in the years of the California rush. They were followed many years later by George Washington Goethals and his canal and the tracks are gone now, underwater. Once there, John R. Giscome and all the other Jamaicans and Chinese men as well built the wide-gauge line on which Americans rode in bearable comfort back and forth between the oceans. A thousand Chinese were employed on the project, two thousand Jamaicans. An old French pamphlet on the Panama railroad: "It is said that upon the railway of the Isthmus . . . there is buried a Chinaman under each crosstie." But John R. went to California himself, goes the story, to look for the gold himself: he walked away, in other words, from his projected mortality as a RR worker, walked away from his work assignment: he got all outside the lines that geography, race, and the languages of white people had made for him and, that way, both entered and failed to enter history. He went on over into Canada.

VICTORIA, 1858
Full shot: A large commercial wharf under a grey, ambiguous sky. Black men and women, a scattering of children, all dressed in mid-nineteenth-century clothing, waiting in line. Two or three white men in uniform, writing down names, at the end of the pier, at a doorway, arched, into a wharfside building.

James Pilton, in his 1951 U.B.C. master's thesis, "Negro Settlement in B.C.," supplies a longish list, an artifact from the nineteenth century, "A Partial List of Coloured Immigrants to B.C., 1858–71," and these three names appear thereupon: "Giscombe, J. (Jiscom?)," "Jiscom, B. C.," and "Jiscom, John R." The title indicates that thirteen-year range but the text suggests that these are the names of people who landed in Victoria in 1858 and 1859. And the list's names suggest the way John R. pronounced the name. When people in Prince George talk about the town off the Yellowhead it's Giscome with a hard "G," which is how my family has always pronounced the name—other Giscombe families differ. When my grandfather took his mysterious trip to Scotland to become an anesthesiologist in the twenties he met people on the boat who told him it was a French name, an Anglicization of Gascogne or Gascoyne. This is a family story, this shipboard meeting: it interested my grandfather enough for him to relate it upon his return to Birmingham, or perhaps he mentioned it in a letter and it caught my grandmother's attention. A "corruption" of Gascoyne? Perhaps its real and true corruption is from the soft "G," the "G" sounding to the ear of some functionary in Victoria enough like a "J" to be written down as that, to the hard Canadian sound that coincides with the sound of my family's preference.

The other name on Pilton's list—"B. C. Jiscom"—is a mystery. It doesn't recur, it appears in no other context that I've found.

THE CARIBOO, 1862
Full shot: A clearing in a northern forest. A troop of ragged white men leading mules, accompanied by dogs, enters from a trail to the right. A voice, one of the troop, emerges from the rabble: "There's the coloured man's house, lads, we turn left here!"

Elsewhere in Pilton: "Negro miners were early in the Cariboo, and by 1862 the 'coloured man's house' on Bald Mountain had become a local landmark." He's vague, Pilton is, but he's likely making reference here to the Barkerville area; I've not been able to find his source. The most famous black residents of Barkerville were probably the barbers Wellington Delaney Moses and Isaac Dickson; the latter, under the name "Dixie," wrote a minstrel column for the *Cariboo Sentinel*. I would think that their fame would likely cause their houses to be known as "Moses' house" or "Dickson's house" (or "Dixie's house"); perhaps the "coloured man's house" belonged to J.L.B. McLean, a miner from Barbados, who lived there in B-ville for many years, who's buried there now. A sometime mining partner of John R.'s and McDame's, an even more peripheral figure than the two of them. The shortcut to Barkerville from Prince George, though, the way that allows you to avoid the pulp-reeking hub of Quesnel by having you climb a ridge above the Cottonwood River and cross the BC Rail tracks cautiously at an unguarded crossing, that shortcut is over McLean Road. As every American is fond of saying, in the future we'll each be famous for fifteen minutes; but perhaps in huge Canada the fame is better measured in terms of space. McDame got a mountain and a creek and a Hudson's Bay post (some buildings of which still stand), Giscome got the portage and a town and those rapids; I recall driving back to Fort George from Barkerville once, taking the shortcut, and thinking in the car, "This is Johnny McLean's five miles of fame."

In October of 1862 John R. and Henry McDame set out from Quesnel in search of gold in the Peace River area but were stopped by ice on the Fraser and wintered in Fort George. It's difficult, of course, to think of this—two men sharing a gold rush cabin through the winter—without remembering

Charlie Chaplin in *The Gold Rush*: its silence makes its images that much more permanent. As I mentioned before, I saw it at the Cornell Cinema years ago: in among the shots of doomed men patiently ascending the slopes were funny vignettes of life inside the winter cabin: in one, Sir Charles's companion's hunger made him visualize the bowlered one as a chicken. The special effects were primitive and, therefore, the moment was extra-funny. We all laughed hard in the auditorium in the basement of Uris Hall.

THE INTERIOR, 1863
Full shot: Canoes pulled up onto a wild bank and overturned, their bellies skyward. The backs of two men disappear into the forest.

In April of 1863 Giscome and McDame set out again and made the "portage of about nine miles" from the Fraser to Summit Lake, paddled north with the current down the Crooked River and got to McLeod Lake in record time. They pushed on and arrived at the Peace, via the Rocky Mountain Portage, on May eighteenth.

THE OMINECA, 1870
Full shot: Sparsely treed peaks in the near distance and, in the fore-ground, some white men wading in a creek, studying its bottom. One black man's among them yet a little separate from them, ambiguously distant.

In 1870 Henry McDame visited the Omineca region in the company of James Germansen and some other white miners. The *Cariboo Sentinel* news article on the discovery of gold on

Germansen Creek lists all the members of the party, identifying him as "Henry McDames (coloured)." Ralph Hall's 1994 book, *Pioneer Goldseekers of the Omineca*, notes McDame's luck and describes him, parenthetically, as "a well known negro miner."

In 1871, from the Mallandaine provincial directory, under "Cariboo Names": "The District of Cariboo contains a population of 290 whites, 685 Chinese, 570 natives, and 32 coloured persons." Under "Other residents, Miners, &c." is listed "Giscome, John R."

THE CARIBOO, 1871

Full shot: Miners, in a mining camp—tents, the smoke from unseen fires, shovels and picks scattered about—clustered around the one miner with a newspaper, reading over his shoulders.

March 25, 1871, *Cariboo Sentinel*, under "Latest from Quesnel-mouth": "Giscome, accused of assaulting Port, has been held to bail by Mr. Ball to appear when called for. Port is either unable or unwilling to give any rational account of the occurrence. A good many think he is shamming. The Indian who is supposed to have witnessed the affray has gone up the river with the Messrs. Trutch and Wright's party." With the money he'd made from his work as a miner, John R. had begun investing in real estate and property mortgages. He'd been carrying—as we say nowadays— William Christopher Port, a.k.a. Porto, for a while and when Port defaulted on his mortgage, Giscome tried to take his horses—the collateral—and there was a struggle. Port was black; there was no interracial aspect to the dispute. One thinks almost involuntarily of Alex Cox's off-handedly ironic 1984 film *Repo Man*. There's irony here too but, unlike Cox's, it's fairly heavy— the named gentlemen in the newspaper piece are Sir Joseph

Trutch, the cartographer whose 1871 "Map of British Columbia to the 56th Parallel" is a frighteningly detailed monument to wilderness's extent, and Mr. G. B. Wright, famous as a builder of roads across that very extent, a gentleman who was born in Jamaica. "The Indian who is supposed to have witnessed the affray" was up on the Fraser with those two, all of them working on the road across the portage named for the man in trouble. From R. M. Ball's letter of July 7, 1871: "I have the honour to forward herewith an order from Mr John [sic] Trutch for the sum of seven hundred dollars on account of the Giscome Portage road."

BARKERVILLE, CARIBOO, 1872
Full shot: Interior of the courthouse. The judge, a white man with a long beard, sits at a table upon which are the inevitable papers. Lesser white men sit to either side of him, whispering to him once or twice.

A year has passed. June 1, 1872, *Cariboo Sentinel*: "An extra stage of this line arrived on Tuesday, 28 inst., bringing an express and the following passengers: Joseph Denny, Chas. Vailancous, Alex E. B. Davie, Mr Brousseau, and John Giscome." He went up a week later, on the eighth of June, before Matthew Bailie Begbie, Esq., Chief Justice of the Supreme Court, and was acquitted. Here one has to think of O. J. Simpson's face on television, that big blank face bursting into a smile behind the squeezed-shut-tight eyes of Johnnie Cochran as the not-guilty verdict was read, that image. This was no "trial of the century" back in Barkerville but it was covered in the June 15 *Cariboo Sentinel* under the headline "Regina vs. Giscome." Port had testified that John R. had hit him with an ax, which my man denied. He testified that, instead, Port had fallen during their scuffle and had been kicked in the head by one of the horses. John Bowron, the librarian and gold assayer, testified on John R.'s behalf. The jury didn't buy Port's story. "Messrs. Barston and Davie for the prosecutor. Mr. Park for the defence."

But here the dates become complicated and speak of a couple of different directions. News came via Lorel Morrison a year after I returned to Bloomington from Fort George: John R. had daughters, two daughters, both of whom were born in Jamaica in 1872: Margaret Elizabeth Giscombe was born on January 30 and Emma Magdalina Giscombe was born on the last day of the year. Lorel had found their baptismal records on a trip to Jamaica and he sent me the Xeroxes; Sarah Page was the mother and, in the records, my man's listed as "John Robert Giscombe, miner, British Columbia, Canada." If Margaret Elizabeth was born in January he would have had to have arrived home—in Jamaica—by May 1871, two months after his arraignment in Barkerville. By the time of Emma Magdalina's birth, John R. had been back in B.C. for at least seven months. It's an inconsistency, a variance and not a misspelling here: the names were recorded at baptism with the "b," G-I-S-C-O-M-B-E.

GISCOME PORTAGE, 1873
Full shot: A small river steamer drifting up to a dock jutting out into the river. Uphill from the dock is a clean two-story building. A line of smoke exits the building's stone chimney; the forest comes almost to its edges.

From *A History of Prince George*, the 1946 tome by Rev. F. E. Runnalls: "In 1870 [Peter Dunlevy] despatched a boat loaded with sundry articles for the Indian trade up the Fraser,

Nechako and Stuart Rivers, and in 1873 he inaugurated annual trips through the Peace River district. To further his trade with the natives, he established a number of outposts, one of which was at Giscome Portage, a place which was named after a negro cook in Dunlevy's employ." The passage echoes, in a fairly obvious way, Father A.-G. Morice's earlier (1906) *History of the Northern Interior of British Columbia, formerly New Caledonia*. From that book: "Ambitious to extend his operations and augment his gains, [Dunlevy] dispatched, in 1870, a boat loaded with sundry articles for the Indian trade up the Fraser, Nechaco, and Stuart Rivers. Three years later, yearning for even greater laurels, he inaugurated his annual trips through the Peace River district, passing through the McLeod Lake region, which had never known the sweets of commercial competition. To further his ends he established a post at Giscome Portage, a section of land named after a man he had for some time in his employ as cook." (The important verbs survive: *dispatched* becomes *despatched* but *inaugurated*, *further*, and *established* make it over the edge whole and maintain, continue to apply. But Runnalls is specific or insistent beyond his predecessor's more graceful sentences and the trader Dunlevy's not a man among men offering sweets to receive laurels in the later account but a white man among the savages and negroes, a Tarzan of the mercantile.)

From the 1874 Mallandaine provincial directory: "Giscomb, John R., miner, Yates St." in Victoria.

MCDAME CREEK, 1874
Full shot: A black man, solitary in a canoe, paddling slowly in a wide but shallow creek through a forest. He is shirtless and sweating and confident in the heat. A riot of birdsong is heard but the day is bright and devoid of movement other than his methodical strokes.

Summer 1874: Henry McDame discovered gold on McDame Creek in the Cassiar District and to mine it formed Charity Company, which consisted of himself and John R., Charles Charity, C. Sharp, T. Parks, and four others.

Three years later, and far away from the Cassiar, Stacey Cooness, a fifty-year-old widower, wed twenty-six-year-old "spinster" Ella Braggs. Victoria, 1877. A photograph of Stacey Cooness as a young man appears in *The Black West*, William Loren Katz's 1973 history; he's handsome in the rather formal portrait and quite well dressed, about twenty years old. The caption's ambiguous and not about him but his parentage: his "black-Jewish mother married George Washington, founder of Centralia, Washington."

On January 26, 1877, Joseph Park died, who had been John R.'s lawyer in the 1871–72 trouble. Drunk, he fell into a flume on the short trail between Barkerville and Richfield. He was forty-nine. *Cariboo Sentinel* references for him in the Barkerville card file list "drunk in court" and "fractured ankle in drunken brawl."

The 1882–83 provincial directory: "Giscome, John R., miner, McDame's creek." (Two photographs exist, taken "ca. 1883," of McDame Creek. I found them on-line at the Web site maintained by the British Columbia Archives—their subject is "Winter Dwellings." The first reveals a loose series of buildings at the base of a low hill: they, the buildings, totter off into the distance and there's snow at the edges of their roofs. One's in the foreground—it's built of logs, chinked together—and a figure stands next to it, apparently surveying the scene below. The other photo was taken either earlier or later in the season: this one shows the snow lying more heavily all around. Deep and crisp and even, goes the old song. The buildings form a crescent along the frozen Dease River, whose great white expanse takes up most of the picture; the creek itself seems to be entering the river at the right edge. From the Williams British Columbia directory: "Communication in the summer once a week by H.B. Co.'s boat from Porter Landing, foot of Dease Lake. In the winter there is only very occasional communication.")

In 1884, McDame, staked by "prosperous" Samuel Booth, found gold again, on Lorne Creek, near the Skeena River. This is the last record of Henry McDame.

NORTHERN COAST, 1884

Full shot: A moving shot of trees along an ambiguous shore—an estuary, perhaps, or a long bay. The wildness of the shore's unbroken by any building, dock, or single light. Storm clouds over the tops of the trees, late afternoon autumn light. Leonard Cohen's voice, faintly, singing "The Stranger Song" (repeating the line "I told you when I came I was a stranger").

1884–85 provincial directory: "Giscom, J. R., Northern coast."

1887 provincial directory, under "Barkerville Directory": "Giscombe, John R., miner, Manson River." And under "Northern Coast, Northern Interior and West Coast Vancouver Island Directory": "Giscom, J. R., Northern coast"— a lot of people listed addresses in this section as Naas River and Omineca, locations on a map, but only John R. listed "Northern coast," a description of landscape rather than a particular, reachable point. Manson River's near Germansen Creek, in the Omineca District. "Northern coast" is the long coastline, unbroken, far away.

1889 provincial directory: "Giscombe, John, miner, Manson River," again and, again, "Giscom, J R, Northern coast." Linda Eversole suggested to me, over lunch at a tea room in Victoria, that people owned property out in the bush while they maintained residences elsewhere, this in explanation of the dual listings during this spate of years. But as we ate, her quite reasonable explanation didn't entirely satisfy me: I mean it didn't touch the thing I noticed—the desolation of the Northern Coast address, that no one else lived there or was even willing to admit they owned a bit of land there, that the address seemed to name the ragged edge of North America itself. (Maybe I was feeling the presence or the possibility of metaphor here; maybe I'm still looking for film quality, maybe I'm stretching for the sort of images one finds on the screen and describes, predictably and inadequately, as "moody"—I think of the way Vilmos Zsigmond photographed *McCabe & Mrs. Miller* for Robert Altman. Faraway, dreamlike, set in the Pacific Northwest. The miners came out of the snow and mist to take their pleasure in Warren Beatty's whorehouse, which was run by Julie Christie, the McCabe of the title, the Mrs. Miller of the title.) Finding Lorne Creek, the site of Henry McDame's last public success, does help: it flows into the Skeena River near the present city of Terrace, which itself is near Prince Rupert, the town from which the Alaska ferries leave. This, Lorne Creek, I figure, is the real location of whatever land John R. worked or owned at "Northern coast." The provincial directories suggest the story—that some sort of affiliation continued between the two men, this based on this address—but they don't give details and the B.C. Archives Web site supplies no images.

VICTORIA, 1892

Full shot: Looking down Fort Street in Victoria. A few brick buildings line the muddy street but there are spaces between them. A horse-drawn milk truck bumps along on one side of the street. The town is young; the street ends at a large public dock. Boats—tall-masted sailboats, steamboats—are seen beyond the buildings.

1891 Mallandaine directory, under "Germansen Creek, A mining camp in the Barkerville division of the Cariboo district. Nearest P. O. Barkerville.": "Giscombe, John R., miner." But in the competing directory—published by Williams—for the same year, that's where the one "explorer" listing occurs. It's a Victoria listing but there's no address beyond that: "Giscome, John R., explorer." It's in boldface, like the one seven names above it for "Gilmore & McCandless, merchant tailors and clothiers," it's indicative of business. (The Census for 1891 backs up the Victoria address over the one for Germansen: it was collected door-to-door apparently, taken down by hand, and in it John Robert Giscome is an impossible fifty years old, his relation to head of household is "L" for lodger, his parents are both born in "Jamaca," his church is the Church of England.)

1892–1899 Williams directories: John R. lived at 122 Fort Street in Victoria. His profession was listed as "miner and explorer" in 1892 and, in the following years, as "miner." In 1899 he would have been sixty-eight years old.

(Negro miners? A few days before I left Vancouver on my bicycling trip to Giscome I stayed up late to watch a CBC double feature on the television, *The Treasure of the Sierra Madre* followed by an embarrassingly bad film of Atwood's *Surfacing*. A cut from the first movie: in the Dormitorio with its name, El Oso Negro, in fading paint on the wall behind them, old Walter Huston, himself a prospector, telling young Bogart that he, Huston, "never knew a prospector who died rich." The hotel's name, The Black Bear, is both that and a specific spot of untranslated language—*Negro*, with its long English "e," *knee-grow*—on the backdrop but nothing as far as the movie goes except *part* of that backdrop, of no consequence to the movie's plot or even to the moment here reproduced between the partners that passed underneath it as if it was a herald or something.)

An 1897 photograph, which may or may not show Henry McDame, was taken at Telegraph Creek, B.C., by F.R.S. Barlee. It's reproduced in an article by his kinsman, N. L. Barlee, about McDame that was published in *Canada West* magazine in 1975. The photo, of "old timers," shows a row of four elderly white men and one elderly black man, the black man identified as an unreadable scrawl beginning with "M" on the back of the picture. McDame is assumed to have died around the turn of the century. The man in the picture is dark-skinned, a little stooped, and has a neatly trimmed but full white beard.

ROSS BAY, VICTORIA, 1907

Full shot: A hillside upon which are a few tombstones—some are large, some are small, and they are at uneven intervals. The camera pans and finds a small group of people under a sideless tent, a canopy, beside which is a large mound of dirt. The camera does not linger here but pans again to find the blue expanse of Ross Bay, Victoria's buildings at the far edge of it. The day is bright and very beautiful: the sun glints on the choppy surface of the water. The sky is cloudless.

John R. Giscome died June 24, 1907. The funeral was put on by "Undertaker Hanna" from the residence of "Mrs. Coones, 201 Johnson St." Captain Travis of the Salvation Army conducted the services, at 2:30 on June 26. John R. had appointed Ella Cooness and Noah Shakespeare executrix and executor of his will; he left the estate to her, twenty-one thousand 1907 dollars after the debts and burial expenses were paid. The tombstone reads: "John R. Giscome, aged 75 years" but if the baptismal records are correct he was just seventy-six, having died two days past that birthday.

In 1908 Stacey Cooness died, his age listed variously at the time of his death as eighty-one and ninety-five. Presumably Ella Cooness nursed them both—Stacey and John R.—in their final illnesses, she was the one to walk them out to the edge.

On February 4, 1911, J.L.B. McLean died in Barkerville. He had been, for years, caretaker of the Richfield Courthouse.

(After we returned from Fort George I wrote to the Quesnel Museum and Archives seeking to verify that the shortcut I'd take on the way to Barkerville really was named for Johnny McLean. No, they wrote back, a local farmer.)

The end of 1913: the "end of steel," the place where the tracks stop, if temporarily, while the rail line's being built, had reached the townsite that the Grand Trunk Pacific had decided to call Giscome or Giscome Station. John R. Giscome had been dead for six years.

In 1934 Ella Cooness died. She had married, after Stacey's death, James Edward Wintworth, a bartender from Montreal, and moved with him to Saltspring Island. She left $1,000 to her husband but the undisclosed balance of her estate went to the hospital at Ganges Harbour, the principal town on Saltspring Island, and to the Protestant Orphanage in Victoria. In an article in *B.C. Bookworld*, John Harris points out the oddness of her name, that one has to read it and think or hear "she-coon," the diminutive—like "hostess" or "poetess" or, of course, "Negress"—of the old racist appellation; John's a short-story writer but oh he thinks like a poet. Some things are inescapable.

.   .   .

A film version? John R. inhabited parts not scripted for him, he became finally—in the geography of Canada—a person out of place. I think it's because his place of origin was not England or Ontario or the United States that he falls so far outside of "history": he did not clear a way for others like him to follow, he was not a "pioneer." To me, as my students say, as I read about him and made notes on what I was reading and listened to old John Aaron talk of him, to me he became the presence of qualification and the demand for compound sentences of description, a symbol of that for which there is no symbol or image—he is, to me, what Olson described Robert Creeley as being, "the figure of outward." Film that one. The headnotes up above are nothing but conventional images and their music is predictable—"The Stranger Song" is plagiarized from the *McCabe & Mrs. Miller* sound track. And what else but "John Henry" for black men working on a railroad? (And I don't know if Taj Majal has a cover of it but he's both West Indian and African-American; "In my house, when I was growing up," he said recently on the radio, "it was both 'you-all' and 'all-you.'")

A film version. In 1985 Michelangelo Antonioni was a visiting professor at Cornell and one evening that fall I went up the hill to Uris Auditorium to hear him lecture and to see the uncut version of *The Passenger*. Watching *Blow-Up* had been an important experience for me in high school—a first "serious" movie—and *Zabriskie Point* gave me a series of images to gauge my years in college against. Both contain a few remarkable sexual moments but it's the profound ambivalence of the main characters that I remember most—what pursuit, what identity, what project is worth anything? Ambivalence and, with it, the stunningly enormous exterior shots, the presence of outside. "If I put a character against a landscape," Antonioni said somewhere, in some interview, "there is naturally a relationship." In Uris Auditorium, one of the Cornell deans made a lengthy series of embarrassing remarks about the university's relationship to the arts and then Michelangelo Antonioni himself came to the podium, shyly thanked us all for coming, and had the projectionist start the film. The uncut version's incredibly long and almost unwatchably painful. The plot's well known and even classic: burned-out Jack Nicholson walks away from his job, his work, his journalist self, and impulsively and awkwardly takes on the identity of another man—another guest at the Dormitorio, someplace this time in northern Africa, another reporter, another white guy—who has suddenly and unexpectedly died. He takes the dead man's wallet and appointment and address books and becomes a passenger on the vector of that man's life.

What the directories and articles and Xeroxes supply is a lot of holes in the fabric of John R.'s life. I know about his money and the record of how he worked, that he was a prospector who did indeed die rich, I know where he lived, his addresses. But these things only begin to say it. When I first met Lorel Morrison he mentioned to me that there was a family story of John R. visiting Jamaica—coming home—and receiving a hero's welcome (this before he—Lorel—had come across the detail of the children). I surprised myself in that conversation by being surprised: it had never dawned on me, in all my thinking of John R., that he might have ever gone back home. My grandfather never returned and I suppose that's signal for me. Now I think of how long it had to take to get from the middle of nineteenth-century B.C. all the way to nineteenth-century Hope Bay, Jamaica, and I think of the incredible physical contrast between the two places—but I have no real understanding of it, and no real images. And the detail of the children, as I put it a few sentences back. And the woman, Sarah Page. And the fact of his having been charged, four thousand surface miles away, with a serious crime and the fact that he went back to face the music, leaving the woman pregnant with a second child, leaving the first daughter. What was in his mind as he journeyed home? Were the daughters really his? I stare at the fuzzy Xerox Lorel sent and see the words, the antique handwriting, and can't get beyond them; my inability seems appropriate.

In this family Katharine's the visual one, I have no skill at making pictures. I have no ability at translating a problem or situation or a place into an image or series of images. But I know when someone is good, I knew that the first time I saw David Hemmings's park in *Blow-Up* and I knew it for sure when I saw Mark Frechette and Daria Halprin in the desert of *Zabriskie Point*. The films are like poetry: nothing's explained but a lot is named and described and juxtaposed. A lot of stuff gets brought up; metaphor descends, it's a presence, and the landscapes are brilliant and unforgiving and blunt. The most irreducible, opaque part of John R.'s story—as I know it—is not his "discovering" the Giscome Portage but this spate of trouble and romance and children and the distance itself between the locales in which those things took place. He's known in the geography and—in the moments when the series of intrigues that history is is broad enough—he's noted there by the two occupations he listed for himself, miner and explorer; you can drive to the geography, you can see displays about the nature of the work when you visit the Provincial Museum in Victoria. But when I think of him on shipboard going home to an island and coming back to a forest I think of the language of that—"shipboard," "island," "forest"—and I run some stock footage past my mind's eye and then I draw a blank and want Antonioni.

Winter in Fort George

Early in March the replies to my broad Giscombe letter began trickling in and were generally disappointing. A number were returned marked UNKNOWN and one had "deceased" scrawled across it. A few people took a stab at my questions but no one knew of John Robert Giscome; the one respondent whose name was spelled as his had been told me that the correct spelling of her name was G-I-S-C-O-M-B-E but that the phone book had dropped the "b" some years ago and that her family had never bothered to call and fix the listing—she said "the 'b' is silent anyway." A young man named Douglas Giscombe phoned from Jamaica to wish me well. I kept the letters stacked, as they came in, on a corner of Vivien's desk, next to printouts of my Fulbright application.

I waited each afternoon for the clunk of mail in the box mounted on the door. 137 South Lyon Street was Katharine's and Madeline's and my northernmost house and therein I, the northernmost adult Giscombe, waited for word that might tell me what I was doing here. And word did come, finally, from three sources—I received a long, lovely letter and some photographs from Icsolene Giscombe, the widow of my father's cousin Johnny; she wrote from Toronto. Susan Buchanan, a descendant of Giscomes, wrote from Winnipeg with a wealth of information. And Lorel Morrison called from Hyattsville, Maryland, just outside D.C. These were remarkable people, I realized as I sat at Vivien's desk sifting through the facts and stories they'd provided me. What was I looking for in all this? Statements of situation, certainly, or the virtual and dubious truth of memory, that sort of stuff. Family? The extended family's a fiction—like religion—to choose to believe in or not: having or not having a particular copulation in common does not equal destiny. But these were remarkable people and over the next few years I made trips and amended trips and journeyed and managed to meet all three of them.

But that winter in Fort George we went out in the car, getting to places rather than to people—short trips out to West Lake and Isle Pierre, slightly longer trips out through Giscome and the funky towns past Giscome. Several trips up to the moose-browsing observation site on the Yellowhead. (It's a platform a little ways off the highway overlooking a marsh and the signs indicate that this is where moose come to graze, but we never saw one.) And at the end of the third week in Fort George we drove down to Quesnel on Saturday intending to go out to Barkerville, the historical reconstruction of the gold rush town. We'd got our usual late start, though, and hadn't arrived at Quesnel until a bit past 3 p.m. and Barkerville was still 80 kilometers to the east: the light would have been more than half gone by the time we arrived, so we put it off for another time. But Quesnel itself was important because it was the place from which John R. and Henry McDame had set out on their big trip of 1862–63, it was the place where they'd been living and, therefore, a town that had some provisional claim in my project as a place of origin. I told that to Madeline as we bombed around downtown past the Pizza Hut and the Kentucky Fried Chicken place. "Where was his house?" she wanted to know.

Oddly enough, I did have some idea about where that might have been—he'd lived on Bouchie Creek, across the river and a little upstream from downtown Quesnel. This from one of Gordon R. Elliott's books about the area: "The name 'Bouchie' has replaced the names 'Henry's' or 'Nigger' for the creek . . . The land where Bouchie Creek enters into the river was taken by H. McDanus, M. McLain, and John K. Giscom in 1862." The "M. McLain" is probably Johnny McLean and "H. McDanus" would be Henry McDame: the creek's two previous names are, apparently, references to him (though the second, "Nigger," suffices as a general description for the whole troupe). Elliott doesn't comment on the blackness of the three men who lived on Henry's Creek but he does become strange about "John K. Giscom": "Moving north Giscom operated a ferry on the Fraser at what became the lumber center of Giscombe." I wonder if he didn't know what "portage" meant.

Anyway, we found Bouchie Creek easily on the map—it bisects the golf course right before it flows into the Fraser. We found the golf course easily as well but it was closed for the season and the road down into it was a swirl of ice. We could have, I suppose, parked and walked in through the snow alongside the icy road but then, likely, the RCMP would have appeared. I've been stopped enough by cops to know I could probably talk my way out, but such encounters are exhausting; one tries not to invite them. And it was a cold day, the air having come, said the local CBC station, "in from Mackenzie." So we stayed in the car and drove up over some roads north of the links to try to double back onto the creek, but the roads all bent on farther north and we found ourselves in a continual ascent into a series of bluffs, away from water level. At the top of one rise we found a dead moose, a road-kill item; Madeline was curious but Katharine, leaning out for a closer look, said that she didn't really want to see it and we spirited ourselves away and turned around a mile later when the road, still rising, turned to gravel. It was a frustrating expedition and as we drove back down into town my mind was full of the necessity of coming back in the spring to traverse the length of Bouchie Creek. Looking for what? A diary buried in a metal box at creekside? I'd know exactly—divinely—where to dig. Like in the movies. Conrad: " 'I glanced casually into the little cabin. A light was burning within, but Mr. Kurtz was not there.'" Anyway, we never went back to Bouchie Creek.

At the bottom of the hill, though, we went into a shopping center to get Madeline the dessert she'd earned by being a good traveling companion. Like Spruceland it was anchored by an Overwaitea store, into which I saw going an old black woman as we were leaving our car. We came close to eye contact across the lot—that is, we looked at each other—and as we walked into another mall entrance I was thinking that maybe we'd stop into that Overwaitea to pick up something for dinner back on Lyon Street; but we got caught up in ordering doughnuts and Danishes at a dessert shop and then in the desire to make it back to Fort George before dark. So I found myself, as we climbed the series of long hills out of Quesnel, having a fantasy of bumping into the woman in the grocer's and her casually revealing herself—in the cereal aisle, say—as a descendant of John R.'s, a product of his year in Quesnel. How attractive a fiction relation is! And what would that do to Quesnel and the whole region up and down the Fraser River? I'd see the hills that much more deeply, I suppose, or I like to think I would, though I certainly can't say how. "The cells try to come to terms with the site," said John Morgan in his poem "Libra"; the poem was about place (Lawrence, Kansas, I think) but the line's a quote from a radio broadcast, a program about tissue rejection. How attractive this story that somehow, out in B.C. or anywhere, there's some great fleshy body to be part of, that I'm consanguine (or at least transubstantiated).

Giscomes and Giscombes

January, 1987: after a sleepless overnight flight in the steerage section of a Virgin Airlines 747 we landed at Gatwick and took the bus up to Oxford to commence a six-month sojourn among the English. I was writing a book, Katharine wasn't gainfully employed, Madeline was a baby, we had some money: therefore England. In Oxford we rented the second place we looked at, an "artisan's cottage" on a short street named Combe Road.

It was a nice little house—two stories, brick, by the Oxford Canal—but I'd liked too Combe Road's coincidence with the second syllable, the suffix, of my last name. The vowel is slightly different—Combe Road had its "oo" sound—but both celebrate the near silence of the "b" and the spelling is of course the same. It's a word, *combe*, that one rarely encounters in America: it's a geographical term for a valley or a ravine but some definitions specify it being a hollow in the "flank of a hill," a recalcitrance, as it were, in the slope. It derives from the Celtic and this name—my name—has always looked British to me because of that ending; lots of Britons have mon-

175

nikers that end with -*combe* and if this particular one, Giscombe, is a "corruption" of Gascoyne, as was suggested to my grandfather, I think that it was an Old World mutation, something from the mess of Europe as opposed to anything that took place down in the islands.

Names have always been a problem for black people in America. "We wear the names of white folks," Louis Farrakhan said when he spoke at Illinois State; our names bespeak the tangles of American culture—miscegenation, issues of property and ownership, the peculiar violence of our past—in the same way our skins do. We don't look like Africans and we don't have African names or African names that have come to us easily through family tradition. Our family names are mostly Anglo-Saxon; Booker T. Washington pointed out that after the Civil War Southern black people typically, as ritual, did a couple of things—they'd leave the plantation, even if only for a few days, and they changed their names. The names they took were common names or names that were common in the white world around them; they were interested in joining the world—the free world—and the names were token of their optimism and forgiveness. But they did shed the patronym of the owner. Anglo-Saxon names, but some have exclusive—or very large—black constituencies. Giscombe has that constituency but its situation's a little different from the story Washington told—it was never a common name and seems to have arrived in any numbers in the States and Canada as a black name from Jamaica during the early part of this century. It may have arrived in the Islands (the so-called New World) from Britain but black people have it now, it's a castle we—black Giscombes—have inhabited, more or less exclusively, for a couple of centuries.

I don't know why Combe Road is so named: there are no

hills or valleys in its vicinity. It's in the part of Oxford known as Jericho—blocks of row houses punctuated by tiny grocery stores, pubs, and huge St. Barnabas. Not an island, but Jericho's got one edge that's water: the Oxford Canal was right next to our house on Combe Road, and beyond the canal and more serpentine was something called the Sheepwash Channel, a backwater of the Thames. We'd feed the ducks in the canal and speak to the people who lived there—quite illegally—on low houseboats. An old woman fished—most days, it seemed—in the channel, mumbling this and that to herself and, as far as we could tell, never catching anything. Across the water was wide, green Port Meadow, a common grazing area since the Bronze Age—we walked there often, and once, hiking across with baby Madeline on my back, I was passed by a tipsy man and his teenage daughter, both on bicycles. He stopped to chat: "Oh when they're young like that you want to keep 'em close," he said, unsteadily straddling his bike and cooing boozily at Madeline, who rewarded him, I saw out of the corner of my eye, with one of her smiles. "Ah, c'mon, Dad," said his daughter, shifting her weight impatiently—but she was smiling too.

This was our England—pleasant, polite, a little foreign, mostly benign. And people were able to pronounce my name after seeing it written down, something that had never happened before. No Giscombes, though, in the Oxford telephone book; there were three or four in the London book but we only went to London a couple of times and I was trained too well to be the sort who calls. This was training I had to overcome years later in order to write to all those Giscombes from our house in Fort George: I was in my forties then, though—during our half year on Lyon Street—, and my child was herself nine and quite independent and growing up and no longer a baby at all. And oddly enough I was a little more reckless in some ways because of those things, a little more confident, a little more wide-eyed and mortal and willing to recognize the simple and common mortality of others.

Toronto, Hyattsville, Winnipeg

Icsolene Giscombe's letter to me noted that her husband and the other Giscome children had reinstalled the "b" in the family name after their father, Charles, died but that she—Icsolene—had never known what the fight was about between Charles and my grandfather, only that her father-in-law had felt very strongly about it. "The story about the B+ and the B− was one I heard of many times," she said, but the squabble itself "is, was, and always will be a dark secret." John had been born in North Bay but she'd met him in Toronto and the two of them had always lived there. After the war he'd worked in electronics—he'd been in the Signal Corps in Britain—and had died two years before I wrote her, and she missed him terribly. In the picture she sent of him, he's trim and, yes, dapper in his uniform sitting in a chair smiling widely over a book with *Negro Folk Songs* in the title. Two of his sisters—Constance and Esther—were still living but in nursing homes; another, Sybil, had died—I remembered her name from the North Bay directories and my shaky memory of her having been a teacher was correct. But Icsolene's favorite sister-in-law was Lucille—she'd been a journalist but her strong and unpopular views, Icsolene said, kept her from working in Canada; she worked in Prague instead, writing in Czech, and, denied reentry to Canada, she died overseas in the sixties. The picture of her reveals that she was very beautiful: her skin had incredible clarity and definition, her eyes were quite sharp; her lips were full and her smile was confident. Icsolene had included a copy of one of her letters from Prague and the writing—an account of a trip to Marienbad and some details about her troubles in trying to recover her passport—was remarkably clear and lively both. She was apparently a big woman, not plump by any means but neither was she wiry; she didn't look much like the pale girl I'd met on the street in North Bay. Her picture was taken in a studio but Johnny's was a snapshot, he's sitting in front of a large, ornate fireplace stove. In the warm hum of Vivien's little under-the-desk space heater I sat in the basement of the house on Lyon Street seeing my second cousins for the first time. ("I can see the family resemblance," one of my students said later, after we'd been back in the States for a while, looking at the snapshot of Johnny and looking at me, "there in the chin." Wishful looking perhaps, my chin having been obscured by this beard—an homage to Fidel—for all my grown years; or perhaps the jawline's more of a presence, visible and defining even through the cloud of hair, maybe that's the similarity she saw.) Icsolene had written me from Toronto, where she'd met John in 1942, where the two of them had married and lived; the listing in the "World Book" I bought was still "J. Giscombe."

When he called, Lorel Morrison was full of questions for me, having been passed a copy of my letter by one of his relatives. This was our first contact and we spoke tentatively on the phone. He'd been working on a history of the family, he said, and I was surprised to learn that he'd seen the two articles I'd seen about John R. The pieces were in small-circulation British Columbia magazines; I'd found them by thumbing through the card file at the archives in Victoria but he was working from Maryland and I don't know what had led him to the *British Columbia Historical News* and the even more obscure *B.C. Outdoors*. He asked about my family and I said I was named for my grandfather who had been a doctor, and this surprised him—"We're just now getting doctors in the family," he said. He asked me to describe my grandfather and I did but then Lorel asked about his ears—were they large or small? Ears? I couldn't remember, and asked why. Small ears, he said, are African; larger ones suggest a European strain in the ancestry. Ears. But when I described my grandfather as a man of great presence and few words and admitted that, to my sister and me, he was somewhat scary, Lorel said, laughing, "Ah, that's family!" He worked for the World Bank he said, in D.C., but he'd been born in Jamaica: his accent was fairly strong, the sound of his laughter—or its timbre—was somehow familiar. He told me the story of his great-great-grandfather, Peter Giscombe, and Peter's brother John Robert—how they'd gone to Panama to work on the railroad across the isthmus and that Peter had returned to Jamaica and married and fathered eight children while John R. had gone on to Victoria and then north. It was a similar story—at least in shape—to the one I'd read in Linda Eversole's article, the story Linda had pieced together from a couple of informants (neither of which was Lorel). The shapes were similar but some of the principal players were different and her story had been skeletal and this story was full or more full and I was aware that yes, this *was* family, that I was finally talking to family, to a member of John R.'s people, possibly to a relative of mine, of both of ours. I stood in Vivien and John's kitchen and took notes. He pronounced the name with a soft "G," which I found interesting after my forty-some years of correcting people who pronounced it that way. Of course, pronunciation varies, I thought as I scribbled, just like spelling does. (And a year after we came back I met a Cornell student, a Giscombe, whose family pronounced the name Gis-COM-bay, as though it were an African name like Moise Tshombe's.) But then Lorel said something that distressed me: in the story he knew from his granduncle—Peter Giscombe's grandson, John Aaron Giscombe—, John R. and Peter were "white English guys," and he mentioned this in a matter-of-fact way. Now, part of my thinking about John R. up in the Cariboo had revolved around his anomalousness—his more or less singular and contradictory (and, therefore, invisible) black self in the bright white history of this very unlikely location. And beyond that, and for me more profound than that and more basic, was that his blackness was part of his Giscombe-ness, no matter how the name was spelled or pronounced: that this be an attribute of the family, part of our makeup. (The direction of the relationship is, of course, important: that blackness is part of us instead of the other way around. This is our family anomalousness, part of what my sister and I long ago dubbed the Giscombe Way, this is how it works; whatever the context, as I've said before, we're contrary and suspicious and, as a given, separate from it. Bigger than it.) I absorbed what Lorel said, but then I was able to remember some things and I stammered out the language of the obituary in which he was described as "the aged negro" and I mentioned the Giscombe names on James Pilton's "Coloured Immigrants" list. We shrugged about it over the phone but I was surprised to find out how upset I was at the possibility of John R. being, having been, a white guy—it's odd because I don't value any kind of racial "purity" and do acknowledge the several white people I'm aware of in my own family's background. (Lorel said he'd send me a Xerox of his in-progress family tree and a week after we talked it arrived in the mail at Lyon Street, a huge, sprawling thing, a map of family names attached to pages of charts beginning with the maroon James Miller, whose daughter Helen Miller married Peter Giscombe: it's the eight children of those two and their descendants that Lorel had tracked. And later he sent the videotape of old John Aaron talking. The old man describes the marriage of Helen and Peter, how they'd met when Peter went to Maroon-town and saw her working in her parents' shop, how her father opposed the marriage and told her that she only loved him "because he had the red skin." Red skin? Redbone, I thought as I played that part of the tape over, redbone, the name applied to the light-complected among us. "White" doesn't always mean "white," I thought there in the glow of the TV set.)

Linda Eversole had crossed paths with Susan Buchanan when she—Linda—was doing research for her article on John R. for *British Columbia Historical News*. Susan, like Lorel, was descended from Giscomes—her great-great-grandmother Anne Clarke Giscome had married a Scottish physician named James Maxwell who had come to Jamaica in 1816 and they'd produced a number of children, one of whom, Alice, was Susan's great-grandmother. When I met Linda Eversole in 1991 she had some letters from Susan Buchanan and she Xeroxed them and gave them to me; I took her—Susan's— address from those and included her in my general mailing to the Giscombes. "We have had no oral tradition of Anne's being of black descent," she'd said in a letter to one of Linda Eversole's associates at the Heritage Conservation Branch, "however we do have a tradition that there was Spanish in the family and this was often used as a euphemism. I have always felt that one should be aware that this possibility exists if one has island ancestry, and if you don't want to know, don't investigate"; she goes on, though, in the same letter, to describe her clan: ". . . if you knew our very large family you would understand why there was never any suspicion that Anne was partly black. I am not untypical with light reddish hair, blue eyes, freckles, and the kind of skin that burns when it thinks of the sun." Miscegenation, for white people, is still a quite taboo subject and this rather casual acceptance of it made Susan, to my lights, a quite unusual person. I'd been interested in how she might answer my query and she didn't disappoint me: she sent a several-page response, the first letter in what became a correspondence. She'd located—since her letters back and forth with Linda Eversole—various parish records of baptisms, marriages, and burials and she sent photocopies of these: from her I learned that her great-great-grandmother was the daughter of James Clarke Giscome, a planter, a white guy, and Jane Skinner, who was described at various places and times as "a free brown woman," "a free woman of colour," and—if she's the Jane Giscome baptized in 1808—"a free black woman." All this was around the beginning of the nineteenth century on the northeast coast of Jamaica in the parishes whose names—St. Mary, Portland, St. George, St. Andrew—I'd heard before as places of Giscombe origin. Of course, the parish records prior to Emancipation (1833) are incomplete— only whites and free black people were allowed the rites of the Church of England and, therefore, a history (or a written-down history). But as I shuffled through Susan's Xeroxes there on Lyon Street, guided by her yellow highlighting, I felt I was present at some sort of dawn (or at the Xerox of some sort of dawn): it looked to me that this liaison between James Clarke Giscome and free Jane Skinner—which produced several children aside from Anne—was the start of the family. That it was with this woman, Jane Skinner, that blackness entered the family and stayed. I liked the off-rhyme of her name—Jane Skinner—and was struck by the resemblance of its sound to the sound of the name of Lorel's *ur*-ancestor James Miller and wondered at the coincidence. And not having yet been to Jamaica and therefore having no picture of it in my mind as place, I imagined her sex with James Clarke Giscome as free-floating, as having no location but time (as though it were the light from a star), as they coupled repeatedly, coming against each other's bodies, committing miscegenation to quite inadvertently produce us all. (I think now that the origin of the family is probably rather more complicated than that, that it may be in fact several origins—but here was a *version*, something that at that moment in that winter in Fort George, with a few pages of facts and names in front of me, I was electing to believe in. But of the several children produced by the Giscome-Skinner alliance only one boy—William Taylor Giscome—seems to have survived childhood and his progeny includes only two boys: boys being important here because of the name. One of those boys, Thomas Welsh, was born in 1847 in Charlestown—my grandfather's father's name was Thomas Giscombe and the child baptized Thomas Welsh Giscome would have been an easily possible forty-two at the time of my grandfather's birth in 1889. Yet Thomas Welsh's father, William Taylor Giscome, was a planter and my grandfather's family was, I think, rather poor and Charlestown is a longish way from Buff Bay. Yet there was a Sarah Giscome buried at Buff Bay in 1829, her color was listed as "Quadroon"; she was, apparently, Thomas Welsh Giscome's aunt—she died young, at eighteen, eighteen years before his birth. Looking like what? Gerald Early, writing about the first black Miss America, the unfortunate Vanessa Williams, said she could "pass for a fairly pronounced quadroon." Another Sarah

Giscome, a widow, died later, in 1832, in the same parish—St. George—in a place called Moore Park that's on no map now, the last Giscome burial in the records of the region. She was fifty-five and Susan suggested in her letter that she was likely the wife of Thomas Welsh Giscome's grandfather's brother Elisha Giscome. Her body's color was listed as "white": in the Xeroxes I had spread out on Vivien's desk she appears as the last white Giscome.)

The "b" began appearing in the name in the 1830s, around the time of Emancipation, Susan said in her letter, but G-I-S-C-O-M-E was, according to all her records she'd come to, the original—or a more original—spelling. Yet she admitted and puzzled over the fact that there seemed to be no more Giscomes anywhere and that that name did not survive in this century except as the name of those remote locations in British Columbia. John Robert Giscome himself was baptized—according to a record she found and sent me—as John Robert Giscombe, at Hope's Bay, in 1848. He occasionally appears as that in the British Columbia records as well but the name's also listed, now and again, as Giscomb, Giskom, Jiscom, and a few other variations too. If I can claim to know anything about him from following his trail through the directories and other public records it's that he was a quite formal man when it came to his name: he appears most often as three words—first, middle, and last names—or as two words joined by the initial "R." and this penchant sets him apart from his fellows in the mining camps. Rarely does he appear as a first and last name only; never is he Johnny or Jack. What did McDame call him when they were out on the trail? Susan Buchanan to Linda Eversole: "I would agree with you, from your material, that J.R.G. was probably a lonely man." He used the G-I-S-C-O-M-E spelling with consistency; he signed his will that way in 1907 and that's the name on the tomb-stone. He was baptized at sixteen going on seventeen and I stared at the figures, trying to imagine him as a teenager—gangly, interested in sex, "doing a man's work," immature—and failed. Baptism records in Jamaica often list the parents but his doesn't.

Likewise are the names of my grandfather's grandparents missing—they would have been born around the same time as John R. but I don't think he was one of my great-great-grand-fathers. His daughters were both born in Jamaica in 1872 and the dates place them somewhere in between the generation of my grandfather's parents, Thomas and Lenora Grossett Giscombe, and my grandfather's own generation. A man named John Giscombe—a blacksmith—died in 1869 and Lorel, when he and I were talking on the phone one time in 1996, conjectured that this might have been John R.'s father, that he came back from Canada for a couple of years, a dutiful son, to attend to the family. Of course, other things were happening then: I don't think Lorel knew about the assault charge when he posited that our man had gone home to help out.

Birmingham, North Bay, Prague

When my grandfather died we all went to Birmingham for a few weeks; my father stayed for over a month. I was eleven—it was June or July and I remember, when I think about then, that the houses in Birmingham were stark and light-colored on the hills in that town, that sunlight stood in the streets like it was the heat itself. It was the summer I learned the phrase about mad dogs and Englishmen. (I didn't understand the lyric as being racial then and went out in the sun proclaiming my dead grandfather's birth as a British subject as permission.) I remember that people had carports—they were the trellis on a slope up from my grandparents' house which sat at the T two streets made, they—the carports—were an open map, a metaphor for something. He died in 1962: the obituary said he'd arrived in Birmingham from his "home island" in 1916 and went on to praise his work as a doctor—I quoted it before, the statement about how "he took a deep and active interest in Negro health in Jefferson County." I bring it up again now because there's a coincidence with Susan Buchanan's great-great-grandfather, the Scottish doctor James Maxwell—the language of the death notices is similar and the dates of arrival and death are both exactly a century apart. From Dr. Maxwell's obituary in the Kingston paper, the *Gleaner*, of May 25, 1862: "He arrived in Jamaica in 1816 and from that time has identified himself with the interests of the island." The coincidence is striking, I suppose, without being remarkable: both doctors had come from foreign countries and made homes in the new land and the language available for describing that fact didn't change much over a century. But then there *is* something odd: after a few years of practice my grandfather decided to become an anesthesiologist and to do so he left his wife and my infant father and went to the University of Edinburgh for a year or, possibly, two years. Perhaps his old school, Meharry, didn't offer a course in anesthesiology then and going to a traditionally white medical college in the States would have been, at best, very difficult. But he probably could have gone to the University of Toronto or to any number of places in London. Yet he picked the school where James Maxwell had studied and neither I nor my father have any real idea why. "Destination's important to me," I scribbled in a note to Susan that winter, feeling close to her as

I dropped it in the Canada Post box near the bike store. But destination—place—is nothing but another version of the question, there's no answer. Sites are specific, all right, we inhabit them and go on.

Twenty-some years after he died I saw a man who looked like my grandfather, or as he might have looked as a young man, this in the London underground. I was near the Victoria and Albert, where actually the tracks are elevated and go across the tops of some low buildings. The man's face was no white apparition, as Pound said, nor was he a gangly test for my heroism, as Césaire put it—he simply had the same high forehead and cheeks as my grandfather had had and the same coppery skin drawn up tight over those, the same squint, the face itself was an island.

Anne Clarke Giscome Maxwell perished when her ship was lost in a storm in the Bay of Biscay; she was on her way to Scotland from Jamaica. Susan's genealogy didn't account, of course, for John Robert Giscome or for my family. Lorel's began, more or less, with John R. and didn't connect to Susan's Maxwells or to my grandfather's people. All truths are partial, I suppose, versions at best. Metaphors for the truth. We all three puzzled about the spelling difference. From my journal of my winter in Fort George:

> The Giscomes were allied w/ the Maxwells—they went "back" to England & Scotland; the Giscombes stayed and became black.

(It's not true, of course, that the only twentieth-century occurrence of the Giscome name is in British Columbia: my grandfather's brother claimed that name as his and listed it in the city directories of North Bay, Ontario. But there's more: I said that Charles Giscome's children reinstalled the "b" in the family name after the old man died but that's a gloss: John did and his sisters Sybil and Connie and Esther did. But Lucille didn't, she retained the old spelling, even as her siblings changed. "She was the only one in the family," Icsolene said in her letter to me, "who dropped the B. I feel that even though she did not see eye to eye with her dad, she had a hidden love for him." The long heart of the family emerges again as a question stated in terms of spelling, represented as a matter of spelling. There's no answer to the question and I fear that there's no answer coming. But at that winter-long moment in the basement on Lyon Street, as I hovered over Vivien's Macintosh, I thought about Lucille in Europe, tried to imagine her life there. That woman, my cousin, hunched over her typewriter in Prague in the sixties, her darker-than-mine fingers on those keys composing in Czech: she was the last Giscome.)

Winter in Fort George

One afternoon downtown at the library I found the complete version of Bruce Ramsey's piece, "John Giscome's Country," on the Local History shelf, bound like a master's thesis. What I said above—that there was never a statue of John R. or a plaque commemorating his exploits in the town of Giscome— is true, but there is Bruce Ramsey's literary appreciation, which was first published, apparently, as a supplement to one of the 1964 issues of the weekly *Giscome News*. I'd seen an excerpt from it years earlier, a bad Xerox of a clutch of pages at the town archive in the museum—this during my second trip to Fort George back in 1991—, but here was the whole of it.

Ramsey's a popular historian in B.C., library shelves all over the province sag with the weight of his books; even Milner Library at Illinois State owns a couple. The whole of "John Giscome's Country" is a rough historical overview of the region itself and contains only a few real points about John R., things gleaned from the *Colonist*, from the *Cariboo Sentinel*. I'd not paid a lot of attention to the piece when I'd encountered it before, having seen its sources elsewhere, but that afternoon the first paragraphs captured my interest:

In the passing parade of B.C.'s exciting history, there march before our eyes many men and women whose names for a brief moment are indelibly stamped in the record and then, just as quickly as they appeared, they pass from our ken.

Such a man was John Giscome (sometimes spelled Giscombe) after whom the townsite and post office serving the Eagle Lake Sawmills was named. We see him in the midst of one of the greatest gold stampedes the world has ever known; we see him engaged in back-breaking toil, sometimes in vain, and at times riding the crest of success. We see him for fleeting moments in the Cariboo, in the Rocky Mountain Trench, in the Peace River country, and beyond to the spreading prairies. And then we lose sight of him forever.

We know nothing of his activities until 1862 when he headed out of the infant Quesnellemouth, now Quesnel. Some writers in the post-Giscome era have described him as being a Negro but there is no concrete evidence on which to hand this decision. His partner was Henry McDame, a Negro from the Bahamas and, at one time, Giscome Portage was known as "Nigger

Portage," but whether this was because of Giscome or McDame is not recorded. The claim he worked on McDame Creek, with Henry, was sometimes called the "Negro Claim." And, so, it is all circumstantial evidence as to his racial background.

He does a professional job for the duration of the piece: in the following paragraphs he takes the narrative back to past perfect, back to the past before the past, back to Mackenzie and Simon Fraser, quoting from the journals of those gentlemen; and then returns to the more recent past, revisiting Giscome and McDame, on whom he spends a page and a half, excerpting from the account in the *Colonist* that describes the first crossing of the Giscome Portage. And because of that, Giscome and McDame's trip looks like, in form (in *status*), something similar to the travels of Mackenzie and Fraser. I was drawn, of course, to the title of Ramsey's piece: his use of the possessive assigns ownership to John R. and makes him, because of that, the patron, the patroon, the *father* of the region. It's a dangerous responsibility to assign, even ceremonially, such ownership—in that person's family name we all proceed, like a family. Black families (in the U.S. anyway) acknowledge the mixture of our ancestry; the mythology of white families is purity. It's for this reason, I think, that Ramsey does that wild little sidestep around John R.'s "being a Negro" by calling such blackness a rumor and identifying McDame as the real and true inhabitant of the woodpile. He lets his readers presume my man's innocence, presume that he wasn't black until it's proved otherwise. Evidence is "circumstantial." His not being *necessarily* black means all the things named for him in the Cariboo are not necessarily black either—what fathers do is put their names on things and people, put their blood into people. People spend money to search out their fathers for down through the father come goods and rank and privilege. Words like *heritage* and *birthright* pop up. I made a clear Xerox of the first pages of Ramsey's essay and came home, stopping at Overwaitea on the way, picking up dinner. I stood in the cashier's line with the white Fort George people, feeling literary and a little smug in that ability to *read*, aware of myself as black, as a Giscombe, thinking this is the heritage, O my brothers and cousins in Canada, I'm what is hidden in the blood.

Giscome, B.C.

Like a family. Relation *is* an attractive fiction and this book's about that, about family as metaphor, about a series of ideas about family and how those ideas roost or came to roost in certain locations. Heritage, nationality, name, geography. "An idea I had and talked about / ," John Ashbery said, "Became the things I do."

But then came Lorel Morrison's phone call about his discovery of John R.'s children, Margaret Elizabeth and Emma Magdalina. I'd always thought of him—John R.—as being profoundly other from all that without even realizing that that was how I was thinking. It's not surprising, I suppose: he'd always been asexual in the references. I'd wondered, vaguely, if he'd been gay. Old John Aaron Giscombe had said something about his having had children with a French housekeeper— "so that side of the family stayed white"—but I'd found no French names among the women from whom he'd let rooms in Victoria and I'd discounted the old man's assertion as rumor, something baseless. (Sarah Page, the mother of record: could she be the white—or "white"—French housekeeper?) Perhaps I'd been overeager to distance John R. from the possibility of descendants; perhaps especially since I was fairly sure I wasn't one. But here came Lorel to complicate my schema, my literary myth based on John R. Giscome, to reveal my own assumptions to me—here were children, a planted field indeed. I see now I'd wanted my man to stay beyond the capture, the thrall, of descendants; that and the lack of photographs of him rendered him conveniently inaccessible through any normal channels. There were no conventional bloodlines, hidden or unhidden, and no family resemblance to claim or lack of family resemblance to wonder over: instead he was a series of references and, more important, he was landscape itself and the way through landscape both. He loomed over life, bigger than it. He was the context for life—it went on quite literally in his name without his having to have much, directly, to do with it. He was aloof in the past and up to the point of Lorel's phone call he'd been, simply enough, an impossible man who several times or, better, ways *outdistanced* his descriptions. Yet he was no hasty symbol or paltry image. The Creeley-esque "figure of outward"? Hah, he was the definitive landscape of the black North itself and beyond even that he was the Giscom[b]e past itself, he was—up to the point of Lorel's phone call—the purest most distant and perfect self with intact borders. An island, an England.

Winter in Fort George

We kept going out in the car, the "good car," the ten-year-old Volvo that started every day, even without a block warmer.

It was still winter, March, but Madeline was off for spring break, so we all went out to Fort St. James, a hundred miles west and north of Fort George, and bought a room in the Chundoo Motor Inn and watched a sentimental Richard Pryor movie—*Bustin' Loose*—on television. Most people we saw in town were from the First Nations but there was a Chinese presence as well. It had been snowing in Fort George and we'd put off leaving for a while, until eleven o'clock, until it stopped and seemed to clear. We went through the drive-through at McDonald's then and headed west out of town on the Yellowhead. Near Isle Pierre I pulled a U-turn to investigate an animal I'd seen out of the corner of my eye in a field off the highway and it turned out to be an honest-to-God timber wolf, *Canis lupus*—it was the long legs that had caught my attention. Katharine watched it through the binoculars as it trotted off, confirming the sighting. The broad chest, the wide face. She'd worked with wolves (as well as with bears) during the years she was at the zoo. Trashy rock and roll was on the radio—"Crazy on You," a song we all half knew. It was the first wild wolf for any of us. We got back on the road then and got to Vanderhoof and took the turnoff there up to Fort St. James: we were thinking we'd tour the re-creation of the old Hudson's Bay fort itself but that was still closed, it turned out, for the season. So we settled in and watched Richard Pryor and looked at the map and the next morning we asked around and found out there was a tourist lodge in Germansen Landing, 140 miles north of Fort St. James, and we called them—having learned from our experience with touring the fort—and the woman said yes, they were open, and that when her husband had gone off that morning he'd taken the rear-wheel-drive pickup (as opposed to the 4WD), so the road should be passable.

This was part of John R.'s range. His address had been, from 1887 to 1889, "Manson River," and the Manson River itself paralleled a length of the road into Germansen. According to Ralph Hall's book, John R. and Henry McDame had prospected on Peter Toy's bar in the Finlay River, east of Germansen, but hadn't thought it would pay enough to make staying there worth their while, and went on. In their trip of 1862–63 they had gone a long way out on the Finlay before turning around and coming back to the Peace—they'd named one of its branches the Vermilion, because of the color, but I don't think the name stuck, I can't find it on any map. All those rivers—the Nation, the Omineca, the Parsnip, the Manson, the Finlay—go to make up the Peace but the Finlay's mostly gone now, disappeared into huge Williston Lake, a B.C. Hydro project.

We bought bread and cheese at the Overwaitea store in Fort St. James and then headed north through bouts of sunshine and light snow. The road was gravel but quickly became hard-packed snow and we drove on for two or three hours, going slow through the many curves, skidding a little on the hills, meeting only two other vehicles, both 4WD pickups. The road was mostly a lane and a half wide with snow piled high at its edges and we pulled off into some truck's big wheel ruts to eat lunch and we pulled off again into a cleared area at the Nation River bridge so Katharine could photograph the trumpeter swans on the open water. Where did John R. live? Presumably there was a settlement that had been called Manson River— that's the purpose of addresses, they're where you can go to get your mail. We came to the Manson River itself and followed it: there were beautiful forested islands when the river swelled into a chain of lakes, the Manson Lakes. But eventually the road left the river and we came to a hill that was difficult: we made it to the top with some effort, skidding back and forth and sideways, and this unnerved us some. The road was curving too in ways that didn't seem to follow the map and this made us wonder what was up ahead: if we *had* missed a turn and got stuck in the snow we could end up in some deep trouble. We'd spent enough time on the winter roads around Ithaca to realize that getting stuck, even with 4WD, was always a real possibility. It was sunny now, at the top of that hill, but that wouldn't last. We sat there for a few minutes talking about all this and decided to turn around and reinvestigate the fork we'd come through a couple of miles back and consider maybe going back to Fort St. James while we still could. I was executing a several-point turn to reverse our direction (the road was still one and a half lanes) when Madeline, from the backseat, deadpanned, "There's a car coming."

It was a couple in a 4WD club cab and they asked if we were going to Germansen and offered to follow us to make sure we made it. We had been on the correct road after all. We got over the remaining ten miles without trouble but we liked having them coming along after us and they turned in behind us to the complex of buildings at Germansen Landing proper just as the sun was starting to fade. We all introduced ourselves then— they were Jacques and Nancy—and shook hands and they went in to check their mail at the general store. Noelle Müller came out and walked us out to the cabin we'd be renting: it was a ramshackle place with a corrugated roof and she and I tried and failed to light the gas stove and I think she was embarrassed by that and promised her husband would be home soon. But there was a woodstove and I made a fire in it and then walked down and bought a package of hot dogs from her and we had beans and franks. We'd picked up a pint of Bourbon at the package store in Fort St. James and a little bottle of lemon juice and some sugar (along with the beans) at the Overwaitea there, so Katharine and I were able to have whiskey sours before dinner. Just beyond the little glow of the whiskey, just past the reach of the fire, was the cold—we could lean back in our chairs and feel the first edge of it—and oh, how that made fire and whiskey so wonderful! Later, Madeline and I went out on Night Patrol: we trudged down the long Müller driveway to the road and then walked across the wooden bridge over the Omineca River; the Müllers' Newfoundland, Bear, went with us. Lots of snow everywhere on earth, lots of stars in the sky. The week before, Noelle said, the neighbor had shot from across the river and killed a wolf on her front lawn. The man had run across the bridge then and dragged the bloody carcass into the store to be weighed. Shaking her head. ("Let me go crazy, crazy, on you-u-u-u- . . ." the song had gone.)

The next day we spent a little time with Scott Müller, who'd come back late. He had taken the 4WD, he said, Noelle had been mistaken, and he looked at our Volvo with rueful respect; he'd have advised us not to attempt the trip, he said. Madeline had discovered and been discovered by the Müller children—four or five blond girls—and as we talked with Scott, inside his store, we saw her run by in their midst, all were coatless in the bright cold. He'd been in Prince George yesterday, he said, buying provisions for the store and taking the oldest girl for her piano lesson. It's a 500-mile round trip; he does it once a week. Mining continues in the area, so, in addition to running the store, he's also the gold commissioner. And the postmaster: the mail arrives on Wednesday morning (though I don't remember now if it comes by truck or by helicopter) and he sorts it and has it set out by 1 p.m.—it's an event, he said, everyone from many miles around shows up. This was everyone's address. There was another black dot on the map, though, Manson Creek: we'd tried to see it the previous day, thinking this might have been the site of John R.'s address a hundred years ago, but had been defeated by a big snowy hill, one we'd had to back down, right after we'd made the turn. "Is there a lot at Manson Creek?" I asked Scott and he looked off into space for a moment and then said if we were looking for land we'd be better off looking right around Germansen itself or at a place a little up the road called Ten Mile—where Jacques and Nancy lived—because there was more of a community, especially at Ten Mile, than there was at Manson Creek, which was full of get-rich-quick types. It took me a second to understand that he'd misunderstood my question, that he'd heard it as a real estate query; he went on talking, based on that, asking if I could make money from my writing and saying that after we'd made the initial investment on a place, we'd find the area was quite cheap to live in. Both he and Noelle were from the States—Indiana?—and had come through here on a canoeing vacation some years ago and returned to stay. Up at Ten Mile, Scott said, we'd find a Stanford economics professor who'd left that employment. And the summer before, a Jamaican fellow had been working at one of the bigger local mining operations. He urged us to stay for the day and to run up to Ten Mile to see what it was like and he even offered to take us into Manson Creek in his 4WD.

I don't know why we declined to spend the extra day and when I brought it up recently with Katharine she didn't know either. We've talked about Germansen a lot since then and it's a regret. We could go back, of course, and likely will, but we have an odd sense of having blown something. But blowing something's nothing but a romantic notion dressed up in a peculiar 1960s argot; and the notion itself of going away off into an extremity—into a place beyond the land beyond—and just never coming back is another one. Somehow the talk with Scott let us see it as a possibility, though. We could just stay there, and why not? Maybe this scared us some, not having a good answer to Why not; maybe that's why we didn't stay for the second day.

We drove back along the Manson River again, but this time we followed it farther east and then went over a hill and crossed the Nation River on a high ice-covered single-lane bridge with nominal sides. Scott had suggested we might enjoy driving over something called the Ice Bridge, a seasonal short-cut across Williston Lake into the small city of Mackenzie—but when we got there we discovered there was nothing to it but some hand-lettered signs pointing to a set of tire tracks going across the frozen lake toward a distant set of smoke-stacks. Seasonal transport. We figured they'd know it was time to close the bridge when the first Volvo went through. We stayed on the road we were on and suddenly there was the

Hart Highway, Route 97, which was startlingly clear of snow and which had an amazingly sharp yellow line down its center. "This is a magnificent car," Madeline said as we went through the gears and got it up to 60. Heading south. I fiddled with the radio and we cruised back to Fort George listening to very hip "Definitely Not the Opera," crossing the continental divide at Summit Lake, a few miles north of the turnoff for the Giscome Portage Regional Park. There was no sign for the divide on the highway, but we knew where it was.

Trains, Airplanes

BritRail

Another British vignette: Madeline and I would often go out walking in the afternoon—from the Combe Road house—and come to the bridge over the BritRail tracks that marked one edge of Port Meadow. It was an old stone bridge, a beautiful arch, and we'd lean across its wide, flat top and watch the trains—so many passenger trains in Britain!—ease out of the Oxford station a mile away and approach our vantage point slowly and slowly roll by under us. The engineers wore ties and jackets; they'd never sound the horn but they'd often wave.

This was not Night Patrol, this was Daddy and Baby—she was one year old then, in the backpack, but she'd stretch over my shoulder and awkwardly point down the track to the distant moving headlight on a locomotive and yell her word for train, a word I never wrote down and can't remember. Sometimes an older man would join us—he was a natty pensioner in his sweater-vest and tie and he praised Madeline's ability as a trainspotter. He'd join us on the bridge or we'd join him; he was often there as, I suppose, we were. "Trains," he said one time, "is a good 'obby."

We went out on BritRail a number of times that year and the trains were comfortable and punctual and I liked that they went so many places on the island. But it was an island, so they never really went very far and the geography never changed all that much—the whole country's in the same time zone—or perhaps the change was something I didn't know how to look for: anyway I think it might have been on the trains in Britain that I felt most foreign, most American. I was there on a fellowship from the National Endowment for the Arts, working, oddly enough, on a poetry book about the South, about Birmingham, Alabama. (The big Midlands industrial city, Birmingham—for which the Alabama city is named—, was to the north of us; we changed trains there once.) Our "artisan's cottage" in Oxford was a row house on a street of row houses and in that house, after I'd finished writing for the day, I'd read *The Guardian*—certainly the best newspaper I've ever encountered—and watch, in the evenings, Channel Four and the BBC; we ate sometimes in the local pubs—the Perch and the Trout—and in Indian restaurants and I enjoyed our proximity to Port Meadow and going birding there with Katharine. But I was thinking of Birmingham and writing about that and my memories of Birmingham were tied up with—bisected by—memories of trains: the first section of the book I was working on is titled "Look Ahead—Look South," for one of the advertising slogans of the Southern Railway Company, and the writing itself is full of references to the Birmingham railroads.

But when I was a child trains were mostly their tremendously physical selves, bearers—because of that—of a certain obvious sexual power but more than that it was how interested I became, as I progressed through childhood, in their capacity to relentlessly, physically cover distance and in that way make space—the unseeable space surface takes beyond, say, a horizon—actual. Verifiable, reachable via the surface itself. And so it was how they connected my Ohio with the South—we'd go to visit my grandparents there on the Hummingbird (on the L&N line) and I'm thinking of that train, the Hummingbird, drifting out of Cincinnati at dusk, out of that border town's station (where Winold Reiss's huge heroic-worker friezes rose over the concourse), and then across the Ohio River there to arrive thirteen or so hours later in Birmingham and how surprised I'd invariably be, stepping down out of the vestibule, at the heat. I remember the "new" L&N station, the one built by the railroad in 1961 or 1962, but not its predecessor, where I, as a young child, got off and then back onto the train God knows how many times. The new one I heard about in my grandparents' talk before it went up, my grandmother's voice in particular in my memory still, saying how they'd promised the colored waiting room would be just as nice as the one for the white people, the voice neither prideful nor resigned but somewhere, I think now, past even irony.

That would have been, probably, 1960. Twenty-some years later, 1982 (four years before Madeline, five years before our house on Combe Road in Oxford, thirteen unimaginable years before our arrival in Fort George), Katharine and I went out West to live in Seattle for six months because I'd won a poetry grant—my first grant ever—from the old Creative Artists

Public Service outfit, the CAPS program. It wasn't all that much money, though, so we had to be careful and try to make it last: VIA, the Canadian passenger railroad company, had a very cheap rate then, so we bought our tickets for their transcontinental train, the Canadian, pleased to discover that we could afford a sleeper. We'd chosen Seattle too because it was cheap or because it was the cheapest of the sophisticated West Coast cities and I'd wanted to be far away from winter, or the kind of winters I knew, had come to know from having spent about all my adult life in upstate New York. My winters growing up in Ohio had been similar: not as much deep snow, but the same bright cold. Years later, of course, we'd embrace winter in Fort George; but that was or would be a stumbled-into embrace—we didn't go there to seek the ice and cold but found it palatable once we did arrive. This time, on my way to Seattle, I was thirty-one years old and simply tired of snow. My original thought had been to go to Mexico, to San Miguel de Allende, but Katharine hadn't wanted to do that—my second- and third-hand descriptions of its bohemian listlessness hadn't appealed. We'd talked briefly then of going South—to New Orleans or Atlanta—but dismissed the possibility because of the fact of our differing races; neither one of us wanted to have that extra to put up with, the fear past the edge of town. My own memories of the South, though, are relatively pleasant: I remember, from my childhood, winters in Birmingham, at my father's parents', the green winter lushness at Christmas or in January—and the one time I nursed a fever all night long there high in a splendid nine-year-old isolation, heat pressing in at my edges from both inside and outside as I lounged in the converted daybed in their extra room, the tiny room they'd made into a library, watching *The Late Late Show*: Robert Mitchum tracked a mountain lion through snow, he was sick and crazed as I was—no, sicker certainly, since whatever it was killed him and I had no fear of that, even at perishable nine—, and then holed up in an ice cave and carved a panther effigy out of a piece of wood, this slightly before dying, while Birmingham sailed through the holiday night unscathed by the thought of snow. It wasn't until the summer I was twenty, 1971, that I read Walter van Tilburg Clark's novel *Track of the Cat*, on which the movie was based; on a hot night in Montreal I finished the book on a hotel fire escape, reading right under the green neon ROOMS/CHAMBRES. Buzzing. Too hot to sleep.

I hadn't known Katharine then, in 1971—we met a couple of years after that, in our first year of grad school at Cornell, and commenced going places together and married in 1975. Going places? We did and still do but I suppose that's my metaphor, it's certainly the metaphor of this book. Katharine's account of these last many years—the stories her photographs tell, her ideas and the things that she's done and wanted to do, the things she's got me into—would necessarily be somewhat other from what I'm talking about here; most of the facts would line up but the emphases would be different—maybe all that's obvious. Going places. February 1982, there was snow and slush all around the CN station in downtown Montreal and, once inside, we went down some stairs and there the train was, all beautifully blue and gold, the high flat bolted sides were clean, almost antiseptic-looking in the dull platform light. Our accommodation was called a "section": we had two bench seats which faced one another and which folded down into a three-quarter-size bed at night. Around nine the porters would come through and make the beds, this being part of their job of running the sleeping cars. I knew about this job— being a porter—because it was legendary, it was the *entry* (as someone described it once) into the middle class for black men in the forties and fifties, even in the sixties, thanks especially to Mr. Randolph's fiery union. It was certainly not the only way in, of course, but it was so well known, so touted, as to be a part of you if you're black and middle-class, even if no member of your family had ever come up that way. A book I'd had as a child—about a boy, a white boy naturally, riding alone, going God knows where, to Grandma's house or something, one of the "Childcraft" volumes—identified the porter as "the colored servant on the train": it was a book that presupposed a white child reader, of course, and so was blind to the mutable and relative nature of class and effortlessly married that "servant" position to race for all time, right there to be sucked in like or with the air of childhood. In the fifties and sixties when my family and I would go back and forth to Birmingham on the Hummingbird all the porters had been black—but Canada's so white, I'd thought that afternoon in Montreal, who'll the porters be and in this the eighties? Black Canadian men, that's who: a profoundly bald no-nonsense man had our car and glided back and forth effortlessly between English for us and French for the ladies in the section across the aisle.

So here we were that afternoon on the Canadian, the VIA flagship train pulling out of the Gare Centrale on time, as they say, into the sunset and Katharine and I up in the very fifties, very Deco-resurgence observation dome drinking Canadian Club from the bar downstairs as the snow flew, O Can-a-da indeed, O Canada! and, later, sharing our table at dinner with a pale mustachioed man about our age going only as far as Brockville, Ontario. We'd actually got on the train, unconcerned about looking like the lower class, with an A&P bag full of enough non-perishable food (and enough Bourbon) to see us at least as far as Calgary but when it turned dinnertime we couldn't resist the dining car (as we'd been unable, earlier, to resist the bar-observation car), despite the restaurant prices. The dining car was fifties too: there was real cloth on the table, the dishes were china, the food was good. We passed the galley kitchen on the way out and stopped to speak with the cook and some of the waiters, all of whom were black, yes even in Canada. And here I came in these the eighties, the darker brother (as Langston Hughes put it), eating in the dining car at the table with the company. One of the waiters, a huge man with thick glasses, studied us hard for a minute, then introduced himself and shook my hand.

We crossed the wild country of Ontario all the second day. It was nothing but forest, frozen lakes, and snow but the train stopped at Woman River and again at Musk—the stations were shacks with snowshoes leaning against them and snow-mobiles parked outside, no roads—and people got on. This was the vaunted transcontinental service and also as close to a class act as railroads in the 1980s came in North America, but out there it was also the only way, in winter, in and out. (Seven years later, when I fell behind schedule in my second bike trip to North Bay and got the train for the final fifty miles I found myself on another classy operation. That train had a name too—the Northlander—and the conductor explained to me, when I questioned her, that the actual train itself had been something called the Trans Europ Express at one time and when that line had gone electric "they sold the equipment to us." The equipment was those Continental coaches with the aisle down one side and the big glassed-in compartments on the other. But the people in the compartments were not particularly Continental, or not the Europeans that one sees in films: my fellow travelers were burly white men with tattoos, burly Indian men with tattoos, stick-thin barely post-teenage mothers with stick-thin kids dressed in homemade duds, cool white high school students with ghetto blasters and enormous rucksacks. This is the other ideal vision: the best equipment for ordinary travelers, fanfare for the common man. That train—which still runs daily from Toronto way up to Cochrane, but with more prosaic equipment nowadays—was full of commoners being transported in grace, with that fanfare, through the woods and abandoned fields that were going-back-over-to-woods of north Ontario. As we went along I developed a crush on the conductor, a confident and good-looking woman—she was a little older than me, a little muscular. I remembered her suddenly, years later, when we went to Jamaica: she was white but she'd worn her black hair pulled back into the severe bun favored by so many Jamaican women; her name was Nancy something, there was a streak of black grease on one of her stockings because she'd helped me load the bicycle. I rode that woman's train from one market town to the next, sitting up in the dining car drinking coffee with a burly tattooed white man on his way home to surprise his mother.)

We had a longish layover in Winnipeg and then the trip resumed and we crossed Saskatchewan in the dark and in Calgary we stopped again and Katharine and I got off and had breakfast in a lovely restaurant in glassed-in downtown. Then we went over the mountains of Alberta—the infinity of white peaks—and entered B.C., the mountains continuing; we crossed the Columbia at twilight on a high trestle and later that evening came to Revelstoke, where snow was piled up to the top of the platform shelters. A loud white man in loud plaid pants got on there and bought drinks for all of us in the club car but it was a sour fun he projected, a general ugliness I saw waiting to burst across the border without tune after, probably, his second scotch. We said our good nights then and retreated to our sleeper; it was only ten o'clock and we were only 250 miles out of Vancouver but it was going to take all night to get there on account of the train having to snake through the Coast Range. We sat up for a bit longer in one of the empty sections, one that hadn't been made up for sleeping, and read and looked out the window some, but the mountains were invisible beyond the glass and we had to be content with our own reflections.

The next morning was grey when I dressed and stepped into the aisle. The crew had changed at Winnipeg and the porters were all white. The sandy-haired surly man who had our car was up and standing in the vestibule where it says DO NOT STAND in French and English, smoking a cigarette. He had the top part of the door open, though, and beyond him I could see that we were traveling along beside open water, the Fraser River, and that the hills in the near distance were treed and snowless; that the air coming into the car around the man's cigarette smoke wasn't frigid as it had been for days. February? When the train stopped at Vancouver we stepped down out of the vestibule and, in that physical surprise at the heat, commenced walking the platform toward the station house, over which flew seagulls. Lugging the carry-ons, sweating in our down and wool by the time we got up past the blue engines that had brought us out there from Montreal. We'd left the East on Canadian National tracks but VIA makes use of both transcontinentals: big ratty letters spelling CANADIAN PACIFIC were splayed out on some sort of wire mesh above the Vancouver station. On the far side, the side that fronted on the street, the bright white and red Seattle bus was waiting—what do you *do* at the end of a line but go farther? I thought, in the parking lot, that I could smell the Pacific Ocean, which I'd never seen then, from way over across town—a raw tartness was in the air—but maybe it was just diesel exhaust from the bus mixing with the diesel exhaust from those locomotives still idling behind the station's back door.

I wrote a lot in the next few months in Seattle. The manuscript that took shape there was titled "Practical Geography" and I finished it a few years later before we went to Oxford, but the book was never published.

The Empire Builder

The book about the South I'd begun writing in the house on Combe Road fared better. That book—titled *Here*—came out in September 1994 and by October I was booked into a series of readings, a little publicity tour, at bookstores and colleges in Washington, Oregon, and British Columbia. (This was the pre–Fort George trip, the trip on which I bought us the green Willys and rented us the house by the Nechako.) So twelve years later I was back on the train—alone this time and on Amtrak—, heading back to Seattle. On the train? Actually it was a succession of trains—by the time the travel agent and I had finished up, the Amtrak ticket was five pages long and it was paper-clipped to a receipt for my reservation for a trip on the British Columbia Railway as well. The price of the same journey by airplane would have been about the same but I've really never cared much for flying and I had some leeway in regard to time. And besides, months earlier, I'd had a vision of myself sitting next to a train window for days reading a book.

I'd arranged to go out by coach on the Empire Builder— that train leaves Chicago every day and arrives finally, forty-something hours later, in Seattle. Or half of it does: Amtrak splits the train in two at Spokane and the half that doesn't go to Seattle goes down to Portland, Oregon. I was going first to Seattle but I'd be returning to Illinois from Portland; I'd get to traverse both forks of the train's route. For the trip back, I'd reserved a sleeper, an "Economy Bedroom"—this in anticipation of coming home tired and a bit frazzled, in a state, that is, where I would be appreciative of the privacy.

The Amtrak coaches are not about privacy. The train at that level's a quite public space in which people are thrown together, for better or worse, for however many hours. You end up eating and sleeping with strangers or in the presence of strangers. Traditional enmities are put aside for the duration. Put aside? At least they're deemphasized or, perhaps more to the point, emphasized politely. Among the passengers a haphazard civility exists out of necessity. And some alliances form. "You know that man who's sitting with us?" a little girl said gravely to Madeline when we were traveling back from Vancouver in 1991. "He's not my dad, he's just some guy my mom met on the train."

The Empire Builder was crowded leaving Chicago but I was lucky and got a window seat, the last one in the Seattle car. Then came the wait as the rest of the passengers straggled on and had to choose who to sit with among those of us traveling alone. I sat by my window and pretended to be reading a novel—Greene's very good *Stamboul Train*—as I kept watch over the new people coming into view, praying more than once, "Not him, please," and "No, no not her." Finally I was joined by a young white woman with African braids and numerous sweaters. She'd been driving around the country in her pickup truck having adventures for a year and was on her way to chill out for a while at her great-grandmother's farm in North Dakota. We talked for a little bit and I looked out the window at beautiful Wisconsin—the light was that incredible diffuse light that clear days in autumn have—and she went off to the bar car and I read and dozed and she came back and I went to the bar car and came eventually back and we both dozed. But somewhere late that night, western Minnesota, I think, we were both in what I recognize as an odd state of wakefulness that occurs after midnight—and after some little piece of sleep—on public conveyances. It's a timeless state. Anyway that's when she and I finally talked about what we did: she showed me photographs of her paintings, I showed her my new book.

She was a good seatmate—smart, undemanding, quirky—but when she got off at 6 a.m. I luxuriated in having the whole thing, both seats, to myself. I kept it all day across North Dakota and Montana and into Idaho but ended up coming into Seattle in the company of a man close to my age on his way to spend the winter with his mother in warm Texas.

Seattle itself was warm and typically rainy but it had been snowing up in Prince George when I got there. I had my adventures—buying us cars, renting us houses—and proclaimed this and that from various podiums and rode various ferries and buses and other trains and finished up, finally, at Reed College in Portland and one of my hosts, Bob Knapp, took me to the Amtrak station, where my little bedroom was waiting for me on the Empire Builder. As we crossed the Columbia and rolled along toward Spokane, where the other half of the train would be joined to us, I was thinking again of my father and how much he'd enjoyed, as a young man, the few times he'd gone off alone—without my sister, Mother, and me—on the Hummingbird. Oddly enough, it's dinner that my father still talks about when he talks about how it was to take that train in the 1950s, his journeys back South to see his parents. (He's part of that generation that left for the North after the war and did well there. Here. I grew up playing with the children of other black doctors, men who'd also come from the South, in those big backyards of the black suburbs south-west of Dayton.) He'd eat dinner alone in the dining car—often it was crab, one of the specialties—and be the only black person there save those waiters who made sure his second bottle of beer didn't appear on the bill. And he'd take that second one back to the roomette or the compartment or whatever the term was then and watch the dark landscape slip on by, travel being accomplished in an ideal, meaning effortless, way. He'd thought about the train for a long while, he told me, and rode it finally for the first time in 1952 or '53. It was something money *could* buy. I'd asked him once about Jim Crow on the railroads in the forties, the bad old days; coaches were segregated, but I'd wondered about the Pullmans and asked him about those, about the compartments where you wouldn't be butting up against white folks anyway. "They didn't like to sell you one," he said, "they didn't like to but they would."

But as we rolled along the Columbia I was thinking that there was something I'd not understood before in the faraway pleasure in his voice, something about the aloneness, when he talked about that train, a thing beyond the racial or, at least, beyond the triumph of money over social custom or regulation. During the last several years I'd traveled in a fair number of sleepers with Katharine and Madeline but this trip back inland from the coast was the first time ever that I'd gone in *singular* comfort, the first time ever that the bedroom waited just for me upon my return from the bar or the dining car. On the Empire Builder there that night in dark eastern Washington I felt a burst of affection for my father. I settled in, put my feet up, and let one of the books I'd brought along to read lie in my lap as I looked out the window at the lights in the darkness and indulged myself in easy, pleasurable thought.

But getting beyond the racial isn't easy; in with the pleasurable thoughts that occupied me on that first night out in my Pullman was my knowledge of eastern Washington's reputation as a stronghold of Aryan Resistance types. Is it really more dangerous than downstate Illinois? I don't know but I was aware of being borne safely through it, aware of the odd mix of safety and pleasure. One did not diminish the other (or add to it)—it's a mixture I recognized at an early age and that I've become almost used to, the presence of some degree of luxury in the face of implicit danger or, better, the presence of some kind of instability just past the edge of a provisional comfort or graciousness.

Some years ago Joseph Lelyveld published an article about his luxurious trip aboard the Blue Train, in unstable South Africa, in *The New York Times*. The article appeared—in the Travel section—just before the end of some aspects of apartheid and I recall that Mr. Lelyveld noted that there seemed to be only one topic of conversation on the train or, indeed, in all the Republic. I imagine he was talking about the conversations of white people—I would think that in South Africa conversations about racism and the law have been typical among black people for a good long time, so typical as not to be worthy of note in an article in the *Times* or anywhere else. He went on to say, though, that it was possible to see the striations in South African society by observing the skin color of the various groups of railroad employees—the striations he noted were the predictable ones. Now, around this time—the mid-1980s, after we'd come back from Seattle—I was doing a couple of things with the anti-apartheid movement at Cornell and through the experience of working in that I came to understand South Africa to be such a volatile, emotional issue for Americans—black and white, leftists and right-wingers—because of that country's profound resemblance to our own. Apartheid itself fell in stages and was gone—at least officially—by 1992, but as I ranged between bar and dining car and coach on the Empire Builder that autumn of 1994, Joseph Lelyveld's words came back to me: it was possible, I saw, to observe the hierarchy in American society by observing the jobs different people do for Amtrak. The conductors are white men, the porters and dining car workers are black. The colored servants are still there in the Pullmans and among the white tablecloths. (Sometimes in Bloomington I'll stand on a certain bridge over the tracks with big Madeline and we'll wave to the almost always white engineer as a freight or passenger train eases into town underneath us; but other days we'll step outside the car to watch the Texas Eagle drift into the Amtrak station over the grade crossing at Linden Street or Broadway, and those are the times the dining car staff waves to us, they lean out from the galley windows to wave back to us when we watch and wave to them from beside the Volvo.)

On the Canadian, Katharine and I had to buy our meals in the dining car but on Amtrak trains those meals are included in the price of a first-class—that is, sleeping accommodation—ticket and eating in that car is a communal experience that both Amtrak and VIA bill as "traditional." The tables all seat four and the steward assigns you to a place when you step into the car. Your dining companions are a game of chance. Yet there's the element of elegance—the white tablecloth, the proximity of the window and its moving scenery, the reasonably high quality of the food—that's interestingly at odds with most notions of chance and the communal. Diners try to make a go of it together, to make conversation with strangers, to accept the company that fate has provided. I took my meals there on my Seattle trip on the Empire Builder, even when I was on the coach on the way out and had to pay extra for them. On almost all occasions I found myself the lone person of color at a table of whites—this is not an unusual conjunction or configuration in my life and I have the ease and confidence that comes, that has also come to me, with my age. I mean I can talk comfortably to most people who are willing to talk to me at all, I can put them at ease. But on my trip out to the Northwest and back, out of that negotiated ease, I think, the topic came up in the talk of my tablemates, again and again: the "rudeness" of the dining car staff. They'd lean across the linen, lower their voices, and say, "They're rude."

Now, I have that cultural commonality with them, the men and women working on the dining car—which means that I'm greeted differently from most of the white patrons and am joked with in ways they are not—, but I'm also a good observer of conventions and exchanges and on my trips on the Empire Builder I'd watched the staff or staffs at work and they'd never seemed particularly rude. Unbending about substitutions, not overly sympathetic when someone would whine about there not being French dressing, maybe a little gruff now and again—but not rude. I'd claim as much in my responses to those whispered complaints, occasionally confessing and, at the same time, lecturing that I had once been a taxi driver (when I was in college) and that that experience had made me forgiving ever since in regard to anyone whose work put him or her in contact with the public (and still claiming, paradoxically, that the staff didn't seem rude to me). Conventions and exchanges? This was race talk or, better, this was race talking. The repeating conversation was itself an unstable exchange: my fellow diners approaching me—as someone who, by virtue of being at their table, was like them and yet who was like the crew, too—with a statement and waiting for a response from me, one that might serve as an explanation or palliative. But the real question, the one I heard underneath all and which I did not answer, was, Why don't they *like* serving us?

My tablemates on this trip out West and back East were, for the greatest part, lower-middle-class white Americans and it occurred to me that the old saw about railroads only encouraging the lower classes to move around the country had some veracity. Amtrak advertising, however, makes it sound like a transcendent act, a way into luxury, a way (implicitly) out of your birth status. Black people have always taken the train—there were those whole Jim Crow cars in the South of not so long ago—and we were much in evidence in the coaches on the Empire Builder. Yet we know that there's no way out of how we were born and I think that Amtrak advertising, in spite of its integrated brochures, is largely lost on us. We just take the train as we always have. But I think my white tablemates were rather eager to be waited on and I think also that they wanted someone to be happy to be doing it. Someone who had less status than they did or was at least willing to embrace a lesser status for the moments it took to serve dinner. There's a nostalgia element built into train travel (or at least the train travel described in the Amtrak brochures), a harking back to that "traditional," to the days when life was, allegedly, simpler. African-Americans weren't so resentful and dangerous back then. It often seems to me that there's only one topic of conversation in our country.

And within that, status is tricky. I come from a relatively long line of middle-class people, even if my great-grandmother, whom I remember, did clean houses for white folks in Birmingham and even if the stories of my family in bondage (slavery time, which wasn't really *that* far back) are very much a part of our present worldview—by this I mean that the long line of my middle-class origins isn't really so long. My cognition of my forerunners having been, in recent memory, the lowest of the low travels with me and yet I'm heir also to that northern childhood of the fifties and sixties, to having come to my majority, that is, black in a nominally integrated culture. It was the era that came at the end of some kinds of segregation and, though we were able to go places, if cautiously, we—my family, my kith and kin—found ourselves part of no American mainstream: the old striations were still very much in place. It's an era that certainly continues: I've realized recently that now, in the 1990s, I'm in the *first* generation of black university professors (or the first generation to teach at traditionally white universities). At the edges of various campuses—my own, places I'm visiting—friendly white people will ask me if I'm a graduate student, though I'm in my forties. And when I speak publicly at a colloquium or town function they'll compliment me on how "articulate" I am. This is also the language of race, or a shape that that language takes: "articulate" is a word every black academic I've ever spoken to at any length knows—it replaces "You're different," a phrase common thirty years ago in the language of proto-liberal whites, but it means the same thing, it means "You're not like the black people we're scared of." It's an act of naïve generosity, I suppose; but I recall that in South Africa the Boers would exclude visiting black Americans—entertainers, writers, etc.—from apartheid by awarding those visitors something they called "honorary European status." Anyway, over here, the topic comes up again and again.

Yet I know it's not really the only topic in our Republic. On my final night on the train I'd gone down to the bar car around midnight and sat at the far edge of an awful scene—a group of young white men, too drunk to hear the terror in their voices, declaiming loudly about the nastiness of women's bodies. "You guys ever smell a yeast infection?" said the articulate one who kept claiming to be an L.P.N. "It's just like when you biopsy someone who's just riddled with cancer." I nursed my Bourbon and read at my book but they were too loud and I'd heard it all before too many times. I bought another little bottle of Jim Beam, pocketed it, and headed back to my Economy Bedroom through the coaches.

There, in the coaches, the lights were turned way down and people were asleep, sprawled over the seats and snoring in any number of positions. Beached animals, their bodies washed up onto this moving shoreline and myself, temporarily upright, moving through them. Soon I'd be asleep too. Madeline learned to walk as we traveled on trains in England, testing her one-year-old balance against the curves, against the lurches, learning to lean her body into the sway of BritRail. I'm a doctor's son, and from there perhaps bodies have always only seemed interesting to me: the act of balance, the physical differences between men and women, the capacities for disease and for healing, the projection of the erotic onto them— bodies—and the forms that that can take. Whatever beauty is or is not. I suppose, though, that I think we Americans are not a beautiful people: we're overweight, we tend to process our hair into bizarre yet unimaginative frizzes, we wear T-shirts that say utterly inane things. Yet the sight of so many of us asleep—women and men of various ages and sizes, a handful of impossibly gawky teenagers, some babies—and together was itself, as a composition, lovely. Sleep's "a blessèd thing" if an easy redemption, a redemption I'm more willing to see, I've realized recently, now that I'm a parent (a status I avoided for much of my adult life), now that I'm accustomed to the feeling of looking in on a sleeping child (though I'm always surprised at the *depth* of that feeling). But it wasn't children I was walking among and I'm father to only one child; I was nobody's guardian here, I was (if anything) a voyeur. Sleep's a kind of nakedness, maybe that's really obvious. All of our bodies lying there, in conjunction, alive, exposed. But I felt a burst of something beyond the erotic, beyond my bad reaction to the boys in the bar car, past the racial: I thought of the trust implicit there among these strangers I was wading through— and recalled that I was one of them on the trip out, asleep and likely snoring next to a woman named Leslie whom I'd just met—and knew that nobody was anybody's guardian, and was moved.

Alaska Airlines

After we'd been in Fort George for a month I took a trip to California: I was being considered for a position at U.C. Santa Cruz and had to go down there and talk to them and let them talk to me. Katharine drove me through the snow to the Prince George airport and I got on an Air B.C. flight to Vancouver, the first of three planes that day. As we were getting out of the car she looked up and saw an eagle drifting over the parking lot and we watched the bird for a minute or so. "It's a good omen," she said, but neither one of us particularly believes in omens. It was a grey morning and I was feeling grim as I watched the mechanics deice the wings. I don't like flying. Eight hours later I stepped off an Alaska Airlines flight in San Jose and was surprised at the heat. A young man from a car service was waiting for me and we drove over the mountains into Santa Cruz. I gave a reading the next day, Thursday, and met people Friday, and on Saturday a lovely man named Tom Marshall, a man close to my age who actually was a graduate student, gave me an all-day tour of the area. On Sunday morning I was back at the San Jose airport for the first leg of the trip back up to Fort George and, as I was going through the security check, I realized that there are no metal detectors at either Amtrak stations or Greyhound depots. San Jose has a rather small air terminal but still there were the armed guards to frisk you and the X-ray technology for your carry-ons, things we've gotten used to. In regard to train and bus travel, though, my thought is that everyone has tacitly agreed or realized that a bomb going off on such a conveyance could have no political advantage for anyone, could hold no national consciousness hostage: if one's to be a successful terrorist one needs to threaten a transport system carrying a percentage of rich folks. In the sleeper back from Portland my fellow travelers, like my dinner companions, had been lower-middle-class people, at least in style and affect. All but me were white, the black people sticking to the coaches. The porter moved among us letting down beds, bringing newspapers, being available—he was friendly to us all but I thought the friendliness seemed forced. Industry tradition dictates that porters, in addition to being black, be nice guys, at least while they're working; I figure the nice-guy part of that combination is included in the job description but I don't know how one competes to be a porter nowadays, how much is unstated. I don't know what it pays or what it costs, only how it appears. Their counterpart in on-the-job temperament would be, I suppose, the women who work for the airlines, the flight attendants. At least in appearance.

Airlines, though, do attract a wider range of travelers. On

my flight out of San Jose I found a family of Mexicans traveling with shopping bags occupying the bank of seats that I thought I'd been assigned to. Actually, through a complicated series of accidents, I'd been bumped up into the next cabin, into first class itself; I was an interloper there on the other side of the curtain, in finally among the white Republicans. I stretched out in the lap of leather-upholstered luxury, ordered a yuppie beer, and gazed around at my cabin-mates; the Mexicans had been friendly as we'd shrugged together over the mysteries of seating but these people did not look back at me. I took stock of my situation, noting the similarities and differences. Many of my fellow fliers that afternoon were plump, though they were wearing good clothes, ones that made fat less of an obvious issue; and their opinions were not emblazoned in print on their chests but were announced on the covers of their copies of *Forbes* and *National Review*—I suppose, though, that the slogans used to sell those journals are no less predictable than the ones available on sweatshirts at KMart. The hair, however, was a little better than what I'd seen on Amtrak; I remembered that young upper-class people (and here I'm drawing from my years of part-time teaching at Cornell) tend to do rather little to their hair aside from cutting it: these were their parents and grandparents with me in the incredibly clear air over California and beautiful Oregon, subscribing to a similar aesthetic.

The flight attendant who'd brought me my beer came down the aisle handing out damp, warm washcloths so that we might prepare ourselves for lunch. I was hungry—I'd missed breakfast that day—and was looking forward to eating in first class, having suffered through airline food on a few previous "dinner flights" when I'd been ensconced back in economy with the other riffraff. Once I'd simply declined the meal when it was offered, much to the shock of my seatmate, a pleasant young white man from South Africa. "But it's included in the price of the ticket," he'd whispered.

Eating dinner on Amtrak, though, is a pleasure, even when it's extra. I also think that it's the moment at which the promise of some luxury and the realities of train travel most often cross paths. In January 1995—after having flown from Seattle to Chicago on the first leg of my mission to retrieve the Volvo and drive it to Fort George—I got on the Texas Eagle for the two-hour trip down to Bloomington; the train left Chicago at six and at six-thirty the dining car steward announced over the PA system that he was about to commence walking through taking dinner reservations and that he'd be going through the Pullmans first. Realizing that I'd never get a seat before we arrived in Bloomington-Normal if I didn't go outside the stated order of things—I was in a coach—I hunted him up and asked if he could squeeze me in somewhere. He looked at me, looked at his list, frowned, and said Maybe. I returned to my seat then but shortly afterward I heard my first name called over the PA system: I was being asked to "report to the dining car." Would this have been different if I'd been a polite white man asking a favor? I doubt it, I think the end product, the bottom line, whatever anyone wishes to call it, would probably have been the same. But what I imagine would be different for the white guy would be the asking itself, the weightless experience of the interracial encounter. What's at stake here, beyond what you get to eat or not eat for dinner? We bring all of what the culture says we are and have been to each one, each encounter, and that's like a gyroscope in a box, it's a terrible and shifting weight to have to pass around, a rolling burden to bear through a conversation. Status is tricky when we meet out there in the instability, out at the bendable edges of our roles. In the dining car, I joined a friendly older suntanned couple on their way to Arkansas and a quietly hip young pale woman going someplace in Texas, Austin or Houston. We talked easy travel talk and I had the red snapper, a fish my mother's mother had often made for us, as we passed through Pontiac, Illinois, where one of the big state prisons is.

Over Oregon the flight attendant reappeared at the front of the first-class cabin with a steamy plate of turkey and dressing in each hand. Or I think it was turkey and dressing: she brought me a tray with a plastic-wrapped turkey roll sandwich on it, apologizing that they hadn't bumped me up early enough for the airline to order the extra first-class lunch. She was sympathetic and charming about it, speaking in a low voice, wrinkling her nose, apparently actually pained at having nothing better to feed me—no one could have accused that woman of being rude. And no one looked at me as I unwrapped the sandwich and ate it. It was my riffraff self, my inescapable economy being having caught up with me, my status being served to me. "I yam what I yam," said the Invisible Man. I was hungry; and it didn't taste nearly as bad as it looked like it was going to.

Winter in Fort George

The night I got back from Santa Cruz we talked for a long time about the possibility of moving there and we talked about it more and more in the following days. California has no racial majority, a fact we liked very much and which we thought might supply Madeline with a more pleasant school experience. There were mountains and big animals and redwood forests and a choice of several beaches on the ocean. The position featured a light teaching load. Houses were expensive, though, and we talked about that and figured we could stand living in some place much smaller because we'd have that access to those trees and that water, to those mountains. I was the second of four candidates to visit the campus; much too soon, we began to wait for the phone to ring.

I went out walking on the tracks one night during the wait—this was no Night Patrol, I was grumpy and stressed out and wanted to be alone. But on the way back I saw a fox ahead of me along one of the rails, so far away at first that he (she?) blended in with the railroad track, seeming to be first a distortion based on nothing but distance and light, and then the fox seemed to be an outcropping of the rail itself—both he and it were black in the whiteness. But, getting closer, I saw him roll in the snow—it was snowing and it was going to snow—and that's when I knew it really was a fox I was seeing and then he or she sat down, finally, alongside the track at attention, the long bushy tail out to the side. I stopped when he sat down and we looked at each other with about forty feet between us. He recommended walking then, so I did too, he on the south side of the track while I walked down its middle, the distance closing between us. When we were ten feet apart he crossed the track before me and drew up alongside, to my north. He stopped and I stopped, a few feet separating us, and we regarded one another. A fear pierced me that he might be rabid—so fearless was he—and I raised my arms at him, which caused him to jump back a little, the correct response. We continued to regard one another then and then one of us, I don't recall which one now, recommended walking, slowly. He stepped into the space between the rails where I'd been walking and sniffed my boot prints, sniffed them thoroughly, and then went off on his way and on I went on mine.

My mother had sung a song to us when we were children:

> Then I saw the fox all weary and grey,
> The huntsman's horn was blowing away!
> Warily, wearily, worn and spent!
> Would I be telling the way he went?
> No not I!

It had been *Vulpes africanus*, the beautiful old black fox, and when I got back to Lyon Street I told Katharine about it and she said, "That's a blessing"—which is a term by which we mean nothing religious but instead an unearned gift, one with no consequences or meaning. We don't put much stock in omens but we're glad for the blessings.

A week after that I got the phone call telling me I didn't get the job at Santa Cruz. I wanted to drive then, to get away from the computer and town, to repudiate all my connections, to be bound to—or reminded of—nothing. It was a Saturday, Madeline wasn't in school. We all got in the car and headed up the Yellowhead and I took the turnoff to Giscome and Upper Fraser and Hansard. The day was cold and there was, of course, snow on the ground: it was a high-ceiling day, a day full of shadowless, dull light. The road to Giscome went up and down the hills I'd cycled before and driven before and at Willow River we banged across the wooden bridge over the river itself and the road was straight then and mercilessly flat all the way into Giscome and I drove through town without stopping. The crews had been out, though, even this far, and the road was clear and smooth under the car: after Giscome it hugs the north shore of Eaglet Lake and then the south shore of Aleza Lake and it crosses the CN tracks a couple of times and goes past a ruined Oblate mission before it comes into the only place of any consequence out there, Upper Fraser, and I slowed finally through that town and we stopped for lunch at the general store—Campbell's soup heated up in a microwave. As Katharine paid I browsed the videos-for-rent shelf and was surprised to find a couple of copies of *Roots*, LeVar Burton looking all feral on the shiny wrinkles of the cardboard box, Kunta Kinte in Canada. There's a big sawmill in Upper Fraser, and when we got back in the car and resumed our trip I looked to my right at the houses of the workers stretching up a little hill in back of the school and the post office: they were prefab things, boxes on the snowy incline, a fate worse, certainly enough, than our big house in Illinois. We'd been figuring we might have to live a ways out from Santa Cruz, in Bonny Doon or Felton or Boulder Creek because of the price of houses in town. Across the street, to my left, was the sawmill itself and the stacks of lumber all around it, the railroad sidings on which lumber cars sat, the continuous noise. Lumber's where the money is in the North. You see a lot of one-armed guys downtown in Fort George. After Upper Fraser the pavement ends but the road was still clear, so I drove on to Hansard and we crossed the Fraser River on the strange bridge they have over it there: it was originally a train bridge, built by the Grand Trunk Pacific about 1912, and trains still use it—but there are boards laid between and alongside the rails, on top of the crossties, and you can drive across it if no train's coming. (A CN worker sits in a booth at mid-bridge and works signals for both railroad and road traffic.) We'd been talking for a couple of weeks about doing a words-and-pictures essay on the Hansard bridge and Katharine had brought her camera, even today, in the hope of getting a money shot of the train coming off the span. I too had hoped to see a train that day, one of the long freights with the massive orange-and-black six-motor locomotives with maps of North America on their sides, big locomotives for the serious grades of the West, but nothing was coming, so we rocked back across the boards and pushed south down the long gravel road toward the Yellowhead; it would have been shorter to retrace our steps but this trip wasn't about objectives and efficiency. The road winds through lumber company land and is bordered by slopes of half- and three-quarter-grown fir trees and signs announcing reforestation and sensible harvest techniques. We came to the ice-covered Bowron River and crossed it on a spindly, one-lane wooden bridge and

I recalled crossing it there for the first time in November 1991, four years earlier, unsure of the road and somehow surprised to be crossing the Bowron. I'd come across the name a few months before in an old issue of the *Cariboo Sentinel:* John Bowron had been the librarian in Barkerville and had testified on behalf of John R. during his trouble in 1871 and 1872. I'd been strangely moved that night, in part because of the surprise of the river's presence: the country was new to us then and here it was as though we were coming across John Bowron's body in the snowy dark, his corpse out there, or the rough shell of him sloughed off like some exoskeleton. There's a moment in *House of Frankenstein*, an old favorite film from my childhood, when the evil doctor discovers, in some ice caves underneath the big old house itself, the body of the monster, in ice. The Bowron was flowing that way, under ice, the water itself was hidden both the first time we came to it and this time as well. "The undying monster," the doctor had breathed and that music was suddenly there. The deeds were behind him, frozen into ice, frozen into the shape of a river and the odd square provincial park, a little farther south, the Bowron Lake Provincial Park. I'd seen his—Bowron's—pistol on display at the Provincial Museum and at the archives someone had handed me a copy of his journal—prosaic, a list of provisions and their cost, kept in blunt pencil. Every European who came out here in the nineteenth century has some kind of geography named after him. And some of the black people too. In 1994 a black bear had tried to eat a German at the Bowron Lake Provincial Park, this was widely reported in the papers in the States, even in Illinois. The German's girlfriend had beat it off with an ax. This day the sky was blank and neutral beyond the reforestation but when we did come to the Yellowhead it—the sky—had changed, had become slate, and we drove back to Fort George under that; twice I thought I saw bears on the roadside ahead but each time the dark curving black shape turned into the shadow created by a big corrugated culvert pipe's mouth sticking out of an embankment.

Darkest Canada: Some Favored Islands and a Peninsula

Black people arrived, in numbers, on Vancouver Island in 1858. Victoria then was a few buildings and mud streets but 1858 was the year of the Fraser River gold rush. The relation—between black folks and gold and B.C.—is a little indirect and hinges on the activities and proclivities of white Americans. American miners had been a presence for a while there in British territory but as more and more prospectors got lucky along the Fraser and as news of that spread south, gold seekers poured across the border. By 1858 the governor of the British colony of Vancouver Island, James Douglas, understood that this influx—those people coming up from the U.S.A. and letting the Stars and Stripes ripple over their camps along the Fraser—could cause some problems down the road. He understood that the American miners would, as he put it, "never cordially submit to English rule, nor possess the loyal feelings of British subjects"; he feared annexation by the States.

Back in the States in the 1850s things weren't good for black people: there'd been Dred Scott and there'd been the

Fugitive Slave Act and in California there was the Civil Practice Act (which prohibited blacks from testifying in courts) and a host of other insults as well. And because of all that the middle-class black community in San Francisco—people who owned property and businesses—prepared to immigrate to a place that would treat them better. They considered three destinations—sites in Panama and Mexico and Vancouver Island—and Douglas, apparently knowing of the unrest in San Francisco, sent word through the longtime captain of the *Commodore* (which regularly sailed between San Francisco and Victoria) encouraging the black Californians to choose his colony. He seems to have understood that numbers of people willing to pledge allegiance to Britain would be an asset if the annexation situation came to blows. A small group of community representatives sailed up from San Francisco to meet the governor and he formally repeated his invitation. The delegation returned with this news and by the end of 1858 six hundred black people had quit San Francisco and come north to Vancouver Island. This is an important—meaning often-referred-to—moment in British Columbia's history: it is, I think, part of the basis for the province's whites' ongoing liberal view of themselves, and the fact of such a wholesale black immigration helps allow the province, and Canada, to claim the moral high ground, to class itself off from the crudeness and prejudice of American culture. Professor Akrigg's 1977 book, *British Columbia Chronicle*, gloats over it: he describes the black immigrants as having "come to British territory in quest not of gold but of something more precious—freedom and dignity in their daily lives." (G.P.V. Akrigg is probably best known for the series of B.C. *Place Names* books that he and his wife, Helen, have published over the years. In the introduction to the current edition they wax sentimental about some old gold-era designations—Nigger

Bar Creek, the several Nigger Creeks, Niggertoe Mountain, etc.—that have been changed and they sneer at the "drive against names that officialdom deems 'racist.'" The 1969 edition, a copy of which I found in the library at Cornell, refers to John R. as "a negro miner" with that traditional lowercase "n" that Caucasian people use when referring to the race of their inferiors.)

John R. was probably among the California immigrants—likely having worked his way to California from Jamaica via Panama—but his fellows were, in the main, Americans and I don't know how much or how little he identified with them. A black friend had remarked to me once that we were fighting the Civil War down here in the States so that John R. *could* be up in B.C. adventuring, but that's not exactly true. John Robert Giscome's national experience is profoundly different from mine and my friend's—we were born in the States and grew up here, as did our parents, and John R. was a Jamaican and, later, a Canadian. His final illness was documented in the *Colonist* in articles that qualified him as "the aged negro" but also described him as "a pioneer," a distinction normally reserved for white folks. A pioneer? He's not mentioned in Crawford Kilian's otherwise useful 1978 book, *Go Do Some Great Thing*, which is subtitled *The Black Pioneers of British Columbia*. The qualifying adjective of Kilian's subtitle is, of course, necessary just as it is or would be before "American" or "university professor." Kilian's American by birth but he teaches at Capilano College in North Vancouver now; it was his book that suggested Governor Douglas's thinking on the black immigrants to me. The black exodus itself, a real-life repudiation at least in part of the popular "Man Without a Country" story, is rarely mentioned in American letters; it's hardly a bump in the bedspread of U.S. history.

One of the families Kilian talks about is the Alexanders, and when I got to Victoria late in the fall of 1991 I'd made a point of calling on Douglas Hudlin, a descendant of the Alexander family. Mr. Hudlin had heard the name Giscombe—"A guy came through here with that name," he said, "in 1858, same year as my great-grandfather"—but didn't know much about John R., just what he'd read in the paper. (Of course, it was in the paper that I'd first read about Mr. Hudlin: a *Colonist* feature article about the early black presence in B.C. had yoked the two of them and a few other people together—the headline had read "Black John Blazed a Trail" and beneath that was a photo of Doug Hudlin.) He pulled out the family album and showed me pictures of his ancestors: I'd seen the one of grim-looking old Charles Alexander before, on the cover of *Go Do Some Great Thing*. I asked how my grandfather might have done practicing medicine here and he mentioned a couple of black doctors, one of whom had learned his trade in jail by ministering to the feet of his fellow prisoners. Mr. Hudlin himself was retired now from his job as a driver with the Sanitation Department and he'd recently taken some pleasure, he said, in getting "offended" when his new, young dentist asked him how long he'd lived in Victoria. "He figured I had to be from someplace else," he said, laughing, "but I'm from here and my people are from here." He insisted on taking me back in his car to the Provincial Archives, where I'd been camped for a couple of days, sifting through documents. It had rained and cleared and the city looked especially sharp: Victoria's a green and pretty place and more than slightly in love with its history—the daily paper's still called the *Colonist* and there are many, many places that serve a high tea at four o'clock and not just to the *turistas* either. On the way downtown Doug Hudlin made a point of blowing his horn to startle a young white man in an orange vest who was absentmindedly directing traffic around a stopped garbage truck. The kid jumped into the air but then smiled and waved. "I used to work with him," he said, shaking his head. I had in my notes to ask him about his reaction to black Americans—our political gambits, the difficulties we have in our communities and with white people, our culture and the ways we're portrayed in the media—but we never got there, it seemed far outside the ken of our conversation, over a border. I'm not really very good at interviews. We'd both been to Nova Scotia, though, and we did talk about that place and our discoveries of black Canadians there.

"I Wish I Was in Shelburne Town!"

Eight years before I met Doug Hudlin, Katharine and I had come into Shelburne, on Nova Scotia's southeast coast, to discover that we had inadvertently arrived during the celebration of the bicentennial of the landing of the Loyalists in 1783. There was a banner across the street featuring silhouettes of men in tricornered hats and at a restaurant that night we were served by bored-looking young women in long dresses. But "Loyalist" itself was a meaningless word to us—something we might have heard sometime during the haze of fifth-grade history lessons, something vaguely British, something colonial— until we read the food-stained article that was paper-clipped to the menu: the Loyalists were, of course, the people we'd been taught to call "Tories," the people who'd sided with King George III against George Washington. They were counter-revolutionaries and despicable, we'd been taught, and I realized, as I read the article, that I'd never thought about what had become of them after their side lost the war. They'd been exiled, we found out in the restaurant, and had come here where they'd been welcomed as heroes, as folks who'd put a lot on the line for their deeply held patriotic values, as people who'd done the right thing. I've traveled in France and Jamaica and Switzerland and extensively in Britain, but I think I've never felt the shock of being an American so strongly as I did in that restaurant there in Shelburne town.

This was an August bicycling vacation. We'd driven from home, Ithaca, New York, to Bar Harbor, Maine, camped next to the harbor itself, got up at dawn, and—leaving the Subaru in the municipal parking lot—cycled groggily onto the Canadian National's Nova Scotia ferry at 7 a.m. We tied up the bikes on one of the car decks and stumbled up the stairs to the breakfast buffet, which had been magnificent: smoked fish, French toast, mountains of sausage and bacon, blue cheese, and a host of other foods as well. We sat next to a window and drank coffee and watched the ocean go by. Soon we were past the three-mile limit and Katharine went down to the casino and lost five or six dollars; I sat in a deck chair and read *The White Hotel*; Madeline was still three years away. Several hours later we came into Yarmouth through a white fog; it was midafternoon when we landed but we set out anyway—we were intending to make Halifax in a week—, but not without first noticing that there was a black population in the town we were riding through. Yarmouth's a small city and we were used to coming into small cities like it in Quebec and Ontario: in such places one typically sees one or two black people or, as often, no black people. Or sometimes you'll see some light-skinned person walking along whose jaw or nose or hair reveals an African ancestor. We're a different kind of presence in Canada than we are in the States and Katharine and I puzzled a little bit over the big numbers in Yarmouth, figuring it must have something to do with Yarmouth being a harbor town, but then dropped it—more pressing was the trip itself out along potholed Route 103, the road that traces the southern coast of the province.

I'd been commuting by bike all spring and summer to my job at Cornell, up at the top of its long hill, but Katharine hadn't ridden much in the previous year, so we moved slowly. We got through a lot of poor towns inhabited by grizzled white people, towns with boarded-up stores and restaurants and with incredible views of the ocean. But at the end of day two we came into big Shelburne and camped in the provincial park on the outskirts and went into town for dinner, where we discovered those Loyalists, and then we walked around a little after that. Bicentennial displays were up in shop windows and one of them featured a few portraits of Shelburne residents whose ancestors had arrived from the States in 1783. I was surprised to recognize an old black man I'd seen earlier that day: as we were entering town he'd come up on us from behind in his car—a rusted-out Ford wagon—and had paced me, staring, for a hundred feet or so; finally he waved and I, of course, waved back. I read some more on the display and discovered Lord Dunmore of Virginia and his promise, on behalf of the Crown, to the slaves: any slave willing to escape and take up arms for the British would be granted freedom after the war was over and order had been restored to the unruly colonies. George Washington wasn't offering anything. Then the tide of battle turned, etc., the ships set out for Nova Scotia, and Shelburne was one of the places the ships came to. A great number of displaced colonists landed in Shelburne in May of 1783 and among them were a thousand black people who'd also thrown in with George III. Loyalists. More ships full of black and white Loyalists came later that year, in August. The black people settled in a place called Birchtown, a little ways out from Shelburne itself; by the next year fifteen hundred people were living there, which fact made Birchtown the largest free black settlement of its time in North America. I don't know what eventually eclipsed it.

But here was our variousness. Back at home the comforting and familiar black presence in the Revolutionary War was still the famous picture of poor old Crispus Attucks being killed by those bad Redcoats and here I was, two hundred Augusts after the fact, on a street corner in Nova Scotia looking at some tacked-together displays that casually revealed an alternative history for us, one I'd not dreamed of and had certainly never encountered in school—I would have remembered, I would have been paying attention. It was the second shock of the day: Loyalists and then black Loyalists. In seventh grade we'd sat through the film version of *Johnny Tremain* and I can still sing the catchy song that the Disney people supplied for it, the one about the rebellious colonists being the sons of Liberty. It had stirred me some there in that darkened classroom in 1964—the civil rights champion President was recently dead but here was the Republic itself embodied in Johnny Tremain, a boy our age, and we overlooked his whiteness (as we forgave so much in those days) and didn't think to look for an *image* of ourselves on the screen but did see and understand that Liberty and related it, in some ways, to our situation with the whites—with "the bigger man," as Jamaicans might say—and took heart. (Or I did, I can't speak for the politics of my black classmates or for the white kids with whom I also went to school.) We could be sons of Liberty too, I thought, in spite of who we were or because of who we were, all it took was a little imagination, a little natural ability at metaphor. That afternoon we watched white actors dressed as "patriots" dress up as "Indians" and toss tea boxes off a boat. Meanwhile and unbeknownst to us, back in the jungle that history is, black people were crossing the lines, going over to the side of George III, and, later, setting sail for Nova Scotia.

The next day we made a little detour and rode "up the northwest harbour" to see Birchtown—it's on the map but there was nothing there that we could see to suggest the place's past. An old house sat at an intersection at the edge of some woods and the steepness of its roof and some other angles made us wonder if it had been built in that period but we didn't know. It was a beautiful house, though, it was high and brown and a little rakish and haphazard-looking and in a gorgeous place. A breeze came in from the water and everything was in bloom. We pressed on to the east then but never did make Halifax: we rode out but turned back and stayed in Shelburne again and the next night at Cape Sable, and, finally (the night before the return trip on the ferry), in a motel in Yarmouth. Yarmouth has a little tourist industry, so we ate well that night and walked back to the motel. At the end of the next day we'd be back in Maine and at the end of two more days on the road after that we'd be back in Ithaca: we were in the process of buying our first house and difficulties had popped up and we had to hurry home and deal with them. But that night we were on foot in Canada and, as we drifted back to the motel, we found ourselves trailing a trio of white girls—eighteen-year-olds, plump cigarette smokers in ragged dungarees—who were talking quietly among themselves until one of them suddenly shouted, "Fuck! Look who it is!" We all looked and up ahead on the sidewalk was a black girl, stopped under a streetlight: she was wearing a green Canadian Army dress uniform and a beret and she dropped her duffel bag as her friends ran to her so that they could embrace her and kiss her more easily.

In what Bruce Ramsey called "the passing parade of B.C.'s exciting history" comes the matter of what breast suckled Sir James Douglas, first governor of the province. W. Kaye Lamb—in one of the 1953 numbers of the *British Columbia Historical Quarterly*—says: "It has been stated that [James Douglas's mother] was a mulatto, largely on the authority of Letitia Hargrave, who referred to James Douglas himself as a mulatto in a letter written in 1842. But Mrs. Hargrave scarcely knew Douglas himself. John Tod, a much better wit-ness, since he knew Douglas well over a long term of years, stated that James Douglas's mother was a Creole. This is a very different term, and does not necessarily carry any impli-cation of mixed blood. It simply means that she was born in the West Indies, or in some other similar tropical region." The governor was born in Guyana, up on the shoulder of South America that hunches along the Caribbean. The O.E.D.'s largely supporting of Mr. Lamb, so much so that I figure he consulted it: the authors are quite specific—"the name having no connotation of colour"—as though in anticipation of that question or perhaps in response to a common misperception. The definition notes parenthetically that some eighteenth-century writers attribute the first instances of the word's use to "South American negroes [who applied it] to their own chil-dren born in America." Among white people the term *Creole* seems to be, according to the dictionary, most often applied to those families that are in some sense or tradition Spanish. (There's Spanish and, as Susan Buchanan pointed out, there's "Spanish.") When I met Michelle Williams in Vancouver she gave me a copy of Garbette A.M. Garraway's pamphlet, *Accomplishments & Contributions: A Handbook on Blacks in*

British Columbia; Governor Douglas is the first photo. He's tall and uncomfortable-looking, mutton-chopped and light-skinned in the rather formal portrait: on the page he is what Lowell said of Colonel Shaw's statue on Boston Commons— "he seems to wince at pleasure / and suffocate for privacy." The caption calls him "a West Indian of racially mixed parentage" but in the text she calls his mother " 'Creole.' " A year before we landed at Fort George I was in a motel room in Indianapolis, stretched out on the bed with the god-box in my hand, watching the Canadian episode of an A&E series, *The Real West*. Suddenly there were people from B.C. talking about places I'd been. Apparently some of the controversy about Governor Douglas's blood is over. The country music singer Kenny Rogers acted as narrator and he intoned that the governor had created in B.C. "a new society, one he would ever hold himself above" and, in explanation of this, on came Minister of Small Business, Tourism and Culture Bill Barlee to think aloud: "I think it went back to his childhood. He *was* half black, I think he felt that; his wife was half Indian, I think he felt that as well. So to make up for that he was a royal personage in B.C." I was in Indianapolis interviewing for a job I didn't want at the poor-relation urban campus of Indiana University. But I'd been interested in the city because of its big black population, including a real middle class: it's a *first* city, meaning here that it's a viable destination for people coming up North over the Mason-Dixon Line and that makes it a border town, a place of influx and mystery, an ambiguous town. So was Victoria. Twenty years after Lamb's article appeared in the *Quarterly* Robin Winks wrote, in *The Blacks in Canada*: "His knowledge that his mother was either a West Indian mulatto or a Creole obviously increased his concern." This an estimation of the governor's welcoming of the California black immigrants in '58. There was Governor Douglas out at the end of a dock in Victoria, said someone in a poem, "welcoming, Creole, pragmatic."

Saltspring Island

But black people had a hard time in Victoria, at least in part because of the presence of so many white Americans, and not everybody stayed there. James Pilton notes: "On Salt Spring Island the situation appears to have been somewhat different, for on the fringe of settlement, any neighbour, regardless of his colour, was a decided asset . . ." Saltspring Island's off Vancouver Island—and several black families were among its first settlers in 1859.

In the 1960s Katharine's aunt Mary had a romance of letters with a man in Canada's Foreign Service, Manson Toynbee. They eventually met and married and Mary Wright became Mary Toynbee and they moved first to Saba, in the Netherlands Antilles, and then to Saltspring Island, where Manson had grown up. Katharine and Madeline and I arrived there on the ferry from Vancouver in August 1991, our first visit. Manson's part of the family that owns Mouat's, the island's department store. He told me that the family had bought its first land on the island from the Harrisons, one of Saltspring's original black families. Mouat's Trading Company had published, in 1978, a collection of photographs, *Snapshots of Early Salt Spring and Other Favoured Islands*, edited and compiled by Manson's brother, Dick Toynbee. The book begins with a portrait of Howard Estes, who had bought himself out of slavery in Missouri and who'd looked for gold in California;

below his picture is a photograph of his big grandson, Willis Stark, standing next to a cabin built by Louis Stark, Howard Estes's son-in-law, Willis's father. But it's Willis's mother (and Howard Estes's daughter), Sylvia Stark, who has achieved a minor celebrity over the years—she was born in 1839 in Missouri and arrived in Canada with her parents and husband in 1860. She endured all the hardships of the pioneer life—primitive living conditions, threats by Indians, loneliness—and lived to 105, independent until the end of her life. Manson recalls stopping by her house in the 1930s, when she would have been over ninety years old, and finding her milking a cow; when he suggested that she should have her son Willis do that chore she'd responded, he said, that Willis had always been sickly. He died in 1943 at eighty-five; she outlived him by a year. I imagine she knew Ella Cooness and her second husband, Mr. Wintworth, late arrivals. One morning at Booksellers Row in Chicago I found a copy of the biography *Sylvia Stark: A Pioneer*, by a mixed-race couple, Victoria Scott and Ernest Jones—it's short and I read it in the car during a slack moment later in the day. The book's full of moral lessons and pastel illustrations but the facts of Sylvia Stark's life—her travels, that independence, her longevity, and her connection to an island off the western edge of North America—transcend those. And the photographs in Dick Toynbee's *Snapshots* collection—the numbers of black faces in the group school portraits, the photo of Willis Stark with a cougar he killed, others—, mute as they are, provide the shape of a documentary of black life in a very unlikely location.

But in the first pages of *Long Black Song*, Houston Baker says, in his own best sage's voice (and I have heard Houston Baker speak), that "the tales of pioneers enduring the hardships of the West for the promise of immense wealth are *not* the tales of black America." I've added the italics but the trouble is that Houston Baker's right, we have other stories, other archetypes. Yet there's the Stark family on Saltspring and my man John R. up in the Cariboo, the Peace, the Cassiar, the Omineca. There are a lot of ways to take the fall, a lot of places to land and find yourself outside history.

The Queen Charlottes

Near the end of George Bernard Shaw's *The Devil's Disciple*, Dick Dudgeon, the title character, calls George III "a pig-headed lunatic." It was one of the religious experiences of my adolescence, discovering the film version on late-night TV—its Claymation sequences, its ironic voice-over, its gallows humor—, and the next day I went out and found a copy of the play itself and committed passages to memory. There's an ambiguous non-white presence in the text in Shaw's description of Dudgeon's illegitimate half-sister, and when we lived in Britain I saw a Channel Four version which did cast a black actress in that role. But the play's not about us.

But maybe George III is, if indirectly, if by marriage. Some years ago I came into possession of J. A. Rogers's three-volume set *Sex and Race*. Dr. Rogers was a race-man, a proponent of blackness, the author of *100 Amazing Facts About the Negro*, *Africa's Gift to America*, and other books. Malcolm X read him in prison. The *Sex and Race* series attempts to document miscegenation through the centuries and even if there are many pictures of "dusky" bare-breasted women with captions such as "Belle of Tahiti" the books are fascinating if one is interested in the talk of miscegenation. The illustration that graces the frontispiece of the first volume is a reproduction of the painting of Queen Charlotte Sophia, the consort of George III—the ancestor of Queen Elizabeth and Prince Charles—, which hangs in the National Portrait Gallery in London. She's youthful in the painting, and slim, almost girlish in her coronation robes. Sir Allan Ramsay painted it before the fifteen children, before the troubles with the American colonies, before George's illness; she looks very much as if she could be one of the young light-skinned black women from Chicago who populate my African-American Literature classes at Illinois State University. She was a German princess, from Mecklenburg, when George married her and two rather slender books about paintings about her—one a collection of caricatures—have been published in the last twenty years. She's just a hood ornament for Dr. Rogers's book; she takes up a single lonely paragraph in the text itself—in the chapter titled "The Mixing of Whites and Blacks in the British Isles" he quotes Horace Walpole as saying of her, "nostrils spread too wide; mouth has same fault," and he—Dr. Rogers—remarks on the clarity of her "Negro strain." The caricatures never focus on this but other pictures of her suggest it (notably the ones by Ramsay, though none to the startling extent of his National Portrait Gallery painting). The authors of the books about her never mention her apparent African ancestry; I wonder if they didn't see it, I wonder at the nature of its density before their eyes.

Off Prince Rupert, B.C., are the several islands that make up the Queen Charlottes and south of those is Queen Charlotte Sound. George Vancouver named the water for his Queen, for her, in 1786 and the islands were named the year after that, though not by Vancouver and not exactly for the Queen herself. The Akriggs note: "In the summer of 1787, Captain George Dixon, after most successfully trading for sea otter off both the west and east coast of these islands, named them after his ship." The companion boat had been named the *King George* and both were owned by a British syndicate in possession of various colonial licenses and permissions. (In a strange act of simultaneity, the Akriggs also quote Walpole, and more extensively, on the Queen's body: "She is not tall nor a beauty. Pale and very thin; but looks sensible and genteel. Her hair is darkish and fine; her forehead low, her nose very well, except for the nostrils spreading too wide. The mouth has same fault, but her teeth are good. She talks a great deal, and French tolerably.")

I first heard of the islands in 1982, when Katharine and I were living in Seattle, and I became friendly with a black man named Rusty who worked at R + E Cycles. He liked riding there, he said, in the Queen Charlottes, because all the roads were well paved and had those wide Canadian shoulders and all the ferries were part of the B.C. highway system and, therefore, free. I thought of him and of our conversation that afternoon in the dusty old R + E store when I found the picture of her. When Katharine and Madeline and I were in Prince Rupert I'd wanted to take a day trip out to the islands but the ferry takes eight hours one way. I'll do it later. The white actress Helen Mirren played Queen Charlotte in *The Madness of King George*, which Katharine saw but she can't recall the character. Fort George was named for George III, but no one in town has much to say about him—that's the remote past and it was an honorific anyway. There's nothing to suggest that either he or Queen Charlotte ever set foot in B.C. Her family has recently been documented, by someone at McGill University, back to "a black branch of the Portuguese Royal House" and there's a Web site, put up by WGBH, dedicated to her and the European context of her African ancestry—it's all about royalty and gene pools and the white British intelligentsia and "abolitionist sympathies." But when I see those islands on the map out there in the blue that represents water I think of her and her wide nose and good teeth, her tolerable French, and of that clarity of her "Negro strain."

Giscomes and Giscombes

Linda Eversole suggested that John R. Giscome may himself have *written* the newspaper account of his trip across the portage, the one titled "Interesting from the Rocky Mountains." I carried that idea around for a while, liking it, but eventually couldn't quite believe in it. I think it was probably an interview—not that that matters, of course: the transcendent detail Linda saw in it is there and I think it is his. And one real writing sample of his does exist: a November 1874 letter to the *Colonist*, a correction of the way in which he'd been represented in print—"In your paper of this morning under the head of 'Cassiar News,' I was made to say that there is any quantity of ground that will pay from $10 to $15 to the hand. I beg leave to state that I never authorized anybody to say the above, although I am of the opinion that the Deloire country will exceed Dease and Thibert Creeks in richness. Yours, &c."

Now, I like stories and have since I'd listen to the ones my mother would make up or repeat when I was a child. I tell my child stories. The oratory has its place, but aside from my mother's stories—and the ones I tell Madeline—there's no particular public tradition of it in my family and I've veered in my own professional life to writing. My grandparents were all born in the nineteenth century—their births came about sixty years after John R.'s and about sixty years before mine; they lived in both our lifetimes—but all four of them graduated from college and John R. himself was literate; these things are facts and they affect me now, here in this century which is itself almost over. My mother's parents met at Alcorn, in Mississippi. Both my father's father and my great-aunt, his sister-in-law, have advanced degrees: Aunt Ollie's 1944 M.A. in English from the traditionally white State University of Iowa makes her profoundly unusual among black women born in the South in the 1800s. I've recently discovered that my grandfather's brother, Charles Giscome, wrote poetry and submitted it, apparently without success, to little magazines in the U.S. We're not storytellers, though; we're a silent family. We suffer in that and whatever pleasure we take we take in silence as well: these are the traditions I'm heir to—silence and writing.

So as I wintered in Fort George, as we drove out into the snowy surround, as Madeline and I walked on the railroad tracks, as I studied the context at the UNBC Library and the Fraser Fort George Regional Museum, I was in search, I see now, of an image that wouldn't war with those traditions—some thing, familiar yet of this place, to which I could fasten my thinking about John R. The museum was a little hopeless: to be fair, I must say that much of the collection had been destroyed by a fire twenty years ago, but the vision guiding its rebuilding has been to celebrate post-1910 development—the histories and successes of white culture in the region. I tried a couple of times to communicate with one of the Native bands out past town but didn't have success—the phone calls were friendly but without consequence. So I found myself in Vivien's study, rereading the things I'd brought with me from Bloomington. Out of that shopping bag of documents—and out of my lonely thinking about my own antecedents—comes the strongest single impression I have of John R. Giscome: it's a particular image of him writing, gleaned from the newspaper story that appeared in the same issue of the *Colonist* as the account of his trip over the portage. The particulars of this second story were also supplied by John R.: it followed, in the paper, directly on the heels of "Interesting from the Rocky Mountains" and was titled "A Fearful Tragedy." In brief, five young men from Ontario, gold seekers, were coming down the Fraser—northeast of Fort George—in October 1862 on a raft of lashed-together canoes. The raft hit a submerged rock and into the water went the Rennie brothers—William, Thomas, and Gilbert—and their friends John Helstone and John Wright. Eventually all made it to shore and it was decided that Gilbert and Thomas Rennie should strike out for Fort George and bring back help. The walk in along the Fraser took them twenty-eight days, significantly longer than they'd thought it was going to, and they arrived at the fort in bad shape and figuring their companions had starved. They spent time at the fort recuperating and they visited John R. in his winter cabin at Fort George on the first day of 1863 and then went on their way south, out of the bush, back to long-third-i civilization, as white people said, longingly, in the Tarzan films I was fond of as a child. But word eventually came to the fort, through Indians, that the missing men had lived for a long while up on the Fraser and that Helstone and Wright had prolonged their own lives by killing and eating William Rennie. In April, when John R. was leaving for the Peace, Mr. Thomas Charles—the factor there at Fort George—asked him to check on the spot where the Indians said they'd seen the two men feasting on the third. He had to bribe his guides to take him to the site and he found two bodies there and buried them but first noted that the gnawed bones had been arranged into neat piles. A grisly image but not the one that's stayed with me. The lasting image, in language from the *Colonist*: "Subsequently on the first lake after leaving the Fraser, Mr. Giscome was engaged in writing a few notes of what he had seen to Mr. Charles when the Indians who had assisted in packing over the portage became vexed, and declared that he was writing to say that they had murdered the last man." I imagine sunlight waning and see water stretching ambiguously outward from the banks and the business of camp being set up and John R. stepping out away from that and sitting down near the water with a pencil and a piece of paper, now writing, now simply holding both and looking off or back over his shoulder, gathering thoughts. All the quiet little physical activities that writing is. The guides did, it turned out, know where the third body was—stripped of clothing and a few hundred yards from the camp on the rapids, nine miles or so south of that first lake. They promised to bury the remains on their way south; John R. was of course pressing north, but in Victoria, later in the year, in the newspaper offices he offered that he had it on good authority that the natives did keep their promise and he offered as well his opinion that "the longest liver" had been killed by Indians—though not necessarily his guides—"for the sake of plunder." Other writers have suggested, in more recent years, that the local tribes found cannibalism particularly unacceptable and may have executed the last survivor for that crime and taken the possessions that he, having relinquished his claim to humanity, no longer deserved to have anyway. *Other writers*. It would be Summit Lake next to which he sat and scribbled notes, "the first lake after leaving the Fraser." I've been to the place, Summit Lake, and driven and cycled around it and looked out across its choppy surface. It must have been an incredible day or couple of days: crossing the portage into new country, interring the remains of some fellow men, discovering the duplicity of the guides—this last, their half-confession, as a response to their witnessing the act of his *writing*, a thing the guides recognized as having some sort of destabilizing power.

The Heart of Darkest Canada

I'd had a vision in 1991, on the road to Giscome, on my cycling homage. It was the day I'd got a good early start leaving Boston Bar and was pushing on north, farther into the canyon, in sunshine. The hills were gradual but quite formidable and by late in the morning the day had become hot. I persevered, making it up the worst slope—Jackass Hill—and resting often. The railroads were a presence: down below the road long Canadian Pacific freights snaked along the west side of the river while Canadian National trains used the east side. Just south of Lytton, though, the two companies switch sides on two trestles: the CN bridge is higher, it crosses over the top of the CP bridge, and the angled, airy configuration forms a rather dramatic tableau above the water. I stopped there, at an empty place alongside the road, to eat a Milky Way and drink some water, and I looked out over the canyon and saw the two bridges and suddenly there, from out of my memory, came Jackie Wilson singing "Lonely Teardrops" and the Isley Brothers singing "Shout." The same line occurs in both songs (and in a number of other songs from back in the day as well): "Say you will." The line—Say you will—was the CP bridge, and the CN span was, differently, the same line: Say you will. It's a request in both songs—no, more than that, it's the same plea. It's a statement too, of desire. I laughed and ate my Milky Way thinking This was black arrival in the North, thinking This is black arrival in the North—myself here out of context, myself in the air a little outside of history. It was a disembodied call and response, odd, specific. A familiar sound, it attached itself to what was available. To my desire.

This is John R. Giscome's problem in black letters, the problem of context, of the lack of a chorus. The problem's how to celebrate the brothers without constituency; we're both we ourselves—individuals—and the mass of us, the culture which grew to support us. Many of my black students at Illinois State will not walk gladly across campus alone, one by one, desiring the context of the knot of us. (A lot of the white students also travel in groups, but those groups report their borders differently.) My sense is that black singularity's especially out of context, is even outside the tiresome romantic archetype of the loner. John R.'s the survival—not the clichéd survivor but the *survival* itself, the Africanism, say, that has survived and entered casually into the speech of others, even whites. Especially whites up there in Canada. "The self persists," Roethke said, "like a dying star." We say, "Blood will tell."

I'm here to reclaim him, I wrote in my journal that winter in Fort George. *This is the dry hump of kinship, my arrival at the public dock at Germansen Landing or Fort George or the Mouth of Quesnelle to reclaim his ass.*

For us? For us but for whom? Black America, pan-Africanism, the Giscombe family in the New World? In *Apocalypse Now*, the film version of "Heart of Darkness," Martin Sheen was a soldier named Willard and he took the trip upriver to find and "contain" Marlon Brando as Kurtz.

Willard's voice-over: "They were going to make me a major for this and I wasn't even in their fucking army anymore." Martin Sheen had gone to my high school—Chaminade—in Dayton but that was before my time and he was known then, of course, as Ramon Estevez. Whose army was I in? Leaning on Ralph Ellison, I wrote:

I've been acquainted for such a long time with ambivalence—
that's why I'm here, up this river in Canada, myself alone.

Winter in Fort George

It took some time for me to get over the loss of the Santa Cruz job but after a while it didn't hurt so bad and the weather itself was changing there on Lyon Street. I'd recommended cycling during the weeks after I'd returned from the interview: there was snow on the ground but it wasn't too cold, about 20 degrees, and I felt myself getting stronger. I'd started off on a flat daily ride—a fifteen-mile round trip—out Otway Road along the CN tracks, along the Nechako, out to where the pavement stopped at someone's horse farm, but soon was making it up the long steep hill to the UNBC campus. And children were appearing on the street and Madeline was bringing girls home and then they'd all go off into the woods and build forts and such. Her friend Diane was with us when we saw our first bear, this on a little Saturday afternoon car trip up the road to McLeod Lake—the bear sat by the side of the pavement munching on something, unperturbed by the Volvo that had stopped ten feet away.

Madeline and I continued to go out on Night Patrol along the tracks and I carried a couple of dog biscuits just in case we ran into my fox; but I never met him again. I finished *Wolf Willow* and, after that, *The Chaneysville Incident* by David Bradley. The former book's largely about collapse, about the end of the borderland frontier and the inevitability of that—the Indians, the white people overlapping, conspiring to close it down. The stench of dead people and dead buffalo. The site, the Cypress Hills where Stegner grew up, is an area in southern Saskatchewan—it's an odd spasm on the plains, a mystical place with its range of low elevations. And like the Giscome Portage it's also a location of the continental divide, an edge, a place to cross over. A way of transgression and miscegenation. The famous psalm of David—"I will lift up mine eyes unto the hills, from whence cometh my help . . ." In the beginning of *Sula* the white people were busy reclaiming the hilly black neighborhood in which most of the book's action takes place, busy gutting it and making it into a golf course. The pasture always gets sold off for that, it's gotten to be an archetype. In spring and summer and early fall human beings with golf sticks swing in B.C. too, on the slopes above Bouchie Creek—née Nigger Creek—in Quesnel: hills, elevations, the practical uses of geography. Rich people live in them, the heights; "up on the Mountain" is the rich white neighborhood in Birmingham. (There is a Mount McDame, the site of an asbestos mine, in the Cassiar District of B.C. but there's no Mount Giscome and there are no Giscome Hills. Instead we have Giscome Canyon, the Giscome Rapids, the Giscome Portage. The canyon's by definition an empty space, a yawn in the landscape, the rapids are low-lying, wide, and treacherous—my great-grandmother, who had worked for the white folks in the houses up on the Mountain and who was not a Giscombe but whose daughter married one, warned, "Watch niggers." The portage was popular because there's hardly a hump there though the trail rises necessarily. It's not a height, it's the absence of one where one's expected, it's an imperceptible crossing. And a combe itself is—as I mentioned before—an arguable critique in the ascent or the slope of a hill, a dissent from being part of the slope. This is us differing with the context. This is who we are, this is the geographic coequal or as close to it as we can get. As close as I can get us.)

David Bradley's novel is about the romance and the failure of research. The speaker, John Washington—a black history professor—, is haunted by the specter of his father, the long-dead bootlegger and backwoods intellectual Moses Washington. But John Washington's a researcher, he has his methods (and his index cards) and attempts to use them to get to the bottom of the mysteries surrounding his father's death and the trials of their ancestors in those Pennsylvania hills. The research methods just skid along the edge of the thing, though, they're nothing but themselves—several trails of three-by-five cards leading to various dead ends, multiple enigmas. People had been telling me for a couple of years that I should read *Chaneysville* because it bore an obvious resemblance to my own interests and project in B.C. and I'd been putting it off because of that. It was also a popular book among my fellow professors and was often taught in various courses—it dealt with research, the business of professors, and its hero was one of us. I was prepared to dislike the novel but found myself taking great pleasure in it—it's a rich book, dense but finely nuanced, and it encompasses stories. That in fact is where the book leads: John Washington learns, by the end, that the index cards will take him only so far, that to get hold of the truth he has to take the leap into the oral tradition and make up a story about the past himself. The long ending of the book is just that and the story's a synthesis, a resolution, a merge of the different kinds of history the book's been celebrating, and it's that merge, I suppose, that makes the novel so teachable. (There's a vague and irritating moment at the very end when John Washington may or may not be dousing himself with kerosene and setting himself alight. When my friend Bob McLaughlin taught the book and came to that one of his students announced—with some disgust, Bob said—that kerosene's got a high flash point, that you couldn't set yourself on fire with it.)

On April 19, back in America, someone blew up the Murrah Federal Office Building in Oklahoma City. We stood in Vivien and John's kitchen looking out the window while we listened to news reports on the CBC—not having television spared us the images of what people are willing to do to one another. We would have watched, we would have had to—if the body's proximate one has to go over and count the exposed bones. Instead we listened to a British Columbia call-in show: "Well, what do you expect?" one caller said in disgust. "Just look at them."

I had to go down there a week later to give a reading at the University of Cincinnati and, with the bombing and its aftermath so much a part of everyone's consciousness, I flew even more nervously than I usually do. But it went all right—the crowd was attentive and the airplane didn't explode and rain its wreckage onto some unsuspecting town in the Dakotas— and on the way back to Fort George I spent some time in Victoria looking things up at the Provincial Archives and visiting with Linda Eversole. I'd discovered, on my first trip to B.C. in 1991, how happy I could be in the library or the archives, happy for days being bookish, surrounding myself in the crisp smells of paper and ink, in the light stink of old documents. Making notes in my blue spiral notebook: no wonder

I'd so easily fallen in love with Bradley's *Chaneysville* book! I did this for a couple of days and then I got the boat back to the mainland and stood on the deck as we negotiated the beautifully narrow passageway out of Victoria's harbor. "Boats at a distance have every man's wish on board," said Zora Neale Hurston. The withdrawal from Victoria is never as sweet of course as it is to come in—this is surely what Harry Belafonte meant as he sang, about Jamaica, "My heart is down, / my head is turning around, / I had to leave a little girl / in Kingston-town." Something elemental there is about water, something about boats—but sailing out of Victoria has always depressed me, it's always been a harbinger of going back to the Midwest, into internal exile, as the Russians used to say. Bloomington has no water to speak of—we drink from a couple of man-made lakes north of town and something called Sugar Creek meanders past a slew of apartment complexes and disappears into a marshy area near the old railroad yards. My friend Bill Morgan recently bought a "borrow pond" next to Interstate 55 north of town—such ponds are created when the highway crew "borrows" earth from people who own land adjacent to the highway in order to construct a hill leading up to the bridge on which a county road passes over the Interstate. The highway gets its hill and the landowner gets a free pond. Bill fishes in his—bass, he says, and channel cats and crappies—while cars and trucks and buses zoom by on 55. We make do with what we have, or try to. But this day I had more water between myself and Bloomington and I was feeling good about that—I had a check in my pocket from the University of Cincinnati and it would more or less exactly cover a passage on the ferry for all of us between Prince Rupert and Skagway. We'd already made the reservation, we were sailing on the sixth of June. And while I was in Cincinnati I'd bought a new pair of Shimano cycling shoes and was looking forward to trying them out before we went to Alaska: I had a May trip coming up, I was going to follow John R. and Henry McDame's route up into country I'd never seen, I was going to bicycle to the Peace River.

A Natural History of Cycling

When I was twenty years old I had an English three-speed bicycle—one of the Nottingham off-brands, a Robin Hood—and I used it to commute from my apartment on Central Avenue in downtown Albany to my classes at SUNY and to my job as an orderly at the Albany Medical Center hospital. At school I was an English major; at the hospital I worked on six and eight, the orthopedic and rehabilitation wards, the bone shop floors. It was motorcycles for the most part that had condemned young men my age into my care. At the end of "Cherrylog Road" James Dickey called the motorcycle "a bicycle, fleshed out" and declared the poem's narrator "wild to be wreckage forever." It was the sort of poem I liked then, even if my work in the hospital had convinced me to stay away from those particular machines. But I understood the impulse, or some version of it anyway: in those days I had more or less decided that the point was to live at some extremity, at places where my mortality might be visible to me. I was typical in some ways, I suppose. I was given to an excess—and, I suppose, my being able now to see it as adoles-

263

cent doesn't mean I regret having given myself so gladly to it.

I worked days and some evenings, and the other orderlies and nurses' aides and I would smoke forbidden cigarettes with the patients during their bath times, wink at their sexual escapades, intervene on their behalf with the nurses. We were the nonprofessional staff, we had no degrees in anything, we had nothing but an aimless, bantering reassurance to offer to anyone. Sometimes that was enough. A man I've mentioned earlier, a patient named Doug, kept a pint of Old Crow in his bedside table and he'd press his call button close to quitting time and on some pretext or another have us in and we'd sip from hospital Dixie cups until 3:30. He was, then, in his mid-twenties—six years older than me—and the first Marxist I ever knew. It was drinking and driving that had got him into a nasty car wreck and thence to the hospital and then it got to be chronic in the following years and got to be the obvious and, perhaps, inevitable tragedy.

But I didn't know then what was coming for him—lots more hospital time and arrests as well, his wife, Judith, leaving—and I don't think that he did either. He was well enough to go home by July and I took him downstairs to sign the papers and to meet Judith, who was coming in with the other car, the one that wasn't wrecked, to collect him. It was a hot, sunny day and we lounged around for a long time down in the parking lot smoking his Kools, watching the interminable construction on the hospital. Finally Judith showed up in her Peugeot, an odd-looking machine even for then with its vestigial fins. She'd hit a deer with it the night before and its hood was dented on the one side—they lived in the next county to the east, Rensselaer County, way up in the first edge of the Berkshires, a place I'd never been. We stood in the parking lot talking about the damage, about French cars, about living in the country. Judith said, "You should come and see us some-time." I said that I'd like that, that I'd try to.

On a drizzly Sunday morning, then, in November of that year, 1971, I set out on my Robin Hood to bicycle from Albany to West Stephentown, where they lived. It was twenty-five or thirty or thirty-five miles, an extremity: I was off on an adventure to see my friend. I pedaled down Central Avenue through its hazardous confluences with Washington and then Western Avenue—back then those were intersections where everyone had the green light—and on out Eagle Street to the new four-lane bridge over the Hudson and then, once across the river, down the first off-ramp into Rensselaer. Sunday morning, no traffic. I followed Route 43 through town and then began to climb and climbed for miles and miles. I was quite unprepared for this and found myself stopping often to rest my legs. Once, on a very bad hill, I was tempted to hitch-hike, to try to get a lift in one of the pickup trucks that had come to be common as I'd gotten farther and farther out from the city. But I didn't, I pushed on instead, and when I got to West Sand Lake, the road leveled out for a while as it went along the north edge of the lake itself. By the time I'd got that far I think the sun had been out for about half an hour, but it's the way the sun looked on the water with the November trees at the far side of the lake that I recall now, nearly thirty years later, with great clarity. And the fact of seeing the lake for the first time from a bicycle did something to me, or at least gave me a specific moment that, later, I could isolate and elevate.

Anyway, I climbed farther then, and the sun went back in and after another hour or so I realized that the daylight itself was starting to wane. The last sign I'd seen was for Stephentown, and West Stephentown was on my side of that but I wasn't sure how far on my side or even how far I'd come. So when I saw a ragged blond child on a beat-up bike going by the other way I hailed him and asked how far it was. He said, "This is it, right here." "Oh," I said, looking around: trees, a few widely spaced houses, a Baptist church. I knew that Doug and Judith lived a mile or so down an unpaved lane—Horseheaven Road—and, for the last hour, I'd been promising myself that I'd call from town and ask for a lift for that last little bit and there were, I saw, no public buildings—except the church—meaning no public phones. But I was exhausted by this time and so I knocked on the door of the church's parsonage, was greeted with a firm handshake by the minister, and gladly granted permission to use the telephone. Doug said he was on his way and I declined the minister's offer of a chair and said I'd wait outside.

It felt strange then being off the bicycle, strange to be still, to be *waiting*. The sun half came out again and in that slant of light and in the sudden stillness there next to my Robin Hood I felt profoundly good. I began to understand that I'd not only made it to where I said I was going but that I'd done something even more unusual as well. Hardly anyone who didn't have to bicycled any distance back then—what we now call the "day ride" (and dress in bright Spandex for) was unknown. And certainly no one black was riding out into the rural north or traveling out into it in any other way for that matter—this hasn't changed much over the last three decades. (I was conscious of myself as an oddity, a likely topic of conversation for the local white people in their cars and trucks, as I was traveling, and conscious of my quantity as a possible threat once I got off the bike—I was glad to find the minister's house but I was relieved, when I knocked, at his handshake. I believe that people who are prone to ask themselves, when confronted with an unlikely situation, "What would Jesus do?" probably won't cause you much physical pain—but you never can tell.)

Doug appeared in that Willys-Overland wagon, crested the hill in it; this was the moment I flashed on twenty-three years later in the rainy forest above Beaver, Washington. He got out and, hobbling on a cane, helped me load the bike into the back of the truck and back we went then down Horseheaven Road to dinner, beer, and a long jag of talking. They were both, Doug and Judith, wonderful and unlikely people and how happy I was to be eating dinner in their house in the first edge of those mountains, so far away from what I'd known.

Seattle to Coles Corner

When I was thirty-one we lived in Seattle and I had my orange Gitane. I'd never ridden in the mountains and figured that now was as good a time to start as any, so I contrived to bicycle over the Cascades—which were visible from a rise near our apartment—to see the Columbia River. I studied the maps and plotted a route that would take me out over Stevens Pass and back in over Snoqualmie Pass and I stuffed my panniers and bungee-corded my tent and sleeping bag to my clunky "mousetrap" Pletscher rack and off I went one afternoon late in May, getting the typical late start but feeling good as I left town, heading north on the Burke-Gilman bike trail—it was a sunny day and everything was crisp and clear.

Halfway to Bothell I met a woman I knew coming the other way, coming home from her job at some troubled-youth outfit. Earlier in the spring she'd been fascinated-from-a-distance by my presence on the street and had once followed me surreptitiously to Kathryn MacDonald's apartment and left, the next day, a note for me at that apartment addressed to "the tall black man with the silver hand." Kathryn had disdainfully brought the letter over to us the next day and I read it (it had begun "Dear Man") and called her to say I was flattered but that I wasn't interested. We'd spoken once after that, when she introduced herself to me in the ice-cream aisle at Safeway, and here she was—our second meeting in the flesh—, stopping her bike in the middle of the Burke-Gilman to ask me where I was going all packed up like that. People whizzed by us in both directions as she listened to my route, biting her lip. She was wearing a plaid skirt and knee socks and Birkenstocks, work clothes. Her name was Ann or Anne and I realized there on the trail that she was pretty, something that hadn't quite registered when we'd met at the grocer's. She looked at me evenly and said, "I could be ready in half an hour." (Katharine's tolerant when I tell about this encounter or series of encounters: after all, I did make the correct response that afternoon—I smiled at her and said I travel alone and off I went on my solitary way. But men like the story very much; the strength of its appeal has surprised me. It gives shape, I suppose, to a yearning we have to be desired or, more to the point, to be chased a little. Desire's complicated. So is race. Something had made me figure she was white when I first read the note—and when I spoke with her on the phone she'd asked me a couple or three times if I was "into music." White women are supposed to desire us, to have this sexual thing for us and our natural rhythm, and a few other times in my life I've met white women who actually did or did aggressively enough for me to notice. We're supposed to have a thing for white women too, of course, and a couple of times I have been invited by brothers to this or that party where "there'll be some white girls there." It's all very complicated; my own longtime marriage to a white woman has kept me—and us—from seriously thinking about living in many beautiful parts of the

United States. I don't know exactly how much it's cost me in credibility among black people; so very many black poets, men and women, have a white spouse, enough so that poets are the biggest interracially married group I can think of—I don't know what it means. Even other black academics—in spite of what Cornel West says about "exogamous marriages"—haven't mated in such numbers outside the race. But in my experience in the black academic middle class, interracial relationships haven't mattered or haven't mattered much. Another black professor I know maintains he's never met anyone, white or black and willing to discuss such things, who's never been to bed with a person from the "other" race. Marriage, though, in spite of whatever else it might be, oozes a kind of respectability; it's hard for anyone to ignore that. But on the Burke-Gilman that afternoon was desire, stated fairly boldly, and oh, the beauty of desire! I wasn't really tempted much by her offer of company in the mountains but oh, how I did like the frank little spectacle of her making it—the offer—, for whatever reasons: it made me glad and alive-feeling as I pressed on into the day. I don't know why I was ever surprised by the strength of the story's appeal.)

I went on up the trail until it ended and then went out on 522 and finally got to Monroe, Washington. I'd come about thirty miles and hadn't stopped except to speak with Ann and I was thirsty and a bit tired. I went into the 7-Eleven store there and bought a can of mango soda, feeling very West Coast, and went across the street to drink it and do some stretches at a bus shelter: I'd been riding fast and hard and my legs were feeling a little tight. But there was a raggedly dressed white man asleep and snoring loudly on the bench in the shelter, so I found another bench nearby, leaned the bike against the back of it, and spread one of my legs out on its surface. An ancient man with incredibly blue eyes—I'd noticed him in the

7-Eleven as I was perusing the cold drink selection—came out of the store with a little shopping bag, walked across 522, sat down next to me, and said, "Long road, ain't it?" I agreed that it was and said that that wasn't such a bad thing. Perhaps it was our conversation that awakened the gentleman in the shelter: he staggered out, looked at us woozily, and fell on the ground. He rolled on the grass next to the bus shelter saying, "Oh shit, oh shit, oh shit!" The old man paid him no mind. "Used to be," he said, "in Wyoming in 1903 you could get on a horse and ride all day and never see a fence."

"That must have been nice," I offered tentatively, a little distracted by the nearby agonies of the drunk.

"It was," he said, "in a way."

The drunk was now sitting in the grass. "Let me tell you about Wyoming," he said. "I was standing next to this little viaduct in Cheyenne once, trying to get a ride, and nobody'd pick me up. Whooo, I stood there two days before I got outta there. Two days."

"I used to do a lot of hitchhiking," I said, remembering that whole stoned, rainy night I spent trying to get out of Montreal twelve years earlier. I'd been leery of the man when I saw him conked out in the bus shelter—white, drunk, dirty. Now here we were telling stories about travel. When I thumbed out of Montreal I was wearing the same clothes I'd been wearing for days. How are we different, and how are we alike?

"I gotta go," I said. It was about four o'clock and I wanted to make another twenty miles or so.

"You got your tipi?" said the old man. Perhaps he thought I was an Indian.

"Tipi hell!" said the drunk. "They got these tents now you can fold 'em up and put 'em in your hip pocket." And to me: "Tell him I'm right!"

"Mine's not quite that small," I said, "but it doesn't weigh too much." I got up and swung my stretched-out right leg over the bike.

"You take care now," said the old man.

"Hey," the drunk said softly and then, softer still, "you need anything?"

I got on Route 2 then and headed east and came to the Skykomish River, where I set up my tipi next to a railroad bridge and made a little fire and cooked a can of beans in it and washed those down with a couple of bottles of Rainier. The next day I cycled over Stevens Pass—it was 90 degrees and I ran out of water and when I got close to the top I realized I was in trouble and sat down on a guardrail by the side of the road and tried to figure out what I should do. I was quite worn out, my lips were cracked, and neither my body nor my head felt right. There was melting snow all around but I'd been told—by friends in Seattle—not to drink it, that the minerals in it would mess up my stomach. Suddenly an older man in a purple jumpsuit came over the top of the hill on a Fuji and swerved over to where I was sitting. "Top's less than a mile to go," he said, grinning. "Water?" I said. "Do you have some extra water?" He gave me one of his water bottles and told me to finish it, that he had lots. I thanked him and gulped it down, the whole pint, and, feeling a little better, I was able to push on and ten or so minutes later I got to the top. I wanted to fill my own bottle then and stopped at the ranger station there at the summit to do that; to get to the station itself I had to walk through a tunnel in the snow and knock on a very ordinary door framed by all that white. The ranger let me in— he and his family were just sitting down to dinner, hamburgers, and they were cheerful and brushed away my apology for interrupting but didn't ask me to stay, which is what I sorely wanted. The summit was four thousand feet above sea level, that's what I'd climbed from Seattle in two days. It hadn't been too bad except for the last ten miles. I came out through the snow tunnel and coasted for twenty miles down the more gradual eastern side of the mountains: that's the way the Cascades were formed, pushed up steeply from the west. I should have been feeling good but I wasn't—I was feeling shaky and weird and when I got to Coles Corner, Washington, I bought a tourist cabin for ten dollars and spent the night vomiting horribly. Sicker than I'd ever been before and sicker than I've ever been since. At some point, some moment of clarity in the middle of the night, I thought about how lucky I was not to have a thermometer because, I realized, the numbers of my temperature would have surely frightened me. I thought about what it would be—104, 105, 108?—and the numbers themselves danced in melting red, Disneyesque, in my mind's eye. But around four I felt the fever leave me like a flock of birds leaving a tree, suddenly and all at once, and in the silence of that I finally slept.

I stayed in bed until midmorning and then got up and stumbled into a greasy spoon called the Squirrel's Nest Café. There I met a man named Jack who put me and the bike in his truck and took me to his house, where his wife, a nurse, told me I had heat prostration and that I'd be OK. He took me to an outdoor store then where a man named Stan, who worked there and maybe owned the place, boxed the bike for me; Stan had ruined his feet in a fall from a high church ceiling—he'd been working, part of a group, on a renovation project and had slipped, as people do, from his perch and suddenly found himself in midair. "But I had it figured out," he said, "after the first couple of seconds"—he'd twisted his body in the air so that he was able to break his fall by striking a glancing blow to a fat man who'd been working below him. The fat man, who'd not been expecting him, rocketed into a pew headfirst and was knocked out but otherwise unharmed. Stan avoided the broken back or the broken neck that might have been his fate had the man not been there, but his feet were severely damaged. Lots of hospital time. Once he woke up, he said, from a light anesthetic and discovered that the men who were working on him had one of his feet off—"I looked down there," he said, "and saw the bottom of my right foot and then there was a hand pushing my head back down." It sounded like a dream to me but I didn't feel like challenging it. We talked on about injuries, about Cornell (where his father had gone), about traveling back and forth across the continent. I sat on a stool in the little back room as he worked; I still felt quite weak and this was companionable, an easy place to be. At two o'clock the Greyhound to Seattle arrived and, my trip over, I took the aisle seat next to a young woman. She was from Maine, she whispered to me, Portland; this was her first trip West. She had a long, pale vacant face and took pulls off a large plastic bottle of Dr Pepper. She was wearing a cotton skirt, boat-shaped black sneakers, and no socks. We went back over Stevens Pass, the bus leaping effortlessly up the slope, and she held the bottle out to me and asked did I want to finish it. I thanked her and declined.

Natchez to Mobile, Memphis to St. Joe

From the journal, April 3, 1995:

11.50 pm at the kitchen table on Lyon St.
Cycled up today into the Arctic & back, 60 mile round trip. I was ambivalent b/c of the weather forecast—60% chance of rain—

but then sd what the hell & took off. Went up Foothills Dr., the 3 mile climb, & then got on the Hart where the ample shoulder starts at Chief Lake Rd. Had lunch at the Salmon R. crossing, sat on a bluff looking down at the water w/ big chunks of ice floating by in it. A man w/ a Vancouver jacket stoppt & askt me if this was "the road to Rupert." No, I sd, & told him to go back to P.G. & pick it up there. "Well I missed the goddamn thing then," he sd, disgusted.

I presst on, first to the BCR bridge & then "just a bit further" to make the whole trip 40 miles & then, finally, I was looking down a hill & thought Do I want to do all this, go on to wherever, down this hill & up the next one? Yeah, I sd, & went on.

Arrived 10 miles later at Summit Lake. Crosst the tracks there & pee'd in a snowbank by the road. I'd pee'd previously on Wright Creek Road. Piss'd in 2 watersheds.

Summit Lake, of course, is the first lake in the Arctic watershed. Wright Creek flows into the Salmon, which flows into the Fraser, and all *that* water gets to the Pacific near Wreck Beach, below the bathing area. The first time we went there—to Wreck—, on the way back from Seattle in 1982, the fashion had been for both men and women to shave all the hair from their bodies. Nothing in the armpits, nothing on the chests, no pubic hair. Now, when I'd worked the evening shift at Albany Med I'd had to shave people for surgery: "nipples to knees" was a common order and that memory gave the beach, or portions of it, an oddly stricken, mortal look. When we'd go there during our sojourn in Vancouver we encountered the body jewelry of the nineties— piercings and tattoos—but there wasn't much of that, really. Most adults at Wreck had very ordinary forty- or fifty-year-old physiques—scarred, potbellied, slack-butted, a little bit scrawny. The body hair starts to thin on its own, becomes less lush on everyone. The weather changed one afternoon when I'd gone swimming alone after leaving the UBC library—some clouds moved in fast and it got grey over all of us there and I pulled on my clothes and headed out. I passed a man who was staring up at the sky and shaking his head. "Another shitty day in paradise," he said, laughing. I smiled and agreed and cycled home ahead of the rain.

I have two bicycles now, the Raleigh touring bike I bought in Britain when the dollar was strong and the lightweight, used blue Gitane I found in a Peoria suburb in the fall of 1993, two years after we got back from Vancouver and two years before we went to Fort George. My Raleigh's fine—it's a model you can't buy here in the States, its frame is that Reynolds 531 alloy and it came with Campagnolo components (which have been replaced over the years, all but the shifters themselves); I've put around thirty thousand miles on it, enough for it to feel like an extension of my body. But I'd had a bad time in the spring of '93—1993 and 1992 were both disastrous years, years filled with illness and family emergencies and midlife crises— and I wanted to affirm my life in some way and the Gitane fit the bill: it's a little lighter, a little stiffer than the Raleigh, the wheelbase is slightly shorter. I had a cheap Gitane, as I've mentioned before, during the seventies and early eighties: I rode that bike everywhere and finally, in 1984, I took it to the U.K. and rode it from London to Edinburgh and then sold it on the street there and bought the Raleigh. I'd always regret- ted selling it—my sentimental side flaming on—and so I was happy when I found the blue bike outside Peoria in a trailer full of bicycles. It's a different ride, it's stiffer, as I said, and more responsive that way than the Raleigh. Madeline calls it my sports car.

(What I told Ann on the Burke-Gilman was true: when I

ride on a tour I do almost always travel alone, and I push myself against the sun and the map. I am not, by nature, a competitive person but this is sport: endurance, muscle, stamina, solitude, all the things "distance" is a metaphor for. The rules are simple: I have to travel far enough to see the country change and I have to make at least fifty miles a day. Fifty's arbitrary but it's my number, I believe in it; I see it coming, watching the digits change on the Cat Eye computer lashed to the handlebar, I get past it. The days tend to come in at sixty or seventy miles and a few reach up into the nineties.)

Miles Davis died while we were living in Vancouver, he died early that fall; the low powered NPR station from Bellingham did a week-long retrospective: our radio was in the kitchen and as I cooked I'd hear staticky versions of some of my favorite songs. "So What," "Human Nature," all of *Sketches of Spain*. I'd seen him play "Human Nature" at the Kool Jazz Festival in Saratoga the year before Madeline was born—much of my 1998 poetry book *Giscome Road* is an oblique reference to that performance, or an homage to it. And even now when I think of Wreck Beach, I hear Kevin Mahogany singing words for "All Blues": "The sky, the sea, / and you, and me: / the sky the sea and you and me / are blu-ue." I'd step into the salt water and be singing that. Mistah Miles—he dead. Shitty days in paradise indeed. Later that fall when I bicycled over the mountains and the desert and got up on the Cariboo Plateau, when I bicycled out on the flat road from the Yellowhead Highway to Giscome itself—my first trip ever to Giscome, accomplished on my Raleigh—I was singing "All Blues," but not the words, just the song itself, under a ragged grey wild-eyed sky all the way into that town.

I had a couple of one-speed, curvy-tubed bikes when I was growing up but I wasn't allowed to ride them in the street, so my relation to cycling was a bit strained. Still, I recall announcing (on the occasion, I think, of receiving the second bicycle for my twelfth or thirteenth birthday) that someday I wanted to bike from Dayton all the way to the summer vacation destination, Gardiner, Maine; and I recall my father's good-natured but knowing response—by the second day, he'd said, you and that bicycle would both be on a train. Now, I have availed myself of trains, now and again, when I've been on a bike tour and I've thought each time I've done so of my father's prediction—partly he was right, after all. But I'm no purist and I've not suffered any by taking a ride when Amtrak or VIA or BritRail has been handy.

(Came back from having cycled to Montreal in 1988 on the Adirondack—that train has no baggage car, so I'd had to sweet-talk the conductor into letting me stow the bike in a corner of the coach itself. After we crossed the border the trackside signals were in bad need of repair and we kept getting red lights and had to creep from one to the next, all through the apple country around Plattsburgh, New York. The day was dark and evil-looking but everybody was good-natured, maybe in response to all that. In line in the bar car I realized the attendant, a black man a tad older than me, was efficiently filling the orders shouted at him while whistling "Blues in the Night" and as I waited my turn I wanted to throw in a rhyming line, to sing a line that would follow one that he'd just whistled. But I'm shy about that joining-in thing, so I just said, after I ordered my beer, that that was one of my favorites, that song. "Yeah," he said, smiling, "yeah, the old songs are the best." The year before or the year before that, on the hip radio station in Ithaca, the apparently white disc jockey had played Mel Tormé's cover and then derided it as "a peckerwood blues"; but I've heard a significant number of black people singing it. The old ones, the old sweet songs, *are* the best, they keep certain things on my mind.)

Fort George to the Peace River

My parents came to visit us in Fort George and we took them up to the Giscome Portage Regional Park and my father made a video of us all on the portage trail. The next day we all went out through Giscome and Upper Fraser and Hansard and had a picnic lunch at the edge of the Bowron River. Madeline and her friend Jessica wanted to explore, so I accompanied them on a short walk out along the water and we found some bear footprints in the mud there. My mother had said she'd prefer not to see any bears but she shrugged at the news of their proximity to our lunch site and finished her sandwich. Another day we took them out to eat at Earl's and my father and I split an order of squid and the waitress—a young woman from Giscome—took us all into the back and showed us the rather impressive series of kitchens. And one evening we drove them the two blocks down Lyon Street to the cliff above the Nechako so they could see the northern lights, which Madeline and I had spotted from our Night Patrol.

A few days after they left I began my cycling trip to the Peace. I was going to have to cross the Rockies to get to it and then I'd follow it into Alberta, to its confluence with the Smoky; I'd come back on the bus. Katharine drove me up to the Salmon River crossing on the Hart Highway and pulled off into the little parking area where I'd had my lunch alone several weeks earlier after having cycled up from Lyon Street. The river had been ugly that day, with lots of ice and big tree limbs in it; I imagine that that's what it had looked like when John R. and McDame got to it in the spring of 1863 and had allowed themselves to be directed to the alternative route farther north—the article in the *Colonist* had described it as "very high" and reported John R.'s opinion that ascending it was "out of the question." But today it was OK-looking—a serious stream but mellow. And the day was beautiful: no wind but blue skies were coming my way. I got the bike off the back of the car and loaded the saddlebags onto the sexy, lightweight Vetta rack and bungee-corded the sleeping bag and tent onto the top of those and made sure the bear Mace was within easy reach, in the handlebar bag. I'd heard a story a few years earlier about a bear coming out of a ditch on the Hart Highway and eating a cyclist—the story's probably a folk legend but it had that one particular, the Hart, and so it was in my mind. Starting from here, as opposed to Lyon Street, meant I had seventy miles to do before my first campsite as opposed to eighty-five. Katharine took pictures of me and I pushed off and went north then, past the portage, past Summit Lake, and along the Crooked River, which had been nameless when Giscome and McDame had canoed it: it was only "a stream running in a northerly direction" in the newspaper article about John R. and they had descended it that way, north. I had lunch with white truckers at Bear Lake, a tiny town whose streets are all named for different bear species, and dinner with natives at the McLeod Lake Hotel—greasy burgers for both meals.

The next day was overcast and dismal and after the Mackenzie turnoff the road was narrow and potholed and there was little traffic on it. I startled a moose that had been browsing at the pavement's edge just as the rain started. I watched her retreat a little ways off into the trees and look at me over her rather formidable shoulder as I stopped and got into my raincoat. A few minutes later it began to pour, great buckets of rain, and in that I climbed Pine Pass in the Rocky Mountains. The road was steep for six or seven miles and the going was heavy—but I had made sure to bring lots of water to drink and the rain had slowed to a drizzle when I made the summit about four o'clock. A mile downhill then and I got to the Azouzetta Lodge. The proprietor was a big man with a mustache and a checked shirt and he had some rooms and they were $24 Canadian and it was "kind of a bunkhouse," he said, and I could, well, take it or leave it. The room had two narrow beds in it, a piece of thick plastic for a window, and a door that wouldn't close—it seemed just fine to me and I gave the man the money and headed down the hall to the showers and stood under the hot water for a long time.

I was forty-four years old and I'd bicycled over the Rocky Mountains for the first time. There was an outside door to the shower room and I pushed it open and stepped into the door-frame as I dried myself. The rain had stopped and the day was bright and clean-looking—a puffy cloud moved by above the Pine River, between the door of the shower room and the mountain. A cool breeze touched me and I let the towel fall and stood there in the mountains realizing how much I liked my body, the portable old site of my being alive. I remembered feeling the same way as I'd stood in the open station door in New Liskeard, Ontario, seven years earlier—I was still the same in this doorway, just seven years older and naked. I leaned against the frame and remembered the women I'd been with. I remembered quitting cigarettes, I thought about asthma, and I recalled losing my arm. I remembered getting drunk and I remembered being stoned. I thought about the East, about the times I'd gone walking in the Adirondacks and Catskills and in the Green Mountains in Vermont.

I dressed and went down to the restaurant then for dinner—a roast beef sandwich and a bowl of soup—and, later, I went out for a walk down the dirt road behind the lodge, being careful to take along the bear Mace. I'd seen an enormous pile of shit at the edge of the lodge grounds—it was sitting there out in the open, next to a nest of rusted machine parts. The next day I did see a bear, a big black bear, in the parking lot of the Gold Nugget, where I'd stopped for lunch; the other patrons and I watched him through the window, all of us talking about how big and bold he was, assuming the bear's maleness, I suppose, because of those two qualities. Anyway, he was gone by the time I finished my cheeseburger but I rode nervously for the first mile or so after that, flicking the bear bell I'd attached to the handlebar and having the Mace at the ready. I got to Chetwynd late that afternoon and the next day I rode through a little snowstorm to lovely Hudson's Hope, on the Peace River. It was the eighteenth of May 1995 when I arrived at the Peace; on the eighteenth of May 1863 John R. and Henry McDame had come to the same stream. I ranged around town that evening, on foot, feeling good and content, after dinner, peering into the windows of the local museum and looking out at the water.

The next day I went on along it. I'd figured the road would be pretty flat since it followed the Peace rather closely, but there was a series of bluffs above the river and the road climbed each of those and at the top of the first one I pulled off to rest in a parking area. It had been drizzling and sleeting a little while before but now the day was starting to clear off and I watched the banks of clouds, blue sky in between them, scud over the river and the hills. I got back on the bike but ran over something there in the gravel and came up with a flat, the rear tire. I walked it back to the bench I'd just been occupying and wrestled the wheel off and then got the tire itself off the rim, when a Volkswagen bus with those green Vermont plates pulled in. The young man at the wheel was from Montpelier, he'd saved some money and was on his way to Alaska: he was going to sell the bus in Fairbanks, he said, and then bike north to Prudhoe Bay. We talked companionably for a while as the day got brighter still and we watched some eagles soaring above the Peace. When I told him about the Giscome Portage he inked it onto his Rand McNally. I declined his offer to split a joint but took him up on the offer of his foot pump and the tire filled up quickly and we wished each other well and I was off. The climb up the second bluff was more severe and the road went through some nasty switchbacks; but the downhill was smooth and straight and I sailed down to river level at forty miles an hour. I was hungry then but there was no place to buy lunch and the can of beans I had with me didn't appeal much. So I began to promise myself an early dinner at a Chinese restaurant in Fort St. John. I was making good time, I was feeling good.

And, even hungry, I was ready for the third ascent: I'd been seasoned by the first two and, besides, I'd figured out that the Alaska Highway likely joined the river road at the end of the downhill that would follow this climb and that would be a straight, flat shot into town. I made it to the top still feeling strong and started to drop down the far side. The road was banked and there was a little curve to it, a slight twist, unlike the hill I'd come down an hour or so before. I was thinking about food—I was remembering having seen an ad for a Vietnamese restaurant in with the Chinese places—and watching the speedometer when something bad happened: I'd been at forty and accelerating and suddenly I was skidding. First I thought the rear tire had gone flat again but I'd had flats at speed before and this was different—I was rocking violently from side to side and I grabbed the brakes and tried to stay upright and keep straight. And though all this took just a few seconds to transpire, from out of nowhere as I struggled with balance and speed and direction came the actual sentence from a *Reader's Digest* article I'd read twenty years before in some supermarket line or doctor's office, something from "Drama in Real Life," the diver saying, "I realized I was being gripped in the jaws of a giant shark"; and I squeezed the brakes and the bike shuddered and kept skidding but I felt it start to slow and I thought, I'm gonna make it, I'm gonna fucking make it, I'm *not* gonna go down, and then I was dreaming: it was a bright day and Katharine was smiling and kneeling in the grass while dogs—Siberian huskies, big puppies—ran around her, their tongues lolling. The dream faded and I became aware that my face was pressed hard into the dirt.

"Try not to move," someone's voice said.

"I don't suppose this is a nightmare, is it?" I said. I realized that I'd been dreaming and that made crash-as-nightmare seem like a logical possibility.

"No," someone else said.

A man said, "The ambulance is on its way."

I was aware then of pain, a dry, familiar, engulfing one. "Oh shit," I said and then, "Pardon my French, please."

People laughed and a woman's voice told me that it was OK.

"Where were you going?" someone asked. I was about to answer when I discovered that I couldn't remember where I was going, that was a blank, and I said so and laughed. But then it occurred to me that that should worry me some and I made myself remember some other stuff—my name, Katharine and Madeline, that I worked for Illinois State University— and I felt better.

"Did anyone see what happened?" I asked.

The woman told me but I wasn't paying attention and I apologized and asked her to repeat it. "Your saddlebags came partway off," she said, "and you were dragging them down the highway. They must have thrown you off balance."

"Oh," I said, "how bad is my face?" That was where the worst pain was and I wondered if my nose was broken.

"Oh, it's not too bad," she said. And a man said, "They'll fix you up good in Fort St. John."

By this time I'd done a quick reconnaissance of all my moving parts—everything seemed to be working and I figured I probably wasn't hurt too badly. My nose? My friend Lynn Powell broke hers once when I was with her—she's not very tall and we were walking and she'd been distracted by whatever we were talking about and had walked, face first, right into a parking meter on College Avenue in Ithaca, New York. It had hurt and it had bled dramatically (and I'd gone with her to the hospital) but it wasn't an important injury; I figured a broken nose was probably going to be the worst of it for me. But when the lads did arrive in the ambulance I told them I was concerned about my back and my neck: too many of my patients at Albany Med had been paralyzed and, though some made remarkable gains, the idea of paralysis has always, since I had that job back in 1971, haunted me: the upper bodies are fine and even muscular, the faces are animated and the intelligence is intact behind those faces—but the legs are perfectly still in the wheelchair and the shoes just never wear out. Cautiously then, they loaded me onto a wooden board and fastened a neck brace on me; they likely would have been cautious anyway. A man said, "I'll take his bike to the hospital in my truck." I made a point then of thanking people for stopping and then I was inside the ambulance and aware we were moving. I remembered being in Montreal, a fall night in the late 1980s, walking down Ste.-Catherine Street, Rue Ste.-Catherine, and an ambulance went by and my walking companion said that thing, "Everybody gets to ride in one of those sooner or later." Yes, yes, yes, I thought, smiling and grim both, I'd put my ride off for how many years? I tried but couldn't remember if it had been 1987 or 1988: my head was swimming, I wouldn't have been able to do the math anyway. What I did remember was how that ambulance had *screamed* down old Ste.-Catherine. "Are the lights and siren on?" I asked the man who was sitting in the back with me.

"No," he said. I dozed then.

And woke up in the E.R. A nurse was letting her fingers search for the snap under my chin and finding it and taking my helmet off: it was a white-and-silver Giro and as it came away I saw that there were a couple of chunks missing and that the plastic cover was shredded. Then she peeled off my shades—I hadn't realized they were still on and I had a little jolt when the room became suddenly brighter and more normal-looking; the lenses were unbroken but they jutted out from the arms at an oblique angle. She dropped them into the helmet. "How bad is it?" I asked her. She said that the doctor would see me in just a bit.

And I recalled being ten and lying on the table in the Emergency Room at Miami Valley Hospital in Dayton. It was the Monday before Easter, 1961: I'd fallen in the backyard and smashed up my arms and there I was in the E.R., lying in some proximity to another black boy, who was unconscious. Who was he, what had happened to him, where is he now? Doctors had come in with the X rays and put them up on the fluorescent panels; I told my father I didn't want to look and turned my head away but he said *Look*, so, obedient child, I looked—the right one was an invisible greenstick fracture but the two bones of the left arm jutted off to the right and looked like the schematic drawing for a railroad switch, for the one set of tracks curving out from the other. I figured I was in some trouble. But I'd known that before, I knew as soon as I felt the bar I was swinging from slip out of my hands.

"Were you hit by a car?" the nurse asked. No, I said, and repeated what I'd been told about the saddlebags. In all my years of riding I've only had the one physical encounter with a car, the abruptly stopped Fiat Spider I rammed into some years earlier: I took some paint off the Spider when I hit it but I'd been lucky, just as I had been today, and there'd been no oncoming traffic to nail me as I flew over the Fiat's trunk and bounced down the pavement. The driver had stopped, as I said way earlier, to let a tall, Mediterranean-looking woman cross in front of him, and now that woman stepped into the street and headed for me, turning her head to tell the young man sitting petrified at the wheel of his sportscar what she thought about all this: "You asshole!" she'd screamed at him. "What the *fuck* did you think you were doing!?" Halfway over she stopped: my handlebar computer had flown off because of the impact and was lying right on the yellow line and she lifted her long skirt and stooped to pick it up. She was wearing sandals with thin leather straps and the skirt was flowered and as I lay there, not injured too badly, putting everything together, starting to hurt, I did see that she was indeed very beautiful.

At the hospital in Fort St. John the nurse worked on my face. This is a hazy place in my memory, one I recall as a series of faraway physical sensations: the warmth of water mostly and the gentle pressure of her fingers. It's funny that I have such strong memories of the crash scene but that the first hour or so at the hospital is such a blur. We talked about something but I can't remember now exactly what it was: I think I told her that

I used to work in a hospital, I think I said something about my fear of paralysis, about how easy it is to get messed up. Once a child had been brought into Albany Med, a boy about twelve who *had* been hit by a car, who'd been smashed against a pizza delivery truck by a drunk driver, and Bob Chase, one of my fellow orderlies, and I had been asked one morning to come over to the kids' ward—which was adjacent to orthopedic—to help change his bed. I was shocked when I saw his legs—they were hideously discolored and there were great gaping holes in them. The nurse whispered to us that he was going to lose 'em and she couldn't figure out why the doctors were putting it off. He was screaming and sobbing as we gingerly turned him and slid the new sheet underneath his body; his mother sat in a corner of the room fingering her beads and yelled over, "Remember what I told you to say!" He sobbed that that didn't help but she insisted and he murmured, "I offer my pain up as a prayer, I offer my pain up as a prayer, I offer my pain up as a prayer," until we left. The next day they took both his legs off.

Much of my life between my arrival at the E.R. at Miami Valley and losing my own arm is an unpleasant blur—they'd knocked me out to set it and I woke up fevered the next morning, Tuesday, in a hospital bed and tried to read and couldn't concentrate. Gangrene'll mess you up. (It actually came rather close to killing me, enough so that my parents thought it important to buy, a couple of years later, a large but tasteful silk hanging for St. Margaret's Episcopal Church. It came from Japan and required Father Cochran to correspond with people over there; I was allowed to keep the stamps for my collection. I think it cost a great deal of money.) I'm not sure what day I lost the arm—Wednesday or Thursday—but I was sitting up in a chair by Sunday, Easter, 1961, and shortly after that I graduated from my private room in Isolation to the children's wing, where I shared my space with a succession of roommates. Notable among them was a seventh grader named Darrel Bryant: he'd dropped a lit match into a bottle of gasoline and his legs were burned terribly. Most kids were in and out quickly—lots of appendectomies and tonsillectomies—but we were long-timers and got to be the old men of the ward both because of our tenure and by virtue of each of us having come rather close to cashing in. Now, though, death's face was behind us and fading and we were getting better: we'd walk unsteadily down the hall together—he had to use a walker—and talk about his experiences back in Intensive Care and mine in Isolation. And we'd talk about getting out.

(But across the hall had been another long-timer, Michael Bullock, a boy who'd been in Cub Scouts with me that winter. He'd been weird in Cub Scouts—he slurred his words and was awkward and inattentive in the meetings—and had left the den sometime in January or February; I don't recall exactly when it was that I was told he had something called a brain tumor. Anyway, he was across the hall from Darrel Bryant and myself and his father was usually there with him; when Michael slept in the afternoons, Mr. Bullock would often come over and spend some time with us. He was a very sweet man, a quiet and generous man; he'd wrangled a leave from his job—I think he was a high school principal—so he could be with his son. One afternoon he popped in and told us—a slight smile on his lips—that Michael had received a letter full of good wishes from President Kennedy. This, of course, became a bit of a human-interest story and Channel 2 sent a crew to the hospital and there Michael Bullock was on the six o'clock news reacting to his note from the Chief. Seeing him on TV was somehow more painful for me than seeing him in person, which I did, of course, every day—his speech was, by this time, total gibberish and his arms and legs flapped wildly and he drooled and the film caught all that and made it real. Darrel Bryant and I watched him on the news that evening in silence as he and his father, across the hall through our two open doors, watched as well. We were getting better and he was getting worse—we knew the cameras weren't going to come back. Darrel left the hospital a week before I did—it was May or early June; when I came out, people said I'd aged, that there was an adult cast to my face that hadn't been there ten weeks earlier. Michael died later on that summer.)

The Fort St. John doctor finally arrived and looked me over and tested me for mobility and arranged for me to be sent off to X-ray to make sure my face wasn't fractured, to confirm his guess about soft-tissue damage. "Have I had a concussion?" I asked. "It depends what you mean by that," he said, and I didn't press the issue. But by the time I got to X-ray I was feeling more with it and declined the wheelchair ride back to the E.R., opting to walk instead. The doctor returned shortly with the pictures of my head and shrugged over them. I mentioned that my hip hurt rather badly and that that was causing me some worry but he pointed out that I had walked back from X-ray and told me to take it easy for a few days but that I'd have no particular lingering effects. The nurse, at his elbow, gave me a little plastic tub of white goo to apply to the road rash on my face. "I've been treated and released?" I asked, sighing, the phrase coming to my lips—an effortless quote—from thousands of news reports. Yes, they said, and the nurse told me there was a cheap motel right across the street—it was eight o'clock and a rich grey color outside. I had to get a couple of things off the bike, so I went out to the ambulance garage then and found it leaning up against the wall: the sexy Vetta rack had simply snapped at the point where its single arm had anchored it to the frame, right above the wheel. With that anchor gone, the rack (with the panniers and sleeping bag still on it) flipped backwards and, held on the bike by the two bolts on either side of the rear wheel's hub, dragged so stiffly on the road surface and forced me into my tailspin. I fingered the place where the arm had separated itself from the frame and thought the words *metal fatigue;* days later I realized that this was the first accident I'd ever had in all my life that hadn't been my fault.

I staggered across the street to the motel. The desk clerk was young and hip-looking and startled, I think, by my appearance— my clothes were ripped and dirty and the right side of my face was badly swollen and swathed with patches of white ointment. "Don't worry," I told her, "I've been treated and released, I'm not gonna die in your motel." Upstairs, I pawed through the phone book: the Vietnamese restaurant, it turned out, was in Dawson Creek, but I found a Chinese place that delivered—I'd promised myself this back at the bottom of the second big hill and I wasn't going to let metal fatigue, an arguable concussion, and a ride in an ambulance get in the way. I phoned them and said I wanted some sort of Szechuan beef with lots of vegetables. The woman who answered the phone had a heavy accent and took offense: she told me that I was obviously from Toronto but that, by God, I was not in Toronto now but in Fort St. John and I better learn to eat what the local people eat, I better rearrange my expectations if I knew what was good for me. The tone surprised me but unfortunately I knew what she was talking about in terms of the food—I'd been in enough Golden Dragons and China Gardens in remote locations in Ontario and B.C. to have encountered the northern predilection for endless chop suey and egg foo young and a very dull dish peculiar to Chinese-Canadian restaurants called hot pot. We compromised: I ordered the take-out— *sans* pot—version of beef hot pot and she said she'd toss in some extra packets of spicy sauce at no charge.

I considered giving myself a couple of days to recover in Fort St. John and then simply going on with the trip but I was shaky and light-headed and Katharine said *Come home* when I called her from the motel. So the next morning I went back to the hospital to retrieve the bike and get it and myself back to Fort George. I rearranged the bungee cords so they held the broken rack in place, strapped on my ruined helmet, and rode stiffly for a mile to an outdoor store. The right saddlebag had some rips in it but other than that the whole rig was in perfect shape: the handlebar computer was working just fine, recording speed and distance—I saw that I'd come forty-one miles the day before. The fellows at the outdoor store boxed the bike up for me and I called a cab to take me and it to the Greyhound station. The bus made a dinner stop at the Azouzetta Lodge and I ate with an older woman from Fort Nelson on her way to Vancouver for a cornea transplant. "We're both traveling alone," she said as she took the chair across from me, "so we may as well eat together"; I was feeling down about my trip ending badly and happy for her company. There were only a handful of people on the bus and the owner appeared after the waitress had taken all our orders—he sat down with a red-haired woman and drank coffee while she ate, speaking quietly with her all through her meal. They touched hands a few times but didn't embrace. He didn't see me or didn't recognize me if he did.

1400 Washington Avenue to 202 Central Avenue, Albany, New York

I can't recall the name of the boy who'd been hit by the drunk driver. But after he'd lost his legs he was transferred to a children's hospital in Schenectady and I decided, impulsively one afternoon, to go up and see him and let him see me and give him moral support. I was at school, on the SUNY campus, out on the western edge of Albany, and I decided to thumb the twelve miles up to Schenectady rather than take a series of buses or bike there: my Robin Hood was chained outside the library but it was already late in the day and I figured I could be more efficient about time if I hitched. I got there without trouble and found the boy in a big rec room, playing some sort of game with the other kids—he was quite adept in his wheelchair and seemed to be doing just fine. He acknowledged my visit but he was engaged, so after speaking with his parents I took my leave and walked down to the big road, Erie Boulevard, and commenced hitchhiking back.

The second or third car stopped, it was a nondescript white man about forty in a small American-built sedan. I was going back to SUNY, I said, and we talked about my being a student and how cold the night was and at some point he began to press me to go and have a drink with him, to come over to his house. The press was not particularly aggressive but it was unmistakable. Straight boys on the road always fantasize about being picked up by women and driven to some secluded place and fucked senseless, but no one I know has ever gotten a ride from a randy woman. Most of us have, however, been picked up once or twice by other men interested in having sex with us. I don't know what connections women make between cars and desire but for men automobiles are ways to get, or at least get to, what we all expect the world to provide in terms of opportunity. I've always figured women knew this about male thinking—put a bag over their bodies, goes the new joke, and their heads are all the same. Anyway, it never surprised me that women rarely picked me up when I was thumbing. I've always been a gentleman, of course, and even my fantasies don't include forcing my affections on anyone. But I am typically in many ways, which is to say straight and male (and heir to the sort of imaginations that straight boys have); I have my fetishes and I've surprised myself on a few occasions, but I usually don't vary too much in who I find attractive and in what situations. I imagine that most people don't stray very far from the set of turn-ons they came to in adolescence. But no one knows what other people, strangers, like. What was this man thinking when he picked me up—I mean what did he *see* when he saw me standing there at the edge of a streetlight on Erie? I was black and young, perhaps obviously a student, I was out on the street. I was big but not all that big. "The tall black man with the silver hand." Whatever I was looked good, I guess, or at least like an opportunity.

So I fended him off all down Route 5 and Fuller Road and finally we turned onto Washington Avenue and the white towers of SUNY came into view. I fended him off but politely because I didn't want to get involved with hurt feelings or embarrassment: to profess desire, even indirectly, puts you in a vulnerable place. I wasn't frightened of him but I saw ways that the situation could turn ugly and I wanted to avoid them; so many of us get so upset about this, about another man looking at us in the same way we're used to looking at women. Eros is eros, boys, everybody gets to play the fool, no exceptions. So the man and I did a dance: Coupla beers, whaddya say? he said, and my response: Thanks but it's been a long day. He said, Why doncha come over, just for a little bit? I gotta get home, I said, not tonight. Back and forth like that. My bike's chained up at school, I said finally, and I want to ride it home. He said, We could put it in the trunk, it'd be no problem. But this was the thing I chose to defend: No, I said, I want to ride home, I've been looking forward to it. He let me out at the SUNY

entrance and I walked over to the library, the customary place
we students left our bikes in those days—my Robin Hood was
the only one still there, chained to the railing. I unlocked it
and pressed the lever for the generator light and went home
down wide Washington Avenue, past the state office campus,
across Brevator Street, into the Pine Hills neighborhood, past
Albany High School and past the brick buildings of the old
SUNY downtown campus and turned left at the Unitarian
church onto Robin Street and rode the two blocks to Central
Avenue and there I was, at 202. It was 1971 and a Cat Stevens
song was popular that year, "Moon Shadow": "And if I ever
lose my legs," the words go, "I won't moan and I won't beg." I'd
always found the song irritating. Offer it up as a prayer. I shoul-
dered my bike and climbed the stairs to the apartment. I *had*
been looking forward to this, to my legs getting me home in
the dark.

Winter in Fort George

The swelling on my face went down quickly and to my great relief since I didn't care much for the way I looked. My right leg, though, was a different matter: it turned black and blue and hurt rather badly. But I wanted to stay active, so I FedExed my busted helmet to the distributor in Montreal and they FedExed a new one to me and a week after the accident I was back on the bike. Riding itself wasn't too painful but stopping for any reason and then getting started again, putting my right foot on the ground (or putting the weight it takes to start off on my right leg), was quite awful. Which fact made it easier for me to ride great distances without pausing for rest and one day, when I returned from a forty-mile jaunt, I found a little Ford pickup truck festooned with Grateful Dead stickers and bearing pale Illinois license plates parked in front of 137 South Lyon Street; Soren Larsen had come to visit.

Soren wasn't the first of my students to come north into the Cariboo—three years earlier, after we'd returned from our semester in Vancouver, Shadd Maruna drove to Alaska and made a point of making the detour to Giscome. He sent us photos of the trip from Anchorage. But Soren came while we were there and accompanied us on a couple of day trips. One was a trip out to interview Laurel Lee Fleury, the woman who guarded the train/car bridge for the CN at Hansard. It feels dangerous—driving down a railroad track over a long bridge—but it's pretty safe: the operator sits in a booth at mid-span and works the signals for both cars and trains. Trains stop a mile down the track while she lowers the gates to block road traffic—usually lumber trucks—from the bridge and then she has to give the fellows in the locomotives the green signal before they can proceed. Sometimes, of course, morons drive around the lowered gates and chug across—for the thrill—with a freight train right behind them, but there will always be morons.

We drove out to her house in Giscome and got there soon enough before her shift for her husband, Kenny DuBois, to take us out in his club-cab and show us their herd of bison. He and Laurel Lee had raised an abandoned black bear cub a few years before and then released her, but she came back at odd intervals, which pleased them; they'd named her Sugar. There aren't supposed to be grizzlies around Giscome but Kenny's found their tracks by the Willow River, down at the end of their property. We drove the twenty miles out to Hansard in two cars—Laurel Lee and Katharine led the way and Soren and I followed in the Swede. We hung out with her for a couple of hours at the bridge, long enough for two freights to come through—Katharine got some pictures and Laurel Lee told us stories. We drove back to Fort George then the long way, across the Bowron River and through the lumber company's forest: we saw a rather handsome black bear a little ways past the river and, when we got to the Yellowhead, we saw a couple of moose. A few minutes after the second moose I was about to point out how the dark curving black shape by the side of the road ahead was not a bear but only the shadow created by a culvert pipe's mouth sticking out of the embankment, when it got up, the shape did, and trotted off toward the woods, *Ursus americanus*.

The next day we went out to the Giscome Portage Regional Park and walked past the Huble farmstead buildings and swung south through some pastures—the area's a common grazing land for the adjacent ranches—and into the woods along the river, heading for the Giscome Rapids. I'd walked here once some years before, alone, and had been startled when I encountered a cow—*Bos taurus*—on a trail: I think she was as frightened as I was as she clambered to her feet—I heard a snort and a second later her massive black head lurched up into view from out of the shadows a few feet in front of me. I'd inadvertently snuck up on the place where she was lying down; the cow ambled off then up the path away from me but it took a little bit for my knees to stop shaking. This time we were prepared: we had the spray can of Mace along and we were all three wearing bear bells. (Of course the joke in the North is that the difference between black bear shit and grizzly bear shit is that grizzly bear shit has bear bells in it.) I hadn't walked very far at all before but today we intended to get to the rapids, which were a couple of miles away. It was going to take some time, though: the trails were not the groomed entities one encounters in state parks but were tangled, barely discernible traces through some thick bush.

I'd realized, as our winter in Fort George was drawing to a close, that there was a very basic hole in my knowledge: I realized that I didn't really know how these things up here came to be named Giscome. I realized—and it was a slow-dawning cognition—that what I knew was the standard stories, the assertions made casually, parenthetically, in books and articles that were always about something else. The town, the story goes, was named by the railroad for the famous portage and this seems quite reasonable and likely—but how was the portage itself named? I'd been satisfied with Father Morice's tossed-off assertion—that it was named by the trader Peter Dunlevy "for a man he'd had in his employ as cook"—but the priest gives no reference for his information (and nearly as little is written about Dunlevy as there is about John R.). But I'd been satisfied with it—I was easy—and had assumed that the rapids had been called Giscome because of their proximity to the portage but now, as we were getting ready to leave B.C., I was starting to have second thoughts. I'd made it down to Barkerville earlier in the winter and had spent a day in its archive—there I'd discovered some paragraphs on the Rennie tragedy by a B.C. writer named Richard Thomas Wright, who, like Bruce Ramsey, has a long list of popular histories to his credit. I hadn't needed to go all the way to Barkerville to find his books but that's what I found when I got there. He gives a particularly lurid recounting of the fate of the Rennies and states that the rapids were named Giscome because that stretch of water was where the initial events of the Rennie tragedy took place and because it was John R. who found the bones in their neat little piles and broke the story. His assertion—even though he doesn't back it up—had made a kind of fragile sense and I'd driven back from Barkerville with that grim connection in my mind; perhaps the rapids were the *first* thing named Giscome and the naming of the portage simply an inevitable follow-up to that. And when I try to fit Father Morice's story—that John R. was Dunlevy's cook—into Wright's, three things occur to me: one, that *cook* is a stereotypical occupation for black people; two, that there's nothing else I've seen to suggest that John R. ever worked as a cook; and three, that his appearance in history as a cook might be tied, in some way, with the fate of the last Rennie, which was to be eaten by his comrades. I mean calling John R. a cook might have started as a joke about the situation. After he'd reported his opinions in the *Colonist*, the other newspaper in town, the *British Columbian*, challenged the story. Its article began tellingly—"But before proceeding any farther, who is this Giscome? All we know of him is that he is a native of Jamaica, West India." The term itself, *cannibal*, has its origins in the Spanish: *Caribal*, my everyday dictionary explains, "native of the Caribbean." The word, of course, predates the arrival of Africans in West India but the wide edge of connection is there. Spanish is a loving tongue, somebody sang. An archipelago of euphemisms. Who's calling the kettle black? asks the *British Columbian*. Here in the States, in recent history, a white fellow, Jeffrey Dahmer of Milwaukee, killed and ate several young men, more than a few of whom were of African descent. When the story came out the detail that appeared in so many articles, apropos of nothing in particular, was Dahmer's employment: he'd worked in a chocolate factory.

I was still hurting from the cycling accident ten days earlier, so I was moving slow, holding us back a little. But the terrain itself was inhospitable to big two-legged walkers like ourselves: the trails were animal trails and creeks were numerous. We stayed close to the river and hacked our way through a lot of thickets and climbed a number of little ridges. Twice I stepped wrong and stumbled and had to stand still each time for five minutes until the throbbing stopped. Finally we heard the rapids, but a moment after that we came to the edge of a large ravine, a biggish creek entering the Fraser, and decided not to attempt to cross it. The ravine made a little bluff, a promontory out into the river, and we could *see* the rapids from it: a line of bright undulation on the river's smoothness. We sat on the ground and looked off at them; Katharine took photographs. They were famous on their own—aside from the Rennies—for being dangerous, the sort of place where your boat would swamp, until the province dynamited a lot of the big rocks out in the forties.

We came back to Fort George and had a late lunch, before Madeline got home from school, at the Pegasus Restaurant in the Spruceland Shopping Center. We all had the same thing, gyro sandwiches with a spicy mayo sauce. The Pegasus was smoky and furnished with molded plastic booths and it was overbright and smelled like the Gateway Diner in Albany, the Garden of Paradise Family Restaurant in Bloomington, the old Rosebud in Ithaca, and a long list of other places as well. We'd made it out of the bush to this and Soren confessed that he had been convinced that we were about to trip over a bear at several points during our walk; those we'd spotted the day before, on the drive back from the Hansard bridge, were the first ones he'd ever seen. We munched our very greasy sandwiches and laughed and talked. No one I've ever spoken to has been quite sure what actually goes into gyros but we can all recognize the taste. The taste of bear meat is supposed to be like that of pork. Human flesh, of course, is also said to taste like pork and people talk of a dish called "long pig" that's popular in—depending on whose story you hear—New Guinea or Borneo or darkest Africa. Or up on the Fraser. But this, I realized there in the Pegasus, was spring and the door to the restaurant was propped open and there was still more water ahead: in a week we'd be on the ferry to Alaska and, once there, we'd turn and drive back to Fort George the long way, through the Cassiar and then over into Alberta, over to the

Peace River. We'd not originally planned to go to Alberta on this trip but I'd asked if we could add it since I'd not quite made it into that province—to that easternmost edge of John R.'s range—on my bike tour and Katharine had agreed. So we'd all get to see the Peace River. The first time for them, once more for me. I still don't know exactly how the name got affixed to the geography here. I can only chart the proximities of the man to the places; I can talk about routes more than monuments. "The Negro speaks of rivers," said Langston Hughes, mentioning the Congo and the Mississippi. "Water's my will, and my way," said Ted Roethke. John R., on his trip on the Peace in 1863, reported seeing, in a day, "as many as a dozen bears on the banks of the river."

The Future

My mother's comment on the future—"We'd all commit suicide if we could see what was coming"—is in fact a crystalliza-
tion of some of the many tenets—the arch fatalism, the irony,
a resigned strength, etc., these in addition to the aforemen-
tioned separateness—that make up what my sister and I
still call the Giscombe Way. (The fact that the crystallizer,
our mother, is not a "true" Giscombe does not diminish this.)
But my days since we returned from Canada haven't been all
that bad.

August 1995

Back in the States from Fort George for two months, I sat on a
Greyhound bus all day and arrived finally at Washington,
D.C., an early evening, early in August. I'd been invited to the
1995 Giscombe family reunion, hosted that year by Lorel
Morrison in the Maryland suburbs. Lorel's mother's a true

Giscombe, she was born Linnette Giscombe, the daughter of Darius Giscombe, whose father, John Aaron Giscombe, Sr., had been Peter Giscombe's son. And Peter, of course, was the brother of John R. I don't normally do reunions, nor do I do them easily: my parents, though close to their parents and siblings, had never been interested in establishing contact with any of our far-flung relatives, so I had no training or example to follow. We went to funerals and—less often—weddings, but those were duties, things to be endured. I was approaching this experience with a little trepidation.

From the journal of July 28, 1995:

Dreamt that the Giscombe reunion was to be held in France instead of Maryland, in Avignon or Lyon. Someplace at the end of the road. I was a cartoon character & went south on the highway from Paris riding a large dinosaur, a brontosaurus like the old Sinclair logo, galumphing down the highway alongside the RVs that the American Giscombes were piloting to the thing.

I arrived and it was a pension, a long rambling bldg. Boys changed clothes in the hall, turning their backs on the throng out of that typical French modesty, casually hiding only their penises. "I know we're not in America," quipped a fellow reunion goer to me. All were white or "swarthy," wch fact made me uncomfortable. Some identified themselves openly as Giscombes but race was "different" in France.

My friend Lester Brooks met me at the D.C. bus station and took me up the road to Annapolis for dinner. We ditched the car and walked out into the burg's preserved, gentrified self, along those narrow streets of old brick buildings and nice places to eat and drink. The ocean—or Chesapeake Bay—was a presence. Lots of young, well-dressed people were out on foot and we'd parked Lester's Cavalier among the inevitable BMWs and Saabs. He'd taught African-American history at Illinois State but had gone over the wall a few years before and returned to the community college in Maryland from whence he came—his wife, Barbara, had hated Bloomington with some intensity and Lester had felt, as most of us here feel, ambivalent about ISU, so when Anne Arundel Community College told him all would be forgiven if he'd just come home he accepted the offer and left suddenly in the summer of '91, just as Katharine and Madeline and I were preparing to go to Vancouver. We'd spoken on the telephone but this was the first time I'd seen him in four years. It had got dark as we'd driven up from D.C. and we walked around town, Annapolis, in that warm darkness, rambling in our talk too about books and students and history, pausing now and then to look out at the water. Finally we went into a seafood place and had drinks and the waitress, a pert Southern white girl, flirted good-naturedly with the two colored boys and we flirted back. I remembered James Baldwin's encounter—described in "Notes of a Native Son"—with a white waitress in wartime New Jersey: she was trying to whisper "We don't serve Negroes here" when he threw his water glass at her, which act caused the seated white patrons of the restaurant to rise "as a man" and come after him. But this was 1995, this was modern commerce, these were the pleasant and conventional gestures, this was the New South.

At the reunion I met African-American Giscombes from Detroit and New York and Connecticut. The family was middle-class and ambitious and connected. The adults were confident, the children were polite. I danced with Lorel's beautiful sister Claudette, I joined conversations about politics and marriage, and I read a statement, at the banquet, about John R. and urged everyone to visit the Giscome Portage site on the Hart Highway. But I see John Robert Giscome as the most unlikely man, the man who is truly out there beyond us a little, the man glowing and visible from the far edge of us. Us? I was a shirttail relative here among true descendants of John R.'s people and here I came bearing *my* John R. like an admission ticket, or like a sword and a shield both. I came bearing a *statement* about some ideas I'd had while I was ensconced in libraries and while I was traveling in B.C. My fellow reunion-goers responded politely, clapping and so forth. But others of us called names, listing the lineage and attachments of the family before and around them, sketching a shape in the air of the room. Some told stories. After I read my piece Lorel led us in singing "Day-O." That old song. We all—myself included—knew all the words. I skipped the final events scheduled for the next morning, Sunday—a groggy breakfast and a church option—, and got the early bus to New York: my sister lives there and she took me to brunch at a Burmese restaurant and then to a play on Broadway. This is the familiar, this is us. But my sister was curious about these other Giscombes: "Was there a family resemblance?" she wanted to know later as we ranged through Times Square. "Did any of them look like us?" No, I said, except for one woman who looked a little like Mom.

But Lorel and I had talked in a quiet moment about the men in the family—when he'd called me in Fort George and I'd described my grandfather as intimidating and silent he'd laughed in recognition of the type. He reiterated that in person, that that's what we were like—someone, a young man passing by, said that it was because of the outside children that Jamaican men were so silent, that they had to be careful not to say anything for fear of slipping and betraying a past alliance.

(At dinner, after "Day-O," we'd sung another song, a clever song about outside children, one with a plot involving a young man who kept falling in love with young women only to be advised, in the refrain, by his father that "The girl is your sister but she don't know"; the punch line, though, is an instruction from the mother to disregard the father's advice because "Your papa's not your papa but he don't know.") But it was more than that and I was struck (again) by Lorel's recognition of it—yes, this was family. I described it before as an impenetrability lying at the heart of things, as a cool silence around the human part of each of us. A tribe has a lot of centers, a lot of stories, a lot of homeplaces and hearts. Here was one I shared with these Giscombes, with John R.'s people, this silence.

Old John Aaron Giscombe, Jr., didn't come to this reunion, so the family patriarch in attendance was a tall, clear-eyed dark-skinned man named Sigismond Giscombe, a lovely fellow about eighty years old, a Kingston man. When, a month or so later, I mentioned having met him to my father, he—my father—knew the name: when my grandfather had died in 1962 he'd left a list of people who should be notified—my father had helped his mother make the phone calls to Jamaica and Sigismond's name, of course, is unusual and therefore memorable. It's French in origin, I think—there was a St. Sigismond—and I don't know how Sigismond Giscombe came by the name but I do know that he's the only one who has it in all of Lorel's big family tree. I called him myself, in 1996, the week before our departure for Kingston: I'd hoped to see him during our trip but he was going to be traveling to New York at the same time we were to be in Jamaica, our planes would pass one another over the water. On the phone I asked a little about the family connection but neither my grandfather's name (which is, of course, my name too) nor his pocket history (Buff Bay–medical school–Birmingham) registered for him. But when I related the story about my grandfather wanting him to know that he—my grandfather—was dead there was silence on the line, the sound of thinking. "Oh," Sigismond said finally, "he must have known me."

March 1996

It was spring break at Illinois State and we were far away. I was sitting on the patio just outside our room at the Mayfair Hotel in Kingston talking to Maurice Giscombe, John Aaron Giscombe, Jr.'s son. I was going to go out into the country to see his father the next day and Maurice had come by to see me; Lorel had given me his name and phone number and bidden me call him upon our arrival. Maurice was a thoughtful, quiet man; he was quiet but not silent—he spoke softly with a casual grace. In our talk I mentioned my old concern to him, that his father had described John R. as "white," and Maurice smiled at that and reminded me that Jamaica was not the States or Canada and that white was different on the island, a different designation. He touched his own ruddy face and said that in school he was known as Red Maurice because there was another boy in class named Maurice, this other boy having a more common, dark skin. I listened to him and as he talked I recalled his father's description of John R.'s brother Peter Giscombe—that "he had the red skin"—and a half picture of what John R. might have looked like formed in my mind. The Blue Mountains loomed past the hotel looking like the Coast Mountains look from downtown Vancouver. Maurice talked about walking in the mountains, about how much he loved the elevations; John Crow birds, as buzzards are known in Jamaica, swooped over the pool—the air was clear, the morning light hung in it, the birds were precise and graceful black "V"s. In the pool swam people from any variety of races and combinations of races—the swimming suits were bright and the skin tones around the suits ranged amazingly. I'm an unambiguous, if light, brown to Maurice's red skin, but it's obvious that we both number white people, a certain concentration of them, among our forebears. I remembered sitting on the Willard Straight deck at Cornell with Rajani Sudan, five years before this—about to leave for the first trip to British Columbia—, staring out at the sweep of Inlet Valley and the blue of Cayuga Lake; if this moment in Jamaica were an American film, what might Maurice's and my light complexions suggest of its theme or content? A drama about miscegenation? I don't think either of us felt particularly tragic. Nothing's neutral, though—value's intrinsic or it gets attached, either way. Skin color is political among black folks in the U.S. as it is in Jamaica, but here in the States "white" means something else. Race is different everywhere, no matter where you go. Value's complicated.

(In the winter of 1997, when I went to Toronto for the MLA convention and arranged to meet Icsolene Giscombe, she wanted to know, on the telephone, so she could pick me out at the subway station: "Are you fair or dark?" In Lorel's extensive notes on the family the word for light complexions is "clear.")

Later, some days after meeting Maurice and back from my interview with John Aaron, I was sitting on David Giscombe's front porch in Kingston and David leaned in close and said, "Only I can tell you what you need to know about your family." I'd been brought to his house by his son Douglas, the young man who'd called me in Fort George when one of his New York cousins had passed a copy of my broad letter down to him. And here I was finally, on the porch, with Douglas and David and a couple of other men, friends. David was ten or fifteen years older than me, an accountant, a big brown-skinned man with a pencil-line salt-and-pepper mustache. And he had one arm, the left one—he'd lost his right to gangrene when he was nine, in a fall from a tree. Lorel had told me that he was one-armed but I hadn't known how closely his circumstances paralleled my own. "We have some things in common," I said on the porch, repeating the line from the poem I'd written two or three years before, an effortless—if giddy—quote. A high literary moment there in Jamaica. Yes, he agreed. He had no mechanical arm and said he'd considered getting one once— "an arm like yours," he said dismissively—but never followed up on it. I noticed he was wearing loafers: it's an old point of pride for me, tying my shoes and neckties. He asked me about my family and I told him my grandfather's name was the same as mine but that his father's name was Thomas and that they were from Buff Bay. David took this in and then turned to the fellow sitting next to him and said a couple of sentences in patois, words and phrases I couldn't understand. The man nodded—he was gangly and had a thick mustache and yellow eyes. David said, to me, "Your great-grandfather was Tommy Giscombe, a short man but very tough. Your great-grandfather and my grandfather William Giscombe were brothers. Their father's name was James Giscombe. My father's name was James Giscombe too—it's one of the names that comes up in the family again and again." Tommy Giscombe was a man of few words, he said, and once he disappeared from Buff Bay with no word to anyone and came back "from over the hill" years later driving a herd of cows. Tommy Giscombe. I took notes as he talked. There is a long valley, David said on his porch, inland from Buff Bay and a place called Belcarres is at the end of it. It's that valley, he said, that the family comes from. I promised him I would come back and that we'd go there together and see the place.

(When I compared David's genealogy later with the Xeroxes Susan Buchanan had sent me there was a very rough coincidence: some names are the same but they're common names—James, William, Thomas—and the generations don't match; for Thomas Welsh Giscome and Tommy Giscombe to be one person David would have had to have jumbled the chronology or Susan's records would have to be incomplete. Both are possible, I suppose. It's a curiosity—whether or not I'm related that way to Susan. Or whether I'm related this way to David—the name I share with my grandfather rang no bells for him and Thomas is a profoundly common name. But David's Tommy Giscombe does sound like my grandfather— short and hard, not given much to speech. Ah, family! When I go back to Jamaica I'll get to the Record Office in Spanish Town and pin all or at least some of this stuff down, I'll whip back the sheets and view the ancestors in their beds, conspiring to make us all. I'll spend days inside reading microfiche. And I'll go up into the mountains with David and see Belcarres.)

May 1996

School was out for summer and Soren Larsen and I flew to Seattle to get the Willys. The deal was that I'd pay our way out there on Frontier Airlines and he would drive it back to

Illinois; I was going farther, on past Seattle, I was going to bicycle to Fort George and return from there, on the train, to Bloomington. Soren had worked with his father restoring a forty-year-old Studebaker truck and was looking forward to the adventure of crossing those states in a vehicle older than himself. But first we were going to the Gifford Pinchot National Forest down in southern Washington State to hike together for a few days.

Katharine had given me Robert Michael Pyle's book *Where Bigfoot Walks* for my birthday and reading it that spring had rekindled my old interest in those stories. Pyle had trudged around in the Gifford Pinchot and his book was an account of that and an overview of the talk about Bigfoot. He—Pyle—is from Yale and perhaps I'm at a point in my life where having gone to an Ivy means something to me. "What I want," he says toward the end of the book, "is a state of brain aloof from arrogant dismissiveness, free from superstition, and rich in question." I heard that kind of talk a lot at Cornell and probably say stuff like it in my classes here. Maybe everybody says it; maybe the difference is that those who hear it in or near a building at Yale or Brown or Cornell are more likely to take it seriously, to organize their lives around it. Perhaps I'm speaking, to some extent, of a rather ordinary kind of privilege. *Where Bigfoot Walks* is subtitled *Crossing the Dark Divide* and it's at least as much a book about metaphor as it is about anyone's search for hairy men of the woods. But the Dark Divide's a real place too, down there in the Gifford Pinchot, and after we got the truck out of Russ Johnson's yard up in Port Townsend we made for it, going south in a light rain on I-5, taking it slow, letting the engine pull us right up the hills, passing the occasional tractor-trailer. I was becoming reacquainted with the machine's feel and noises: I'd driven it back and forth a couple of times between Seattle and Port Angeles, resting my arms on the huge steering wheel, but this was the first long trip and I was falling in love all over again. There was no radio but Soren had brought a cassette player and we listened to his Grateful Dead tapes: I'd always been fond of "Jack Straw" and "Friend of the Devil"—and "Sugar Magnolia" contains the lines, about the title character, "Well, she can dance a Cajun rhythm, / Jump like a Willys in four-wheel drive." We never used the 4WD, though: we got off the highway and went east on a paved two-lane, arriving just past dusk in Cougar, a very small town at the edge of the forest. We went a little ways out of town and camped beside the truck and the next morning came back into Cougar for breakfast.

The place was deserted except for the waitress and a fellow sitting with her at a back table. She made us our pancakes and he kept the coffee coming. He was friendly, of indeterminate age, a nice guy, and we went back and forth with him, bantering a little bit; he said some things about the decline of the town, sighing over that, but then he got elliptical: he began dropping references to his medical needs, suggesting that they were special or at least uncommon enough to require him to make regular excursions out to Vancouver, Washington, not saying exactly what the needs were or what other demands— aside from the road trips—his illness was placing on him. There were places in his talk for us to fill in the blanks, places where he was declining to make the final connections, and we figured, because of that, that he was likely talking about HIV—all illnesses, I think, have social values attached to them but HIV/AIDS has all the complex sexual stuff—the taboos—as part and parcel of itself. He sighed often as he talked and the sighs themselves seemed like invitations to us to press or to half-reveal something in return; perhaps he thought we were a couple. He looked healthy, but that's meaningless, of course.

We finished our coffee and waved goodbye and drove then way up onto a ridge and left the truck and struck out on foot into the forest. We were in the vicinity of Mount St. Helens and after a while we crossed a river of odd smooth rocks; Soren had recently taken a course in geology and squatted down and identified them as volcanic. "These cooled very quickly," he said, hefting one, "this was a lava flow." I remembered the eruption and how the scientists had said that we in the East might notice a difference in the sunsets that year—I'd shrugged at this until I was driving across Syracuse one evening and saw the sun going down behind the twin blue bulbous steeples of Assumption church on the north side. "It was like God was drooling on 'em," I said to Katharine when I got home and she smiled at me indulgently. Soren and I climbed and climbed and fairly suddenly we were in the snow and we climbed farther in that, through some drifts, and finally came to what we decided was probably an official campsite, a place where trails came together. We dropped our stuff and made a little fire and some gray jays came to hang out with us—yes, this was a camping area. We were on a small bluff and we sat there before the flames with our backs against a tree for a long time, sipping at cans of Olympia: we watched below us for animal movement in the trees, and we looked up to the ragged crater edge of Mount St. Helens moving in and out of the clouds.

The next day it was snowing and we came down to where it was raining and walked in that for a long time. Sometime around noon we were startled to see a group of large, identical black-and-white umbrellas bobbing toward us: it was a group of clear-eyed people in their sixties and seventies out for an organized hike and we stopped and talked for a while in the rain. In the outdoor community in Illinois one hears talk about the fucking wind and, in winter, the fucking cold. Even in good weather people go to the shopping malls to walk for exercise. What is it that begins, "As I was a-walkin' one mornin' for pleasure . . ."? Some cowboy song. Katharine and I lived in Seattle for six months and though there were lots of jokes about the climate and lots of T-shirts that read *Seattle, may it rust in peace!*, we never once heard about the fucking rain.

But this rain had got our down bags wet, so we hiked back to the truck and, city boys at heart, drove to the Laundromat in town and put them in a dryer. There we ran into the fellow we'd met the day before at breakfast and this time he seemed a tad less veiled. The town used to have a gay community, he said, and there were dances and people came in from elsewhere to attend them, but that all changed, gradually, over a period of recent years. It was still a pretty tolerant place, though, he said. Perhaps this was the point where we were supposed to come out if we were gay. Or perhaps he'd figured we were probably straight but decent fellows anyway, good enough to pass time with in a laundry. We asked about Bigfoot and he chuckled over that and said he'd lived in Cougar for a long time and there were black bears back in the hills but that was about it. We were the only people in the Laundromat; it was humid but outside the weather was clearing off, sunlight was glistening in the puddles. We all chatted companionably as our friend folded his duds—a few pairs of underwear, socks, a couple of shirts. He was someone who lived alone, I thought, looking at the clothes—he folded them neatly, as I'd been taught to fold my own clothes, and then dropped them into a cardboard box. Laundromats have always made me think of mortality. People keep coming, he said, to look for Bigfoot, and some young women, he said, had made some plaster casts the week before. He smiled again and said it was probably good for business.

That day we went back up on the ridge intending to camp at an easy roadside place we'd seen the day before and get an early start for Portland the next morning. Soren's girlfriend was coming in on the airplane from St. Louis and he wanted to be there to greet her. We set up there—at the roadside place— but, as we were doing so, we realized it was full of very bad vibes: it was, apparently, a location where young people came to party and I've slept in such before and sometimes bad things happen during the night. We talked about it and shoved the tent into the back of the truck and went a mile down the road to a less popular site, a little clearing at the end of some wheel ruts that curved off away from the pavement. It was dusk, the forest loomed around us, and as I went out into it to gather wood I found myself walking deeper and deeper in, aware of the pull of the trees, aware that there were animals nearby or that there might be and that I was moving noisily in a strange, western forest. I was loving this, I realized, loving being here. I went back to the truck in a little daze of excitement, yapping at Soren about the feel of the woods and how if-there-is-a-Bigfoot-then-this-*is*-his-place and from all that we got to the conversation we'd had with the man in the Laundromat about Bigfoot being a boon for business and from there we went to the old idea of story, the meta-story beyond the story itself. Bigfoot's the series of stories—good for business in Cougar, WA, the funky sexual Bigfoot that R. Crumb created for Zap Comix in the seventies, all the myriad stuff on the Bigfoot ListServ (<bigfoot@teleport.com>) and Web sites, *Harry and the Hendersons*, all the tall tales of close encounters with shadows and bears, and the other stories, too, the ones that don't quite reduce to anything familiar—and, that way, he really *is* always just past the fire's glow, it's utterly true and basic and profoundly human. Soren said that perhaps the stories were measurable, that is, that their quality might be useful as an index or a gauge, something to quantify the spiritual or psychical health of a culture—the stories would have lean years necessarily and fat years. How's Bigfoot doing this year? Bigfoot! We gender him, discuss with others the problem of "belief" in him: Bigfoot's real, he's socially constructed. Like sickness or health, like the varieties of race and race's combinations. We laughed loud in our recognitions around the feeble light Soren's lantern cast, we were loud at the edge of the shadows; the Dead sang on the tape deck, sounding tinny in the big woods.

And here we were, guys who were rich in a lot of ways, guys who could laugh in the forest—we had lives to go back to, women who were waiting for us to show up. And we would and did show up for those women—we were connected to the world, suspended in it, and yet, in many ways, masters of our fates. Straight, middle-class, male. Americans. (It's that combination of statuses, I think, that web of comfortable constructions and suspensions that sometimes allows me to forget about being black for hours at a time.) We had and have, I hope, long lives still ahead of us. But no one knows what's coming in the future. Is someone going to be there in our final illnesses to do our laundry and then walk us out to the very lip of everything we know, out to the gape of some kind of open mouth? Where will the dark catch up with us and how?

We ate freeze-dried chicken-something then and, after dinner, we both walked a ways out into the forest and stood quietly for a few minutes—out away from our vehicle, out of sight of the road, out past the fire, out where the story starts. This was different from the more dramatic place we'd stayed the night before, under the crater of the famous volcano: this was our makeshift, drive-up campsite, easily accessible and "convenient" and, for that reason—in my thoughts as we approached it—, mundane and inconsequential. But these woods were damp and full of a certain quality of noise—they felt alive and we were alive too but different, in between the trees. We had climbed to the other campsite, using a Forest Service map, and achieved it, the one just under Mount St. Helens, but this one was exhilaratingly fecund-feeling and anonymous—unnamed—and this one had pulled me out over an unanticipated edge.

We split up the next afternoon in Portland. My old friend Lisa Steinman teaches at Reed and she and I met for dinner that evening and the next day I was on the Coast Starlight to Seattle and several days after that I glided down the hill and across the Fraser into Fort George itself at rush hour. So strange to be back: the cycling trip had been long—592 miles, nine days on the road from Seattle—but devoid of the kind of adventures that might have made it memorable. I camped where I camped before, ate where I'd eaten on previous trips. I suffered no flat tires, no episodes of heat exhaustion, no broken flanges or flaming descents—but neither did I have any unexpected encounters with people or animals. Fort George itself was pleasant: I talked long into one night with Peter Thompson, a boatbuilder from Barbados, and I went out walking with Vivien and John and Barry, making it to the top of Teapot Mountain. I washed and dried my rank, road-weary clothes in the machines in the basement of the Lyon Street house, but Vivien surprised me by taking them out of the dryer and folding them.

I was going to get the Skeena out of Fort George and meet the Canadian at Jasper and take that as far as Winnipeg and then get the bus over the border to Grand Forks, North Dakota, and catch the Empire Builder to Chicago. And the Texas Eagle, finally, to Bloomington. I'd have three hours in Winnipeg between the train and the bus and I called Susan Buchanan and asked if she was free for lunch downtown. She was Susan Bethune now, having married a Californian, a man named Ed Bethune—on the phone her voice was husky and precise. It was more or less exactly the voice I expected from having read her letters, and two days later there she was herself at the train station wearing the blue flowered skirt she'd told me to watch for. She had a stack of papers—Xeroxes of correspondence, photographs—and she and Ed took me out to lunch and then we talked in the plastic seats of the waiting room at the VIA station. I looked at the pictures of her great-uncles, four brothers who were the grandsons of Anne Giscome. Handsome men, dark-complected if the standard is European. One had lips that were quite full, quite "sensual," and Susan remarked wryly on how "Spanish" he looked. J. A. Rogers, in an offhand comment on a portrait of Simón Bolívar, suggests that the lips are "the last trace of Negroid ancestry to disappear."

In the train station, Susan talked about James Maxwell and Anne Clarke Giscome. The "oral tradition" in her family had made them quite real to her and as she spoke of them to me—pointing out and speaking aloud a descriptive line in a letter here, furrowing her brow over a mysterious qualification there—they became present for me, not mysteriously, but because they were so present for her. I listened. A few weeks before I'd left for this trip Lorel had sent me an updated, expanded version of his family tree, one that cautiously—with parenthetical ?-marks—posits that I'm descended from Anne Clarke Giscome's brother William, that Thomas Welsh Giscome and Tommy Giscome are indeed one and the same. I've never been particularly interested, as I said somewhere up above, in the "costume drama" of the past. But my connection to Lorel and Susan—my relation to them, the relation I've forged with each of them—has complicated that sort of principled dismissal, they've softened my hard line a little. My desire to visit the records house in Spanish Town is, I think, token of my ongoing correspondence with the two of them. It's a new type of desire for me, something to place alongside my old wish, which has always been to disappear into landscape; this, of course, is what John R. did—"the definitive landscape of the black North itself," I call him someplace above this. His name, my name, "the countenance of that man's woods." Yeah, yeah, yeah. But family was different, a complex and graceless series of connections, almost a religion with its various orthodoxies, shamans, atheists, mysteries, schisms, ecstatics and heretics, its sex, its pieces of the true cross. Its myths and their imperfect relation to the flesh and names. John R. Giscome and Peter Giscombe and Charles Giscome and Anne Clarke Giscome (and all the other Giscomes and Giscombes) and James Maxwell and James Miller and Jane Skinner and Lorel Morrison and Susan Bethune talking to me in the train station in Winnipeg.

And Winnipeg itself—as Susan handed me a Xerox of a letter from the McCleary sisters—suddenly seemed like a strange place for me to be touching the cloth. The waiting room was a little shabby and a trio of plump older women were smoking in another part of it—the dry smell of that reached us; outside, the day shimmered. Everything—islands in blue water, Africa, Europe—seemed possible. Far away yet possible.

"What is Africa to me?" Countee Cullen had asked. What is any of it? Susan's talk sketched a shape in the stale air; her lips were thin and her skin was quite pale—as she'd described it in a letter to Linda Eversole—, perhaps especially so in the fluorescent light of the VIA station. Lorel Morrison is quite dark. "I suppose I could be described as fair," I told Icsolene Giscombe on the phone a year later in Toronto; the standard—unspoken but understood clearly between us, people of different citizenships and ages who had never met—being African. I felt an odd shiver there in Winnipeg, one not unpleasurable.

Soren broke down in Walla Walla and ran out of expertise sooner than he'd figured he would; he couldn't find a competent mechanic and ended up towing the Willys to Bloomington behind a U-Haul truck, which was not cheap. In Richard Matheson's novel *I Am Legend*, the narrator—the human survivor of a worldwide disease that turned everyone else into vampires—kept himself equipped with a Willys because they're fairly dependable and easy to fix. The novel's outline is typical future-as-hell genre but inside it's much more thoughtful than the genre usually allows. It's another book about metaphor: the narrator spends most of his time dispatching vampires but they finally outsmart him—by using a woman—and capture him and schedule him for public execution at which long point he realizes that *he* is the monster, not them. That is, in the stories they tell and will tell after his death, he's the legendary predator (from whence comes, of course, Matheson's title). I found the book in the trash when I was eleven or twelve and my job was to take the cans out and burn the paper—I rescued it and read it and it helped me understand some things. The film version—*The Omega Man*—was disappointing and starred Charlton Heston; he drove a Mustang. These many years later, when I think of my hunt—through newspapers, correspondence, conversation, etc.—for traces of John R. and how unsuccessful and frustrating and contradictory most of it has been, I'm tempted to think of him as something a little bit greater than human. A monster? Maybe a saint instead of a monster, a personal legend (in either case). The temptation's always to construct in our own image, I suppose, to make the supernatural being—be it god, saint, or vampire—both resemble and exaggerate our capabilities and proclivities. The famous Bigfoot film, the one taken in the sixties by Roger Patterson, shows such an unlikely-looking monster, one so awkwardly human, that it's set a standard for description and reference. The film's quite amazing: the monster is doing what Auden said we all do, walking dully along.

May 1997, Giscome Portage

Two years after we'd quit Fort George I met John Harris and Vivien Lougheed and John's son Wes in Jasper and we all cycled south over the Icefield Parkway, crossing Sunwapta Pass and then Bow Pass and arriving finally at Lake Louise. We split up then and they continued south over to Radium Hot Springs and I went west to ride across Rogers Pass but we reconnected in Revelstoke, B.C., and, through a complex series of bus and automobile transfers, all drove back to Fort George together, back to 137 South Lyon Street. I sat up drinking red wine with Vivien in the kitchen, then slept in what had been Madeline's room. We all rested up for a day and then I went out to the Huble Farm with the president of the Giscome Portage

Heritage Society and, standing next to the Fraser River there, read a dramatic monologue about John R.'s 1863 trip through the place while a friend of the society videotaped me. I'd composed the piece myself but I'd written it quickly (the night before) and delivered it woodenly. I'd been thinking that such a thing might have enough historical value to outweigh what I realized—even as I was keyboarding it—was going to be its lack of artistic integrity. I don't know what's become of the tape—I suppose I hope it's been lost. I think my impulse—to present something in an accessible and popular style—had been a good one but the execution itself had been shoddy and I rode back to town in the president's very nice car feeling that I'd betrayed John R. both by scripting words for him and by scripting them poorly.

The next day, though, I went back out there with John and Wes and Vivien and we walked the portage trail itself. I'd never done this (and neither had they); it was May and the day was warm but the path was well shaded and soon we were wading through deep snow. As we walked John pointed out trees that had likely been here when John R. and McDame had come through and the trees—spruce and Douglas firs—seemed almost cartoonishly huge and dark and brooding. There would certainly have been snow on the ground back then, I thought, and more than this, since it was April when they made that first trip. Where are the snows of yesteryear? I tried to imagine what it must have been like but this afternoon, with 1997 snow in my Shimano cycling shoes, all I could think of was something strange—the tropical forest set through which white actors had walked with cinematic awe in *King Kong*; when we crossed a creek on a plank bridge I remembered the log on which the actors had got over a ravine only to encounter Kong on the far side. It was quite the intervention on my part, this sudden and compelling memory of a peculiar film with much racial baggage, and I laughed to myself—at myself—in the snow, in my wet shoes. I was walking where John R. had walked and even here, in this quite specifically Giscome place in the geography, the imagination of all that just wouldn't kick in.

In my searches up here and in Victoria I'd turned up a few receipts for John R. Giscome, a welter of addresses, a paternity listing, a handful of other things—these are the footprints, proof of his having been at the places I visited in B.C., but the man himself had eluded me. All historical figures elude us, I suppose; even autobiography tells the reader only what the author wishes her to know. I have no story to tell, finally, on John R., my kinsman, my old arrivant. I can't make the leap, I won't imagine a life for him, I'll not try to craft one out of my learning. I've always disliked historical novels and persona poems—more than that, really, they've always offended me. (The memory of my own poor performance at the shore of the Fraser certainly doesn't help—it's simply another log on the fire.) I've budged some on family and ancestry and the project of family trees—there's a consciousness, I've learned, in that endeavor that's profoundly human, that at its best bespeaks curiosity and is specific and finite. But in the more public world of historical novel and docudrama the dead have no opportunity to refute the animation foisted on them. So I've tried not to be a Frankenstein here in this writing (or I've not tried to be); I've not tried to make John R. Giscome into someone. He *was* someone and then he died. I see his literacy, I see his curiosity, I see his care with his name and his wise choices with his money. I don't know how or why he could leave his daughters, I don't know what his friendship was like with Henry McDame—what pleasure did that bring him and what duties? A few years ago, halfway through my forties, I began to worry for the first time about what I should arrange to have done with my journals—the saga handwritten into a succession of blank books since 1977, the ongoing account of my consciousness and adventures, the true story on which this book and the poetry books are based—after I've breathed my last. I'd been planning, without giving the matter much thought, to leave instructions that they be burned or even do it myself if I was of sound enough mind by that time (which I reckon should occur, barring incident, in forty years or so); but that idea strikes me these days as terribly final, as a sure way to be really dead. Friends have suggested that I will them to Madeline; perhaps I'll do that.

The Grand Tour

It was the end of winter in Fort George and we were on our way to Alaska.

We arranged for Madeline's absence from Quinson School and on Sunday, June 4, we drove out the Yellowhead to Prince Rupert. 740 kilometers, 460 miles. The day we left started out hazy and humid but the light changed as we neared the water, becoming sharp around Terrace and then simply, unambiguously *clear* when we got close to the little city—Prince Rupert—, to the northern coast itself. We spent the next day hanging out in Rupert—I did a radio interview on CBC, we went to bookstores and museums, we ate—and that light persisted and made the town look squeaky clean for all the time we spent in it. And in that light we drove onto the ferry on Tuesday morning and were off, leaving the land, heading north via water.

This was the final trip out from Fort George (or the final trip before the big trip back East, back to the States). My project around John R. was coming to a close and this was a last hurrah: when I'd applied for my Fulbright I'd said that I wanted to pull together "a book that will obligate me to trace and travel as much as I can of his routes in the Cariboo and Cassiar Districts and in the Peace River country" and this Alaska jaunt was part of that travel and tracing. In the late nineteenth century one of the best ways to the Cassiar was by *this* route, water, up along the coast to Wrangell—called in those days Fort Wrangel—and then down the Stikine to the head of navigation at Glenora. Hoagland's *Notes from the Century Before* begins with Telegraph Creek—a newer town adjacent to Glenora—and the area nowadays is connected by a good road with the nearby Cassiar–Stewart Highway, Route 37. This water route—the Stikine and the channels between Rupert and Fort Wrangel—could have been the way John R. and McDame got to the Cassiar, so our trip on the ferry was to the point and at least vaguely "authentic." (In fact, on a whole-hog authenticity impulse one afternoon earlier in the year, I made some telephone inquiries as to how much it would cost for us and our car to arrive at Telegraph Creek or Glenora from Wrangell via the Stikine River; I had an image in my head of the Volvo lashed to the deck of a small steamer and us clinging to the rail as the boat negotiated rapids, a romantic/ironic mishmash of "Heart of Darkness" and Richard Wright's final journey—he took his Oldsmobile—to France. I ran into enough dead ends on my quest, though, to understand that the idea was so weird that doing it would probably take a great deal of money.)

We got to Wrangell that evening and the boat had a bit of a layover, so we piled off to see what we could see. Everything had been a fort back then—Fort George, Fort McLeod, Fort St. John, this. At the ferry slip I bought a dollar raffle ticket from a plump teenager who was trying to be elected queen of something and we walked a ways toward town, half looking for the Stikine River. Some little fires were burning on a hillside and Katharine took photographs of that scene as we walked. The road wound up another hill, across from where the fires were, and into a neighborhood of prefab houses: it was dark, close to midnight, and most of the windows were dark too but one was lit and inside that house we saw a trio of twenty-year-olds watching TV. Or the two young women were—the man, shirtless, was passed out on the couch, his mouth open, his chest smooth and very white. Fort Wrangel. We went back to the boat without finding the river.

From the journal of the next day, June 7:

11.10 & still half-light as we drift into the sunset toward Juneau. In the forward lounge of the Malespina. This & all the boats in the fleet being named for glaciers.

"Skagway's where all the history is," sd someone a bit ago, disparaging Haines, meaning—by the praise of Skagway—the Chilkoot Trail. As tho' history was concentrated in a finite number of places—here's where they did this, here's where they did that, our national mythology. I think of Charlie Chaplin. To go into that general history, the subject of popular books & films, a national nostalgia to disappear on into.

I'm going north toward or into (I hope) a specificity, a few patches of ground, a vista, a now as well as then.

The next afternoon we drove off the boat into Skagway: it's in an armpit of the coast, at the end of something called the Taiya Inlet, it's as far up into the cleavage of the continent as the salt water extends. There's of course a little strip of the United States there—the hinge of the Alaska panhandle—and just beyond it to the north is a little strip of British Columbia and just past that is the Yukon and the Alaska Highway.

Skagway itself was a tourist trap, a successful—or at least ambitious—marketing of the story of the gold rush, and we got through it quickly, stopping only for gas and to get some Canadian dollars from a bank. There was a profoundly distressing American feel to Skagway, one that hit me hard, I figure, because of our months away from the mother country, because of our winter in Canada—it reminded me of Galena, Illinois, and Cooperstown, New York, towns we'd visited recently, secluded and stately and "preserved" towns both, and in lovely locations, towns whose economy depends on tourist trade: what's for sale in those places is a series of crystallizations—vistas, trinkets large and small, easily digestible exhibits, ambience—of a cultural past, of the "us" several generations back that we've inherited. Galena, home of U. S. Grant, and Cooperstown, home of James Fenimore Cooper (and the Baseball Hall of Fame), are in some sense our fathers' houses, the houses of two of our many fathers; gold-rush Skagway's the house of one of our rakish and disreputable and hard-drinking but much-loved uncles. How to celebrate John R. and McDame, though, how to herald the brothers without a past, the brothers who ranged and rambled and to whom there are no cultural monuments, for whom there is no cultural moment? "Where was his house?" asked Madeline as we came into Quesnel back in the winter. Older Americans in shorts clogged the sidewalks of Skagway and young families crept along in their minivans, turistas from the lower forty-eight with U.S. dollars in their pockets. North to Alaska indeed. We rolled north again, back toward the Canadian border.

But as we rolled Katharine announced that she was sick, her tone communicating something familiar and unpleasant. Is it diverticulitis? I asked, knowing it was. "Not yet," she snapped. We had been intending to turn right on the Alaska

Highway and head toward the Cassiar and camp that evening someplace near Watson Lake, and this changed that. Diverticulitis is, essentially, an inflammation of the large bowel and antibiotics will usually knock it back but if you don't treat it that bowel can perforate and it can kill you—it's Katharine's chronic disease, no one knows where it comes from, but it appears about once a year as if to remind us about mortality. So when we got to the Alaska Highway we turned left instead of going right and soon we came to Whitehorse, capital city of the Yukon Territory, where we rented a room at the High Country Inn and got Katharine an appointment with an M.D. the next morning. She actually had antibiotics with her and had commenced taking them, but this was being safe—probably overcautious but undeniably safe—, running it by the professional before going out into the bush. She crawled into bed with a book and Madeline and I went over to the municipal pool, which happened to be next door; I sat on the sidelines while she made friends in the water with a girl her age who had a real tattoo—a heart on her shoulder with a script inside it that read "Mom and Dad." The two of us went out to eat after that and had bad Chinese food at a roadside place at the edge of town—the other patrons were a couple of extended young families, ragged blond twenty-year-olds with babies and assorted sisters and brothers and friends, all jammed into and overflowing from a single noisy corner booth behind us. All—excepting the babies of course—were quite drunk.

We stayed on another day and night in Whitehorse. I got up early that second day, while Katharine and Madeline were still sleeping, and breakfasted alone in the restaurant downstairs from our room; I sat at a table next to that of a big inter-racial family group, a gathering apparently in honor of the matriarch, a black woman of what I took to be a well-preserved seventy-five or so. I sipped my coffee and charted the connections: her daughter who was married to a white fellow, that couple's children, a couple of her other daughters, the white fellow's brother or sister, and that person's spouse, their children. Middle-class, polite, apparently happy. Sober. It was an unlikely group to be chowing down alongside of in the Yukon and I smiled, remembering the maxim about finding someone black there before you no matter where you were, pleased to see it fleshed out again. "Big Mamma," goes Sherley Anne Williams' poem about Sterling and Daisy Brown, but then it questions itself, "Mamma to who?" These were Canadians, though, the argot that came in snatches from their table was different; race was different. Mother to whom?

Katharine was beginning to feel better and when we went to the doctor he shrugged over the diverticulitis and said Keep up the antibiotics. The next day we were back on the road.

From the journal:

Alaska Hwy was full of RVs. Passed along big rivers & long Teslin Lake & got finally to the Cassiar–Stewart Hwy. Started down toward McDame, thought better of it after a mile, & returned to the intersection for gas. The Indian man we'd passed up hitchhiking the first time down the road was swimming in a roadside pond the 2nd time we saw him, making the question moot. Pressed 60 miles or so down thru Good Hope & made the turn-off to McDame. Drove across one stream—gravel over some overflowing culvert pipes—& stopped at the next one wch was deep & fast. M & I crosst it & walkt a ways, M complaining of bugs & fear of bears, & we returned. (She'd crossed, crouching, on a branch laid over the water: I'd followed but fallen in. A tad deep to chance with the Volvo.) Some Indians came by in a blue 4WD pickup, young man w/ a set face at the wheel. We drove on out & down to Mighty

Moe's Campground & were there met by Mighty Kevin, the mgr, gawky white kid on a mtn bike w/ panniers full of "my library." We talkt abt animals—grizzlies across the river, wolves coming through "in some #s"—& I askt abt McDame. He ran & got me pix of it, one of wch he let me keep, Polaroids, an abandoned HB post. He puts canoeists in at the campground & picks them up there, at McDame; the pix are given them so they'll know where to get out of the Dease. Indian burial ground across the R. from it. Sweet young man, made sure we were comfortable. He took M out for her first canoe lesson, showed her a loon's nest & beavers gliding across the H$_2$O. Beans for dinner at 11 o'clock: it was still light tho' everyone was asleep but us & some Germans.

Saw McDame's Creek for the first time, from the Cassiar–Stewart, & we weren't sure it was it: K sd Maybe that's the Dease. But it rushed (it's very fast) around a ♥-shaped island in our view of it from the road, a bifurcation there far below us.

The next day we stopped on the highway and walked down to the stream on a long, straight trail from the road—from a turnout with a marker that informed passersby of the creek's name, a marker we'd somehow not seen our first time through—and ranged along the creekside for a ways. Henry McDame had been out on the Dease and found gold at the place where this then-unnamed creek entered the river; he left the river then and followed the creek up through where we were walking and he found more and more of it. John R. and Charles Charity and a handful of others joined him there and, later, a lot of miners came. I think this is where John R. got rich. Madeline lost her ring—an onyx item we'd bought for her on the Alaska Highway—and we looked for it unsuccessfully in the gravel at the water's edge and then moved on.

From the journal:

The interpretive sign on McDame Creek makes no mention of Henry McDame, only Albert Freeman (was he black?) & his big nugget find. And R. M. Patterson's Trail to the Interior abounds w/ references to McDame Creek but never a ref to Henry McDame himself tho' other people are identified, people w/ places named after them.

McDame & Giscome are aberrations in what has come to be called history & understood & accepted as the heritage of this area. Heritage mixed up again with inherit, w/ forefathers. Foremothers? At the Prince George RR Museum we saw the photo of "the First White Woman Arriving" here, stepping off a river steamer: implicit in the caption is that no longer will the white men here copulate w/ Indian women, that white females + a European culture make civilization. Local civilization's adulterated by location a little, altho' such adulteration only shows the Europeans' hidden racial strengths, things to display in the face of the unruly wilderness—this is, I think, important for white Canadians: to live in the wilderness & still be white.

We made it, that long day, to another Summit Lake, not the one come to by John R. and McDame at the northern end of the Giscome Portage but one in the Rockies. The campsite was prosaic, right next to the highway, but we went for a good walk up onto the mountain above it and the next day drove down to Fort St. John. The newspaper, the *Colonist*, had described how, in May of 1863, John R. "made up his mind to try his luck down the Peace River" and it went on to tell how he and McDame had built a raft and arrived that way, via water, at this place, Fort St. John. My own arrival at this venue—via ambulance—had been somewhat less happy and my sense of town was limited because of that; but we bombed around some in the car and I showed Katharine and Madeline "my" hospital and we searched for some remnant of the Hudson's Bay Company's fort until some kids at a gas station told us that it had burned down five years ago. We ate an early dinner at McDonald's then and headed east. From the journal:

Pushed on into Alberta down a switchback hill across the Beatton River, wch I mistook for the Peace, realizing the mistake some miles later. Loitered there at the beautiful green girder bridge, K taking pix of the span, of the river, on my information that this was the Peace.

Up from the river then & across flat Alberta. A different, wilder flatness than Illinois, forest at the edge of the big picture(s) or perhaps it was the knowledge of having come out of the mtns recently or the violent descents to the Peace (& the Beatton). Saw a family of red foxes—Vulpes fulva—playing in a field: startling, sharp red in the weird Alberta light & startling too after the black foxes of Fort George. Smoke blew across the road—from a forest fire? Gas flame on a chimney at the turn-off for Fairview.

At the store at Fairview I met a black man in coveralls & fantasized later about him being a McDame. Big man w/ a scraggly beard. He & the white woman at the counter agreed that the best place to camp was at Ft. Dunvegan itself on the Peace & he sd "20 minutes, I just came over from there."

We made it back down the road south from Fairview then, past the flame, and came down a long hill to the Peace in the dark.

It looked like a movie set for a campground: manicured bushes evenly spaced around each private pull-off, & the pull-offs were covered, on their floors, w/ gravel, w/ a layer of gravel. M dinna like it, it was deserted. Made 2 or 3 circuits of the whole place & decided on a pull-off nr the river, set up the tent there. I walkt over to the bushes to pee & found bearshit on the gravel & squatted down to look at it & there was M beside me. "Is that bear poop, Daddy?"

Yes, yes, yes but don't worry, etc. Told her a b.t. story in the tent &
then K went in to say goodnight to her & she was scared, wanted us
both in the tent with her but K came out & sat w/ me at the picnic
table & identified the odd gronk noise I'd been hearing (& identify-
ing as bullfrogs by the river) as "Ursus americanus, a maternal unit
and 1, possibly 2, junior units."

She'd worked with them for years, hosing out their cage, bringing them food, photographing them; her identification of their noise was beyond question. Bears for Baudelaire, "*Mon semblable—mon frère.*" And here they were, finally, a presence around us, another family marked by their sounds, by their conversation with each other, saying what to one another? Things about food, the facts of foraging itself, a sound or series of sounds to mark the edges of the process. We listened to them and discussed—in euphemisms for still-awake Madeline's benefit—what we should do. Black bears are rarely predatory; the one that tried to eat that German over at Bowron Lake was an exception—an aberration—as was the one that did eat three boys at Algonquin Park in Ontario in the seventies. Those boys were fishing at various points along a stream and the bear took them one by one. The first victim had been black and some of the local investigators had hypothesized that bear had mistaken him, initially, for another bear and embraced him as that only to be disappointed and then interested. Why is it that black people are frightened when the police stop us on the highway?

The Ontario boys had come to Algonquin together but had split up to fish and we were all together—three big, strong humans in a group—and Katharine said she thought that the danger to us was pretty minimal; but we agreed that maybe we should pull the car in closer, position it to be an escape hatch in the unlikely event of things getting hairy. Not wanting to alarm Madeline, I called to her in the tent, asked if *she* would feel better if I moved the car closer in, and did so, positioning the front passenger door right next to the mouth of the tent, when she said that yes, she'd like that. I left the keys on the floor and, feeling a great deal better myself, sat down at the picnic table again and poured a Dixie cup of Bourbon for Katharine and one for me. We'd bought the bottle in Fort George before we left for Rupert but this was the first time we'd opened it. "Thank you, Daddy," came the little voice from the tent.

At the table the dry, papery taste of the cup touched the bite of the Bourbon. A toast to wilderness, to the bear, to all pursuits. Bears are an easy metaphor, though: mistaken for Bigfoot, resembling humans. Katharine's Bears for Baudelaire is a joke about the temptingness of that resemblance; their shapes, when you see them bounding across the road at dawn or in the headlights, are the shapes of old men, stooped and still big as some old men are. Mostly, though, they're a hidden presence in the trees: toothed, unseen, a little unpredictable, black. Black bears, but there are all those different colors of black bears. John R. saw lots of them every day on his trip out here, on these banks of this old river. Still, what might the ungainly ancestor be like, how might he appear in a dream or alpha-state vision, as what just beyond sight? Compared to *what?* sang Les McCann. (There's a funny moment in At-wood's *Surfacing* in which the narrator watches for her lost father to improbably appear or reappear, unrecognizable. At the bottom of the page what comes is a bear: "It materialized on the path, snuffling along bulky and flat-footed, an enormous fanged rug.") Forebear, fur-bearer, the bear before. The Invisible Man said, "Call me Jack the Bear."

But these were real bears in the neighborhood, unseen but unhidden, a metaphor for nothing in particular. We survived our night among them and in the morning we packed up camp and drove the half mile over to the Fort Dunvegan historical site. John R. and McDame had been "kindly received" by the Hudson's Bay factor at the fort, a Mr. Shaw, when they came through in 1863 and I'd been hoping that some remnant of the structure had survived. It was gone, of course, but a new visitors' center stood on the place where the fort had been and we went in and wandered through the displays of photographs of the old days; the place had an acidic smell to it, the staff was aloof. We came out and found a path that led to an old Oblate mission with a huge statue of Mary-Mother-of-God that tilted out over the Peace; Katharine photographed that.

That afternoon we got to the village of Peace River, which is at the confluence of that river with the Smoky. This was the stretch that it had taken John R. twenty-four hours to cover, from Fort Dunvegan to here; we'd meandered, eating late breakfast/early lunch along the way and drifting through the farm towns—the day was grey and hot, threatening rain but delivering none. Peace River's a lovely, haphazard little city in the hills and we parked downtown to let Madeline spend her travel money at a hardware store that sold toys. We were going on that night to Grande Prairie, going to get a room in a motel and then, the next day, cross Pine Pass and drop down into Prince George. We'd see the Smoky on the way to Grande Prairie and that would cover the extent of John R.'s push eastward. (From the *Colonist*: "They followed up Smoky River some distance, not liking the appearance of the country and finding nothing more than occasional color.") It was all water, everywhere we'd gone—we'd traveled along the Manson River on our trip to Germansen; we'd visited John R.'s

McDame Creek address in the Cassiar. We'd gone south to Quesnel and spent an afternoon looking for Bouchie Creek. Now here we were in Peace River but this was it—winter in Fort George was over and when we got back to the house on Lyon Street we'd have to start packing up to go back to Bloomington.

We headed out of town, stopping at the town museum on the way. I'd given a talk about John R. at the Prince George Genealogical Society and had brought printouts of that to distribute to all and sundry on this trip; the Peace River Museum was the first open archive we'd come to. From the journal:

At the museum in Peace River we spent time w/ Albert Kilkenny, asst curator, who Xeroxed my article abt JRG's 1863 trip & remarked on the paucity of "colored" travelers through here. We talked back & forth & he insisted on giving us "the 5 minute tour" wch took half an hour & we talkt some more then. Good fellow. "Don't belittle your friend's trip up here," he sd. "There was nothing here back then, you'd go days without seeing anybody."

I askt Why forts? For fear of Indians? No, he sd, fear of animals. Into these forts up here came JRG & McDame, Island men, colored men from the Islands. What was in Giscome's mind?

There'd been a break in the grey weather while we were taking the tour: it wasn't exactly sunny but it was bright, the afternoon was full of a sourceless light. In that, we practiced throwing spears on the lawn of the museum and Albert Kilkenny took a photo of the three of us with the Peace River itself behind us, flowing north. Katharine has it on her desk now. There's a lot of sky in the picture: clouds with a blue tinge to them hang in the whiteness and both the highway bridge and the CN bridge are visible at Katharine's right shoulder. It's a beautiful location—the bluff above the river, more hills in the hazy distance, the bridges. Madeline kneels on the ground between us wearing the dark blue T-shirt we got her at the campus store at the University of Northern British Columbia; it fits her like a tent in the picture but now she's graceful in it in her sixth-grade class at Bloomington Junior High. We're all three smiling goofily and we're all grubby.

We shook hands goodbye with Albert Kilkenny and pushed off south for Grande Prairie. We'd been on the road for a lot of days and I was looking forward to taking a shower.

Postscript

In spring of 1998 we sold our house on Vale Street and that summer we left Bloomington, Illinois, and moved to State College, Pennsylvania. I teach now at Penn State; that university's English Department approached me in 1997, we courted for a year, and now Katharine, Madeline, and I live there. Here. As I type this I'm looking out the big back door of this cedar and stucco house, over the porch rail, into the woods. This is a new suburb and the house is new—built in 1975—but the woods come to within a few yards of the back door. This—where we live—is a valley in the Appalachian Mountains; Katharine thinks it was a bear that pulled down the lilac tree next to the porch—she found arguable claw marks and the tree's branches had been quite close to one of our bird feeders (which hangs from the bottom of a second-floor deck). Birdseed attracts 'em, said the people at the pet store. We righted the tree and tied it to the porch rails with a rope and it seems to be doing fine.

Of course, I stayed at Illinois State and in Bloomington much too long to have left easily. Friends—the people I taught with, the people who lived around the corner, students—made my life rich there, in that place, and made leaving a much more complicated event than I'd figured it would be when I was applying for other jobs. And landscape? I talked so much, during those years, about the dull oppressiveness of the flat but I did realize, at some point, that I knew what a town looked like when it was eight miles away and what it looked like when it was five miles away; and, at a later point, I realized that there was pleasure in this kind of seeing. I must acknowledge that the prairie is part of me.

So is British Columbia. The province's landscape is final, as Barry McKinnon has said, the continent ends with British Columbia. Whenever I recall that landscape—the snowy mountains, the Peace River, the desert around Spences Bridge—I immediately remember the joy of coming into it for the first time. And the joy of crossing it and recrossing it. But my life—and my family's life—was good there, due, in large part, to the efforts and kindness of Prince George people.

This is, apparently, what it is to age. One has more people and more places to return to.

Into and Out of Dislocation was supported by a Fulbright Research Award from the Council for the International Exchange of Scholars and the Canada-U.S. Fulbright Commission. (I'm especially indebted to Karen Adams at the C.I.E.S.) I first went to Prince George and Giscome in 1991 when I was living in Vancouver and working on *Giscome Road*; that time was given to me by the Faculty Research Grant Program of the Canadian Embassy to the United States, the Illinois Arts Council, and the Fund for Poetry. (The Vancouver poets George Bowering and George McWhirter were both very helpful at early stages of this book.) I began writing prose on my first computer, which I purchased with money from a 1988 grant from the New York Foundation on the Arts. Many years on I'm still grateful to those organizations and people for that support.

I thank Ethan Nosowsky, my editor at North Point Press/ Farrar, Straus and Giroux, for talking with me and listening to me and guiding the pieces of my manuscript into this book; and I thank Elaine Chubb (also at Farrar, Straus and Giroux) and Kent Sedgwick (in Prince George) for keeping me honest about distance, song lyrics, and historical detail. I'm very grateful to Paula Deitz and Frederick Morgan of *The Hudson Review* for their generosity and for their encouragement early on in this project.

And I need to acknowledge here my relationships with Susan Bethune and Lorel Morrison. Because of their correspondence, conversation, and insistences I have touched the cloth of family in ways I'd not imagined when I began this book. Lorel's 1999 compilation, *The Prism: A Partial Saga of the Giscombe Family,* is a testimony to love, memory, perseverance; Susan's long letters have guided me. My far cousins— you've brought me out past my own edges.